Hands-On Microservices with Kotlin

Build reactive and cloud-native microservices with Kotlin
using Spring 5 and Spring Boot 2.0

Juan Antonio Medina Iglesias

BIRMINGHAM - MUMBAI

Hands-On Microservices with Kotlin

Commissioning Editor: Kunal Chaudhari
Acquisition Editor: Nigel Fernandes
Content Development Editor: Francis Carneiro
Technical Editor: Diksha Wakode
Copy Editor: Safis Editing
Project Coordinator: Devanshi Doshi
Proofreader: Safis Editing
Indexers: Tejal Daruwale Soni
Graphics: Jason Monteiro
Production Coordinator: Aparna Bhagat

First Edition: January 2018

Production reference: 1240118

Published by Packt Publishing Ltd.
Livery Place
35 Livery Street
Birmingham
B3 2PB, UK.

ISBN 978-1-78847-145-9

www.packtpub.com

To my friend Juan Antonio Breña; his motivation and passion is an example, pushing me to a level that I thought was not possible. Without him, this book would never exist. To Sergio Valera, whose inspiration and vision will be something that I'll always remember, no matter how far apart we are nowadays.

– Juan Antonio Medina Iglesias

`mapt.io`

Mapt is an online digital library that gives you full access to over 5,000 books and videos, as well as industry leading tools to help you plan your personal development and advance your career. For more information, please visit our website.

Why subscribe?

- Spend less time learning and more time coding with practical eBooks and Videos from over 4,000 industry professionals

- Improve your learning with Skill Plans built especially for you

- Get a free eBook or video every month

- Mapt is fully searchable

- Copy and paste, print, and bookmark content

PacktPub.com

Did you know that Packt offers eBook versions of every book published, with PDF and ePub files available? You can upgrade to the eBook version at `www.PacktPub.com` and as a print book customer, you are entitled to a discount on the eBook copy. Get in touch with us at `service@packtpub.com` for more details.

At `www.PacktPub.com`, you can also read a collection of free technical articles, sign up for a range of free newsletters, and receive exclusive discounts and offers on Packt books and eBooks.

Contributors

About the author

Juan Antonio Medina Iglesias began his career 20 years ago as an indie game developer and worked abroad four countries since then, from embedded software to enterprise applications. He has a lifetime's dedication to software craftsmanship.

Since 2006, he works at Santander Technology with a talented group of professionals who performed one of the biggest transformations in the banking industry.

Nowadays, he works as a Senior Engineer in the Digital Transformation team within Santander Technology UK.

I need to thank Victor Herraiz and Neil Cannon my official reviewers and to Francis Carneiro my Content Developer Editor. They have done a great work with the content of the book and the example code.

I must as well thank, David Albone, Rachel Warburton, Alan Taylor and Khurram Mahmood for the unofficial reviews and feedback on the chapters.

About the reviewers

Neil Cannon has been developing Android applications since 2010, following many years working on server-side Java. After trying the Kotlin 1.0 beta, he moved away from Java and has written as little Java as possible since.

Víctor Herraiz Posada is a senior software engineer with more than 15 years of experience in designing and developing complex distributed systems for companies such as Santander Group and Mapfre.

He is passionate about teaching and training. He has given courses and talks on accessibility, quality control, design patterns, and programming languages. He loves physics, metal music, playing guitar, video games and old sci-fi movies, books, and comics.

> *I would like to thank Juan Antonio Medina Iglesias for asking me to review this insightful book. Microservices with Kotlin is quite a journey through the challenges that many companies have to face.*

Packt is searching for authors like you

If you're interested in becoming an author for Packt, please visit `authors.packtpub.com` and apply today. We have worked with thousands of developers and tech professionals, just like you, to help them share their insight with the global tech community. You can make a general application, apply for a specific hot topic that we are recruiting an author for, or submit your own idea.

Table of Contents

Preface

With Google's announcement of introducing first-class support for Kotlin in their Android ecosystem, Kotlin is realized as a mainstream language.

Microservices helps with designing scalable, easy-to-maintain web applications, and Kotlin allows us to take advantage of modern idioms to simplify our development and create high-quality services.

With 100% of interoperability with the JVM, Kotlin makes it easy to work with the existing Java code.

Popular Java frameworks, such as Spring, Jackson, and Reactor, have included Kotlin modules to take advantage of language features such as null safety and type-safe declarative builders.

This book will guide the reader through designing and implementing services to having the production-ready testable code, creating easy-to-maintain and lean code that will be shorter and simpler than a traditional Java implementation.

We will discover the benefits of using the reactive paradigm in order to take advantage of non-blocking techniques and take our services to the next level of industry standards.

During the journey, we'll consume NoSQL databases reactively in order to create high-throughput microservices.

In this book, we will demonstrate how we can create Cloud-Native microservices that can run in a wide range of cloud providers, and how we can monitor them.

We will create Docker containers for our microservices and learn how to scale them.

Finally, we will deploy our microservices in Openshift Online.

Who this book is for

If you are a Kotlin developer with a basic knowledge of microservice architectures and now want to effectively implement these services on enterprise-level web applications, then this book is for you.

What this book covers

Chapter 1, *Understanding Microservices*, introduces microservices and their principles. We will review Domain-Driven Design, Cloud-Native microservices, and Reactive architecture.

Chapter 2, *Getting Started with Spring Boot 2.0*, helps develop our first microservice with Kotlin using Spring Boot 2.0. We will take a deep dive into the Spring Boot and see how we can use IntelliJ IDEA to build our microservices.

Chapter 3, *Creating RESTful Services*, expands our Cloud-Native microservices to become RESTful APIs, introducing different Spring components.

Chapter 4, *Creating Reactive Microservices*, creates non-blocking reactive microservices. We will learn how we can use Spring WebFlux and project Reactor to build reactive microservices.

Chapter 5, *Reactive Spring Data*, focuses on how we can use reactive Spring Data to perform operations against NoSQL databases such as MongoDB. Then, it looks at how we can enhance our reactive microservices creating reactive CRUD operations for our REST APIs.

Chapter 6, *Creating Cloud-Native Microservices*, outlines what Cloud-Native microservices are, and how we can easily build with Spring Cloud.

Chapter 7, *Creating Dockers*, informs how to install and configure Docker to create, publish, and run containers, and how we can integrate this when we build our microservices with Maven.

Chapter 8, *Scaling Microservices*, showcases how we can Docker swarm to create our own personal cloud, and how we can scale and control our microservices.

Chapter 9, *Testing Spring Microservices*, covers how we can test our microservices using JUnit using SpringBootTest. We will learn how we can test our microservice in a more expressive way by using Kluent to do fluent tests.

Chapter 10, *Monitoring Microservices*, discusses why monitoring is a critical part of any production-ready system, and how we can provide microservices that can be monitored and controlled using Spring Boot Actuator and JMX.

Chapter 11, *Deploying Microservices*, explains how to deploy our microservices Dockers in OpenShift Online, and how we can integrate GitHub to do automatic deployments when our microservices code changes.

Chapter 12, *Best Practices*, goes through industry best practices that we can use to create our microservices.

To get the most out of this book

To get up and running, users will need to have the following software installed:

- JDK 8
- Maven 3.5+
- IntelliJ IDEA CE 2017.3
- Any Zip Extractor
- Any Browser
- Docker for Windows or Docker for Mac (Not Docker toolbox)
- For some examples related to Windows, you may need Cygwin or Windows Linux Subsystem

Download the example code files

You can download the example code files for this book from your account at www.packtpub.com. If you purchased this book elsewhere, you can visit www.packtpub.com/support and register to have the files emailed directly to you.

You can download the code files by following these steps:

1. Log in or register at www.packtpub.com
2. Select the **SUPPORT** tab
3. Click on **Code Downloads & Errata**
4. Enter the name of the book in the **Search** box and follow the onscreen instructions

Once the file is downloaded, please make sure that you unzip or extract the folder using the latest version of:

- WinRAR/7-Zip for Windows
- Zipeg/iZip/UnRarX for Mac
- 7-Zip/PeaZip for Linux

The code bundle for the book is also hosted on GitHub at `https://github.com/PacktPublishing/Hands-On-Microservices-with-Kotlin`.

 When this book was written, the current snapshot version of Spring Boot 2 was `Spring Boot 2.0.0 M7`. The code bundle and examples are up to date with that version. Eventually, `Spring Boot 2.0.0` will be finally released and the code bundle will be updated accordingly.

We also have other code bundles from our rich catalog of books and videos available at `https://github.com/PacktPublishing/`. Check them out!

Download the color images

We also provide a PDF file that has color images of the screenshots/diagrams used in this book. You can download it here: `https://www.packtpub.com/sites/default/files/downloads/HandsOnMicroserviceswithKotlin_ColorImages.pdf`.

Conventions used

There are a number of text conventions used throughout this book.

`CodeInText`: Indicates code words in the text, database table names, folder names, filenames, file extensions, pathnames, dummy URLs, user input, and Twitter handles. Here is an example: "Mount the downloaded `WebStorm-10*.dmg` disk image file as another disk in your system."

A block of code is set as follows:

```
package com.microservices.chapter2

interface ServiceInterface {
  fun getHello(name : String) : String
}
```

When we wish to draw your attention to a particular part of a code block, the relevant lines or items are set in bold:

```
<build>
....
 <plugins>
  <plugin>
   <groupId>org.springframework.boot</groupId>
   <artifactId>spring-boot-maven-plugin</artifactId>
   <configuration>
    <executable>true</executable>
   </configuration>
  </plugin>
....
</build>
```

Any command-line input or output is written as follows:

```
mvnw spring-boot:run
mvnw compile
```

Bold: Indicates a new term, an important word, or words that you see onscreen. For example, words in menus or dialog boxes appear in the text like this. Here is an example: "Select **System info** from the **Administration** panel."

 Warnings or important notes appear like this.

 Tips and tricks appear like this.

Get in touch

Feedback from our readers is always welcome.

General feedback: Email feedback@packtpub.com and mention the book title in the subject of your message. If you have questions about any aspect of this book, please email us at questions@packtpub.com.

Errata: Although we have taken every care to ensure the accuracy of our content, mistakes do happen. If you have found a mistake in this book, we would be grateful if you would report this to us. Please visit www.packtpub.com/submit-errata, selecting your book, clicking on the Errata Submission Form link, and entering the details.

Piracy: If you come across any illegal copies of our works in any form on the Internet, we would be grateful if you would provide us with the location address or website name. Please contact us at copyright@packtpub.com with a link to the material.

If you are interested in becoming an author: If there is a topic that you have expertise in and you are interested in either writing or contributing to a book, please visit authors.packtpub.com.

Reviews

Please leave a review. Once you have read and used this book, why not leave a review on the site that you purchased it from? Potential readers can then see and use your unbiased opinion to make purchase decisions, we at Packt can understand what you think about our products, and our authors can see your feedback on their book. Thank you!

For more information about Packt, please visit packtpub.com.

1
Understanding Microservices

Microservices and their continuously evolving architecture have become one of the most used approaches in enterprise applications. In this book, we will try to get an understanding of what they really are and the principles that they are based on. Using Domain-Driven Design, we will reinforce those principles to maintain a clean architecture that can evolve with our applications.

Since microservices have no static architecture, we will discover how the new reactive paradigm could change the way we create them. And, finally, we will have an overview of cloud architecture and why we should create Cloud Native microservices.

In this chapter, you will learn about:

- What a microservice really is
- Understanding microservices principles
- Using Domain-Driven Design for a clean architecture
- Non-blocking reactive microservices
- Cloud Native microservices and their benefits

What is a microservice?

Microservices are modular, loosely-coupled services that provide a fine-grained protocol. They physically separate concerns and allow us to design, develop, test, and deploy them independently.

Due to their modular capabilities, they can be created by small cross-functional teams that are embracing the benefits of agile methodologies and the DevOps culture. They are also an ideal candidate for continuous delivery and deployment.

 DevOps is a software development and delivery process that emphasizes communication and collaboration between product management, software development, and operations professionals.

They are easy to understand and connect well with other services, making integration of complex applications a lightweight task. They can be scaled, monitored, and controlled independently so that they fully benefit cloud architectures.

Understanding SoA

Microservices are an evolution of the **Service Oriented Architecture (SoA)**. So, if we want to understand what a microservice is, we need to understand what SoA is. SoA is based on having application components communicating through a set of services, a discrete unit of functionality that can be accessed remotely. Services are the foundation stone in SoA, and the same applies to microservices as well.

As described in SoA, a service has four properties:

- It logically represents a business activity with a specified outcome
- It is self-contained
- It is a black box for its consumers
- It may consist of other underlying services

To understand these properties, let's look at an example of an application using SoA:

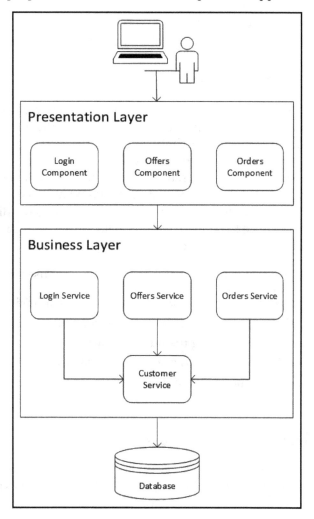

SoA application example

In this typical n-tier architecture, the application is divided into three layers:

- **Presentation layer**: Holds the UI for our customer
- **Business layer**: Has services implementing the domain logic for our business capabilities
- **Data layer**: Persists our domain model

Each component includes the logic to interact with the customer in a specific business activity and to do so, uses the services provided by the business layer. Each service represents the realization of a business activity. For example, you log in to the application provided by the login service, check offers provided by the offers service or create orders via the orders service. These services are self-contained in the business layer, and they act as a black box for their consumer—the components don't know how the services are implemented, nor do they know how the domain model is persisted. All the services depend on the customer service to obtain customer data, or return customer information, but the client does not know about these details.

This approach provides several benefits to any architecture that uses it:

- Standardized service contract, allowing easy integration with components
- Reusability, allowing services to delegate responsibilities to each other
- Business value, implementing the business capabilities
- Hides complexity; if we need to change our database, the clients are unaffected
- Autonomyl; each of the layers could be separated and be accessed remotely

Differentiating microservices from SoA

Microservices architecture evolves from SoA, but it has key differences that we need to understand. Let's recreate the previous SoA example with a microservices architecture and review the differences and benefits for this type of architecture:

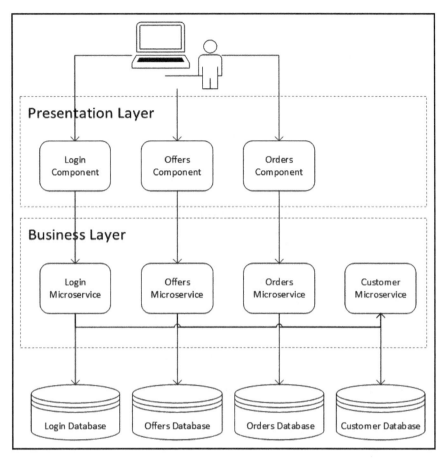

Microservice application example

In this architecture, the layers are not bound together, as they are purely divided logically. Each microservice is completely decoupled from the other services, so even our UI components could be completely separate, deployable modules. These microservices own their own data and they could be altered without affecting each other. This is a capability that will stand out when facing continuous integration or delivery, as we could provision data for our tests and pipeline, without affecting other parts of the application.

Because of their independence, they could be very specific. We could use this benefit to build that expertise into our teams. An expert team that controls the domain logic from a business capability could effectively deliver better value to our products.

We could vary the range of development languages, platforms, or technologies to build each microservice. As they are completely independent, we could use a different database for each different business need, or perhaps use certain technologies that will give us the agility required to adapt to certain requirements more easily.

Since they are modular, we could deploy them independently and have different release cycles. When we need to monitor them, we could create different alerts or KPIs based on the nature of what they do and how they are done. It may not be the same for a microservice used in our accounting process as one that just provides content for our marketing banners. For similar reasons, we could scale them separately; we could have more servers for some microservices, or just more CPU or resources for others.

 Taking advantage of how we can control and monitor microservices independently will grant us the ability to optimize scaling.

The infrastructure for microservices is usually simpler, as there are not as many complex servers to manage, configure, monitor, and control, no huge database schemas and, since the expertise within the teams is higher, more things can be easily automated. This will make DevOps culture within microservices teams a common practice, and with it we will gain even more flexibility within our products.

As microservice teams are usually small, there is a common understanding within the industry that the optimal size for a microservice team is one that could be fed with two pizzas. Whether or not this is the reality, keeping your team small will help to maximize the value of this type of architecture.

If we look at SoA and then microservices, what we can see is a natural evolution. Microservice architecture takes the advantages of SoA and then defines additional steps in that same direction. So, we can definitely say that:

"Microservices are SoA but all SoA are not microservices."

From the monolith to microservices

So, why did SoA evolve into microservices? Perhaps one of the reasons was due to the monolith. There was a point in time where applications were small, and the presentation logic was usually coupled with the business logic. Then, the domain model got complex and many software patterns arose. Most of them were focusing on one thing: Separation of Concerns.

Separation of Concerns (SoC) is a design principle for separating software into distinct sections so that each section addresses only one concern. But software is not the only thing that needs separation; the architecture needs it as well. Things like SoA are designed for that, as it allows us to hide our complexity behind black boxes to make our architecture more modular, and with the ability to handle the complexity that we require.

We may create a complex data store in the mainframe based on detailed business rules, or on a powerful database with a deep schema, complex stored procedures, views, and relationships. We can choose frameworks and tools to easily orchestrate all these parts. We probably also need a powerful **Enterprise Software Bus (ESB)**.

An ESB is a software component that is in charge of the coordination, mapping, and routing of services. The overall idea is to have a very powerful component to easily orchestrate messages. In order to create complex applications, services were designed using most of these elements, creating complex relationships.

From services calling each other, to views querying several tables, pulling data from different business domains. And finally, merging in our ESB several of those elements with business rules to produce new services.

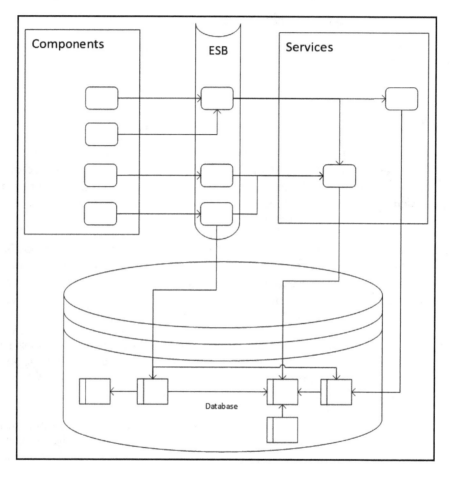

Complex SoA application

Changing one service, or a table in the schema, produces a knock-on effect in the whole application, resulting in those relationships and dependencies needing to be changed, whether they're services, mappings, or even screens as they are all bundled together. In many cases, this causes long release cycles as handling that level of complexity is not an easy task. And nor is the development, configuration, testing, nor deployment.

Even scaling the application could be affected, whether it's a bigger database, more servers for services, a bigger ESB for handling more messages. Since they depend on each other, it is not easy to scale them separately. All of this means that our architecture is coupled and we have created a monolithic application.

Monolithic applications existed before SoA and, in fact, this was one of the things that SoA helped to handle, decoupling the clients from the business domain. Unfortunately, trying to implement SoA drove many applications back to it.

Does this mean that doing SoA will produce a monolith? No. In fact, before the concept of microservices, many architects and developers started to adopt patterns and architectures to handle this problem. This evolved into what we call microservices today.

There were people doing microservices before that name existed; they just called it SoA.

Microservices principles

Defining microservices principles will allow us to build scalable, easy-to-maintain enterprise applications. We will focus on benefits and downsides when we review them. We understand that sometimes there could be some disagreement in some of them; however, we encourage you to review them all. Finally, we know that there are probably dozens or more principles that could be included, but we chose the ones that made most sense in the context of this book.

Defining design principles

We need to choose a set of principles when we design microservices; each of them will have their own advantage that will be reviewed later on in this chapter, but defining them will also allow us to have a consistent approach for different kinds of problems, and will help others understand our architecture.

The key principles that we are going to define are:

- Modelled around business capabilities
- Loosely couple
- Single responsibility
- Hiding implementation
- Isolation
- Independently deployable
- Build for failure
- Scalability
- Automation

Modelled around business capabilities

A well-designed microservice should be modeled around the business capabilities that are meant to be implemented. Designing software has a component of abstraction and we are used to getting requirements and implementing them, but we must consider how everyone, including us, will understand the solution, now and in the future.

When we need to update, or even modify our microservices, we need to abstract back to the original concept that defined it. In that process, we could realize that something was not as we originally understood, or that our design could not evolve. We may even discover that we have to break the boundaries of our business domain and we don't implement the original capability anymore, or that actually it is implemented across a set of different non-related microservices. We could end up coupling our microservices together, and that is something that we want to avoid.

The domain experts of these business capabilities have a clear understanding of how they operate and how those capabilities are combined and used. Working with them could make our microservices understandable for everyone, including our future selves, and will move our services to become not just an abstraction, but a mapping of the original business capability.

Work as closely as you can with your domain experts, it will always benefit you.

We will deep dive more into this topic in the *Domain-Driven Design* section of this chapter.

Loosely couple

No microservice exists on its own, as any system needs to interact with others, including other microservices, but we need to do it as loosely coupled as we can. Let's say that we are designing a microservice that returns the available offers for a giving customer, we may need a relation to our customer, for example, a customer ID, and that should be the maximum coupling that we may accept.

Imagine a scenario that for a component that uses our offers, the microservice needs to display the customer name when it displays those offers. We could modify our implementation to use the customer microservice to add that information to our response, but in doing so, we are coupling with the customer microservice. In that case, if the customer name field changes, for example, to become not just a name but is separated into surname and forename, we need to change the output of our microservice. That type of coupling needs to be avoided; our microservices should just return what information that is really under their domain.

 Remember that our domain experts could help us in understanding if a business capability owns a function; probably the experts in customer offers will know that the customer name is something that is a handle in another business capability.

We need to take care of how we are coupling, not only between microservices, but with everything in our architecture, including external systems. That is one of the reasons why every microservice should own its own data, this including even a database where the data is persisted.

Single responsibility

Every microservice should have responsibility over a single part of the functionality provided by the application, and that responsibility should be entirely encapsulated by the microservice. The design of the microservice should be narrowly aligned with that responsibility.

 We could adopt Robert C. Martin's definition of the principle applied to OOP that said: "A class should have only one reason to change"; for this principle, we can say: a microservice should have only one reason to change.

If we realize that when we need to change a business function within our application, it modifies several microservices, or that a change cascades into non-related microservices, it is time that we reconsider how we design them.

This does not mean that we get to make microservices that do only one operation. Probably it is a good idea to have a microservice that handles the customer operations, like create, find, delete, but probably shouldn't handle operations like adding offers to a customer.

Hiding implementation

Microservices usually have a clear and easy to understand interface that must hide the implementation details. We shouldn't expose the internal details, neither technical implementation nor the business rules that drive it.

Applying this principle, we reduce the coupling to others, and that any change in our details affect them. We will prevent the technical changes or improvements that impact the overall architecture. We should always be able to change when needed, from where we persist our business model, to the programming languages or frameworks that we use.

But we also need to be able to modify our logic and rules, to adapt to any change within our domain without affecting the overall application. Helping to handle change is one of the benefits of a well-designed microservice architecture.

Isolation

A microservice should be physically and/or logically isolated from the infrastructure that uses the systems that it depends on. If we use a database, it must be our database, if we are running in a server, it should be in our server, and so on. With this, we guarantee that nothing external is affecting us and neither are we affecting anything external.

This will help from deployments to performance or monitoring, or even in building our continuous delivery pipeline. It will facilitate how we can be controlled and scaled independently, and will help the ops functions within our team to manage our microservices.

We should move away from the days when a failure in some parts of the architecture was affecting others. Containers are one of the key architectures to effectively archive this principle. We will learn more about this in the *Cloud Native microservices* section of this chapter.

Independently deployable

Microservices should be independently deployable; if not, it probably means that there is some kind of coupling within our architecture that needs to be solved. If we could meet other principles but we fail at this, we are probably decrementing the benefits of this architecture.

Having the ability to deliver constantly is one of the advantages of the microservices architecture; any constraints should be removed, as much as we remove bugs from our applications.

 We should take care of deployments from the beginning of the design of our microservices and architecture; finding a constraint on this area at late stages could have a big impact on the overall application.

Build for failure

It doesn't matter how many tests we do in our microservice, how many controls are in place, how many alerts could be triggered; if our microservice is going to fail, we need to design for that failure, to handle it as gracefully as possible, and define how we could recover from it.

"Anything that can go wrong will go wrong."

– Murphy

When we approach the initial design of a microservice, we need to start working on the more basic errors that we need to handle. As the design grows, we should think of all the edge scenarios, and finally what could go really wrong. Then, we need to assess how we are going to notify, monitor, and control those situations, how we could recover, and if we have the right information and tools for solving them.

Think of these areas when you design a microservice:

- Upstream
- Downstream
- Logging
- Monitoring
- Alerting
- Recovery
- Fallbacks

Upstream

Upstream is understanding how we are going to, or if we are not going to, notify errors to our consumers, but remembering always to avoid coupling.

Downstream

Downstream refers to how we are going to handle, if something that we depend on fails, as another microservice, or even a system, like a database.

Logging

Logging is about taking care of how we are going to log any failure, thinking if we are doing it too often or too infrequently, the amount of information, and how this can be accessed. We should take special care about sensitive information and performance implications.

Monitoring

Monitoring needs to be designed thoughtfully. It is a very problematic situation to handle a failure without the right information in the monitoring systems; we should consider what elements of the application have meaningful information.

Alerting

Alerting is to understand what the signals are that could indicate that something is going wrong, its link to our monitoring and probably to our logging, but for any good design application, it is not enough to just alert on anything strange. We require a deeper analysis on the signals and how they are related.

Recovery

Recovery is designing how we are going to act on those failures to get back to a normal state. Automatic recovery should be our target, but manual recovery should not be avoided since automatic recovery could fail.

Fallbacks

Think about how, even if our microservices are failing, we can still respond to whoever uses them. For example, if we design a microservice that retrieves the offers from a customer but encounters a problem acceding to the data layer, maybe it could return a default set of offers that allows the application to at least have some meaningful information. In the same way, if we consume an external service, we may have a fallback mechanism if that service is not available.

 Fallbacks are a common pattern to prevent a problem within your architecture affecting other parts of the system. If we have a good fallback, our application could work until that problem is fixed.

Scalability

Microservices should be designed to be independently scalable. If we need to increase how many requests we can handle or how many records we can hold, we should do it in isolation. We should avoid that, due to a coupling on the architecture; the only way to scale our application is scaling several components together or through the system as a whole.

Let's go back to the original SoA application example and handle a scenario where we need to scale our offers capability:

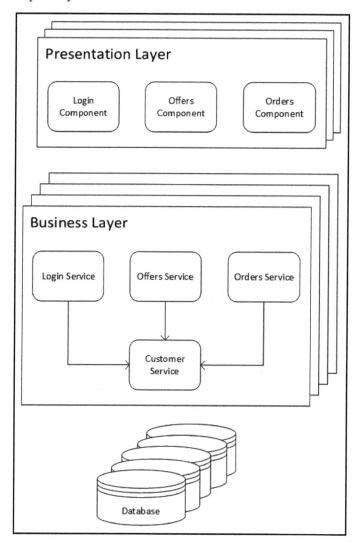

Example of scaling a coupled SoA application

Even if what we need to scale is our offer capability, due to the coupling of the system, we need to do it as whole. We will increase how many instances of the presentation and business layer we have, and we increase our database either with more instances or with a bigger database. Probably, we may need to also update some of those servers as the resources that they require will increase. In a microservices architecture, we could just scale the elements that are needed. Let's view how we could scale the same application using microservices:

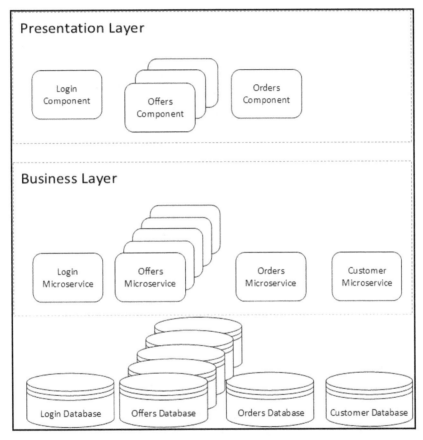

Example of scaling a microservice application

We have just increased what was required for the offers' capability and to keep the rest of the architecture intact, we need to consider that in microservices, those servers are smaller and don't need as many resources due to their limited scope.

In a well-designed microservice architecture, we could effectively have more capacity with less infrastructure since it could be optimized for more accurate use and be scaled independently.

We will review more about this topic in the *Cloud Native microservices* section of this chapter.

Automation

Our microservices should be designed with automization in mind, from building or testing to deployment and monitoring. Since our services are going to be small and they are isolated, the cost to automatize them should be low and the benefits should be high.

With this principle, we benefit the agility of our application and we prevent unnecessary manual tasks having an impact on the system. For those reasons, Continuous Integration and Continuous Delivery should be designed from the beginning of our architecture.

Domain-Driven Design

Using **Domain-Driven Design (DDD)** in our microservices will help us meet our microservices principles, but DDD will also help organize our products teams in ways that will benefit the value that we give from this type of architecture. But first, we need to understand what DDD actually is, and how we could apply it to create a clean architecture.

What is Domain-Driven Design

Domain-Driven Design is a software development approach to connect to an evolving complex model bounding into a core domain.

The term, **Domain-Driven Design,** was created by Eric Evans in his book with the same title.

When we approach a complex system, we usually abstract it to a model that describes the different selected aspects of the system, and how we could use it to solve problems. When multiple models are in play, and the code base of different models is combined, the software becomes buggy, unreliable, and difficult to understand. It is often unclear in what context a model should not be applied. The domain is the sphere of knowledge that the users of our system understand, and what they use to interact with our software; they are the domain experts.

In DDD, we define the context within which a model applies; explicitly set boundaries in terms of team organization, usage within specific parts of the application, and physical manifestations such as code bases and database schemas, keeping the model strictly consistent within these bounds.

Ubiquitous language

In DDD, we should build a common and rigorous language between developers and users. This language should be based on the domain model and will help us have a ubiquitous and fluid conversation with the domain experts, and will prove to be essential when approaching testing.

Since our domain model is part of our software, we should be precise to avoid any ambiguity and evolve both model and language as our knowledge as the domain grows. But when creating software, the usage of the ubiquitous language should not be only in our domain model, but also in our domain logic and even architecture. It will allow a ubiquitous understanding by any team member.

Creating tests that use the domain language help any team member to understand our domain logic.

Bounded context

When a domain model grows, it becomes complicated to have a unified domain model. Sometimes, we face a situation when we see two different representations of a concept, for example, let's examine the concept of family in a large model.

In a shopping platform, we may have the concept of products families, for example, our fabulous 32" LCD screen and the classical 24" CRT screen are part of the screen family. On the other hand, our speed offers and last day offers are part of our limited timed-offer family.

We could see that family may not be exactly the same thing on products and offers, probably they both have a unique name on their model, but in each context they may have a totally different model and logic.

In DDD, we separated them in to bounded contexts, a boundary that surrounds a model. This keeps the knowledge inside the boundary consistent, ignoring the outside world so we could still have our ubiquitous language for our domain model.

Context mapping

In a large application designed for several bounded contexts, we can lose sight of the global view. It is inevitable that the various bounded contexts will need to share or communicate data between each other. A context map is a global view of the system as a whole, showing how our bounded contexts should communicate with each other.

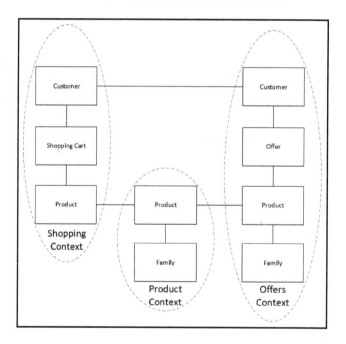

Context map example

This is an oversimplified example that shows three bounded contexts and how they are mapped. In the product context, we have our product and the family that it belongs to. Here, we will have all the operations for this domain context in it and it does not have a direct relation dependency to any other context.

Our offers bounded context has a dependency on the product domain context, but this is a weak relation that should purely reflect the ID of the product that a particular offer belongs to. This context will define the operations that contain the domain logic for this context.

In our shopping bound context, we have a weak relation with the product that belongs to a shopping list and will have the operations for this context. Finally, both offers and shopping concept have a relation with the customer that probably belongs to a separated bounding context.

Using DDD in microservices

Now that we have a clearer understanding of what DDD is, we need to review how we are going to apply it to our microservices. We could start with the following points:

- **Bounded Context**: We should never create a microservice that includes more than one bounded context: it is better if we can map that whole context to a single microservice, something that indicates that our context is really bounded
- **Ubiquitous Language**: We need to ensure that the language that our microservice speaks with is ubiquitous, so the operations and interfaces that are exposed are expressed in the context domain language
- **Context Model**: The model that our microservice uses should be defined within the bounded context and use the ubiquitous language, even for entities that are not exposed in any of the interfaces that the microservices provide
- **Context Mapping**: Finally, we need to review the context mapping of the whole system to understand the dependencies and coupling of our microservices

After reviewing these points, we will notice that we are in fact fulfilling the main principles defined before. Our microservices are modelled around business capabilities, our context domains, are loosely coupled as our context mapping shows, and have a single responsibility as a bound context should. Microservices that implement a bounded context could easily hide their implementation, and they will be nature isolated, so we could deploy them independently. Having those principles in place will make it easy to build for failure, having scalability and automation. Finally, having a microservice architecture that follows DDD will deliver a clean architecture that any team member could understand.

> The ubiquitous language of a well-designed bounded context will make many tasks easy in a microservice life cycle, from working with the domain experts to tests or any tasks for the ops function of our team.

Reactive microservices

Reactive programming is currently a trend topic. This is mainly because of the benefits to implementing software using this new paradigm. Spring Framework 5.0 included numerous changes to give the advantage of this programming model and many new components of the Spring family have evolved to support it. In fact new Spring libraries have been created to add additional support to applications interested in what is called the reactive revolution. Additionally, Spring has rewritten the core of the framework, using reactive technologies that will allow a better technology for the applications that use them. In this section, we will understand the basics and principles of reactive programming and how we could apply it to create reactive microservices.

Reactive programming

We are quite familiar with imperative programming: in our software, we ask to do something and expect a result and meanwhile, we wait, our action is blocked expecting a result. Consider this small pseudo code as an example:

```
var someVariable = getData()
print(someVariable)
```

In this couple of instructions, we will set the content of a variable from the output of a function that will return data; when the data is available, we will print it out. The really important part of this small piece of code is that our program stops until we completely get the data, this is what is called a blocking operation.

There is a way to bypass this limitation that has been used extensively in the past. For example, we could create a separate thread to get our data, but effectively, that thread will be blocked until completion, and if different requests need to handle this, we end up in the situation of creating a thread for each one, possibly using a pool, but finally we will reach a limit of how many of those threads we can handle. This is how most traditional applications work, but now, this could be improved.

Let's see some pseudo code for this in reactive programming:

```
subscribe(::getData).whenDone(::print)
```

What we are trying to do here is to subscribe to an operation and when that operation is complete, send the result to another operation. In this example, when we get the data, we will print the results; the important part of this is that after that sentence our program continues, so it could process other things; this is what is called a non-blocking operation. But this could be applied not just to a single result, we could subscribe into a reactive stream of data, and when the stream starts to flow, it will be calling our function that will be progressively printing the data that we receive.

 A reactive stream is a collection of data that will continuously flow as soon as it is ready, so imagine that instead of querying a database for some results, the database starts sending results as often as it is ready. Many modern database drivers support these concepts.

This new programming model allows us to have high-performance applications to process way more requests than in a more traditional blocking model. This approach utilizes resources more effectively and this could reduce the amount of infrastructure required for our applications. But now we need to understand what are the real principles of reactive programming.

Reactive Manifesto

In 2013, a working group of experts from some of the biggest software companies in the world published the Reactive Manifesto that set the basis of how reactive systems are understood and work, this manifesto is available on `https://github.com/reactivemanifesto/reactivemanifesto`.

Let's review what the Manifesto said:

First, the Manifesto introduces the current landscape of modern applications, focusing on how this demands a new kind of system that needs to respond to way more data and faster than before, and has to be scalable, resilient and fault tolerant. The intention of the Manifesto is to have a coherent approach to those problems and define reactive systems and what benefits we get from them. Many of those topics were discussed in our *Microservices principles* section, so it probably is a good idea to review them, but now we need to do a deep dive of how reactive systems are defined in the Manifesto.

If you would like to sign the manifest or have a PDF version in any language you could go to `http://www.reactivemanifesto.org/`.

Responsive

Modern applications should respond in a timely manner, but not only to the users of the system but also to the responsiveness of our problems and errors; we are long way away from those days where our applications would freeze when something was either taking longer to answer or failing for unknown reasons.

We need to help the users have a seamless and predictable experience so they could progressively work in our system, and doing so with consistent quality, so they will be encouraged to use the system and remove our past stigma with randomized user experiences.

Resilient

We cover much of this topic under our build for failure and isolation principles, but the Manifesto indicates as well that if we fail to have resilience, we tend to affect our responsiveness, something that we should handle.

Some of these issues could be handled, as well as applying correctly our scalability principle, since we could archive resilience by replication and replication, depends on our scalability.

Elastic

Reactive systems should be elastic, so they effectively apply the scalability principle to stay responsive under varying workloads, but more internally, the system itself may have the capability of increasing or decreasing the resources that allocate.

In the older architecture, planning resources was part of our architecture; we design thread pools to handle our request with certain capacity, and we prepare our servers to be able to manage this.

In reactive systems, our services could dynamically fetch more resources if required and free them when they are not needed.

Message-driven

Reactive systems use asynchronous messaging to flow information through the different components with very loosely coupling, that allows us to interconnect those systems in isolation. We could think of this as if we are connecting streams through pipes, one service could subscribe to another to get some information and the second service could be subscribed to a couple of additional services to combine the data and return it back to the original service.

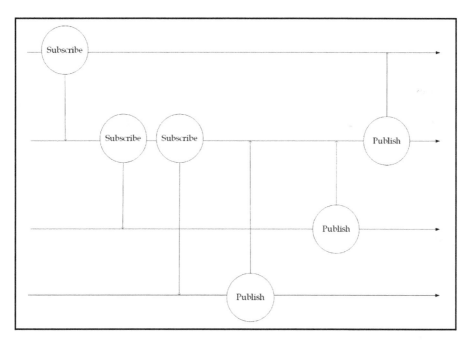

Connecting streams

Each of those services does not know why or how that information is used, so they have little information about the dependencies. This allows us to replace those pieces easily, but as well as handling errors in case of failure, we could simply just create a stream of errors with other receivers that will handle and process them.

But the manifesto speaks about applying back pressure; we need to understand that concept further.

Back pressure

Back pressure is produced when a reactive system is published at a rate higher than the subscriber could handle, in other words, this is how a consumer of a reactive service says: *Please, I am not able to deal with the demand at the moment, stop sending data and do not waste resources* (for example, *buffer memory*).

There is a range of mechanisms for handling this, and they are usually close to the reactive implementation, from batching the messages to dropping them, but right now, we don't need to get into the details, just understand that any reactive system must deal with back pressure.

Reactive frameworks

There are several reactive frameworks that we could use to create reactive applications.

Let's list the more important frameworks:

- Reactive Extensions (`ReactiveX` or `Rx`)
- Project Reactor
- Java Reactive Streams
- Akka

Reactive Extensions

Reactive Extensions is probably one of the most popular frameworks to create reactive systems and support a wider set of platforms and programming languages, from JavaScript using `RxJS`, to Java using `RxJava` or even in `.Net` platforms using `Rx.Net`.

It uses the observable pattern to perform no blocking operations; most of the major reactive systems have been built using `Rx`.

More details can be found at: `http://reactivex.io/`.

Project Reactor

Project Reactor is a JVM reactive library that follows the reactive streams specification and provides a high-level library to easily create reactive applications. Spring Framework 5.0 uses Project Reactor extensively.

More details can be found at `https://projectreactor.io/`.

 Reactive Stream is an initiative to provide a standard for asynchronous stream processing with non-blocking back pressure. You can refer to `http://www.reactive-streams.org/`.

Java reactive streams

Since Java 9, we now have an implementation of reactive streams in the Java platform, some projects are migrating existing Rx code into the new Java 9 libraries.

More details can be found in: `https://community.oracle.com/docs/DOC-1006738`.

Akka

Akka was created by Jonas Bonér, one of the main authors of the Reactive Manifesto, to create a toolkit in the JVM, using Scala, to create concurrent and distributed applications. Akka emphasizes in the actor-base model and has been proven to support high scalable distributed applications.

More details can be found in: `https://akka.io/`.

Reactive microservices

Now that we have a better understanding of reactive systems, we need to consider why we should create reactive microservices. If we look at microservices and remember what drove SoA into microservices, we could view what we need to create more complex applications and produce a better system for our users driving the architecture. With the new reactive programming model, we could create fast and non-blocking software that will utilize better the resources of our infrastructure. We could provide better responsiveness, and we could simplify our development to create highly reusable services that could be connected loosely with each other. And considering how aligned the reactive systems are with our principles and the extensive support of frameworks that they have, we conclude that the way forward for modern microservices is to become reactive.

We will explore more of this topic in `Chapter 4`, *Creating Reactive Microservices*.

Cloud Native microservices

Cloud Native microservices is an approach to building microservices using the advantages of the cloud computing model, focusing on building our microservices and allowing our cloud to deploy, manage, and scale them.

Cloud architecture focuses on how, and now where it will give us the agility to deliver value to our products constantly, but first we need to understand what cloud computing.

Cloud computing

Traditionally, organizations need to take care to provision specific infrastructure for their services. Whenever our applications need to scale, we need to buy more servers for them, many times using costly hardware provided by different vendors, and tanking a considerable amount of time to configure them within our systems.

That infrastructure approach usually is tied to a static capacity, so if we have a peak of load in our app, we need to buy more servers, and after that peak is gone, part of our infrastructure is unutilized, sometimes producing more costs just to maintain it or recycle into new services, and because configure isn't easy, probably we keep it as-is until the next peak comes in. Cloud computing is about using common and cheap hardware to create resources that could be used to dynamically deploy and run multiple applications that can be scaled either automatically or manually.

In a traditional architecture, we may have a database that has a certain capacity and is running in a particular server; if we need to scale it, we either upgrade the server resources, or we buy another server and configure. In a cloud, we create a database server and we scale the number of instances dynamically, and we get rid of unused instances if we don't need them anymore. The resources freed on the cloud could be used for creating or scaling other applications, and the cloud capacity overall could grow just by adding more conventional servers to it.

This approach allows organizations to go to a pay-as-you-go model for their infrastructure, instead of up-front buying servers, they could pay whatever resources their need for a specific period of time. Cloud applications are designed to easily be configured, since the overall idea is to have services that could be easily spawned in a short time. Cloud Native applications will use some kind of system, either provided by the cloud platform or the application itself, to be configured when new instances are created. Since we need to have services running in our cloud that could easily spawn and destroy, the majority of cloud use some kind of containerized applications.

Containers

Containers is a virtualization method that allows an operating system to run an application in isolated user space, controlling and limiting the resources for each contained application. For an application that runs on a container, it will work as if it is running in its own operating system. Most of the containers will not know that they are hosted on another operating system. This allows the host operating system to spawn or destroy those applications without affecting any part of the system and preventing impacts of one container to another.

Since these containers are running on a hosted system, when they need to start they will be faster than in a normal virtualization that requires a new operating system to boot. However, this implied that we could not spawn a container with a different system than the running host, so we could not run a Windows application as a process in a Linux host. Docker is probably the most used container system for cloud applications, however different cloud providers may choose different systems to run their applications. We will learn more about this topic in `Chapter 7`, *Creating Dockers*.

Deployment models

Organizations could choose different deployment models when creating cloud applications, let's review the most common models:

- Private cloud
- Public cloud
- Hybrid cloud

Private cloud

Private cloud is a cloud infrastructure for a single organization, and usually hosted internally in a self-hosted data center. They are usually capital intensive, and require allocation of space, hardware and environmental controls. Their assets have to be refreshed periodically, requiring additional costs. They usually need to be built and managed internally so they are not fully benefited from *focusing on the how, not where* concept.

Public cloud

Public cloud services are delivered in a network that is open for a public audience through a services provider that operates the infrastructure and their data centers. Providers manage access control and security for the organizations that use these services and usually allow connection through the internet, but organizations could choose to use direct connections, if required. They could be seen to be more expensive than a private cloud in the pay-as-you-go model, however considering the cost to build, upgrade and maintain a private cloud that is not always the truth.

> Keep your servers upgraded, security patched, with resilience and reliability is neither easy or cheap, think on the overall benefits of public clouds.

Hybrid cloud

Hybrid clouds try to take the benefits of mixing private and public clouds. An organization could choose to have a private cloud and linked to a public cloud to handle a peak of capacity or additional resources. Some organizations may choose this approach because a critical part of their business needs to be managed in-house in a private cloud but going to a public cloud for other matters.

Service models

There are several service models than can be offered to organizations by different cloud providers, sometimes more than one could be targeted by different products on the provider.

Here are the most common:

- **Infrastructure as a Service (IaaS)**
- **Platform as a Service (PaaS)**
- **Software as a Service (SaaS)**

Infrastructure as a Service

The most basic cloud service model offers computing infrastructure, virtual machines, and other resources, as a service to their users. They usually provide a high-level API or frontend to take care of low-level details such as networking, data partitioning, scaling, security, backup and so on. All of these are usually delivered as raw elements, so the cloud users need to maintain, patch and configure the different servers created by the platform.

Examples of these platforms are:

- Amazon AWS
- Google Compute Engine
- Microsoft Azure Virtual Machines
- Red Hat OpenStack

Platform as a Service

In this service model, the cloud platform provides services that allow customers to develop, run, and manage applications without the complexity of building and maintaining the infrastructure. Often this is facilitated via an application template system, that allows easy creation of new services. For example, providing a standard template for an application type, framework or even programming language.

With this, we could reduce complexity and the overall development of the application can be more effective, and maintenance and enhancement of the application are easier. Usually, the cloud will provide capabilities to patch and configure the different servers.

Examples of these platforms are:

- Google App Engine
- IBM Bluemix
- Microsoft Azure Cloud Services
- Pivotal Cloud Foundry
- Red Hat OpenShift

Software as a Service

In the SaaS model, users gain access to application software, because of which this model is sometimes called on-demand software. All the elements required for that software to run are managed internally on the platform. The cloud users do not need to take care of anything on the platform, neither the cloud, since everything is managed by the provider and is usually a pay-per-user basis.

Examples of these platforms are:

- Google G Suite
- Microsoft Office 365
- Salesforce

Cloud Native microservices

Now that we have a better understanding of cloud computing, we need to think why we should build Cloud Native microservices. If we have been following our microservices principles, we could easily deploy them in a cloud and take advantage of those platforms to benefit further from the microservices architecture. Our microservices could easily be scaled and managed, and since their isolation is a loosely coupling, they could easily fit in containers.

When we create microservices, we could make them cloud aware, and try to benefit from not just being microservices, but becoming Cloud Native applications, so they could fully benefit from the cloud computing model. Spring Cloud provides an easy to use the framework to make our cloud services independent of the cloud platform that they are hosted on and take the full benefits of the platform.

We will expand this further in Chapter 6, *Creating Cloud-Native Microservices*.

 While this book was written, the current snapshot version of Spring Boot 2 was Spring Boot 2.0.0 M7. The code bundle and examples are up to date with that version. Eventually, Spring Boot 2.0.0 will be finally released and the code bundle will be updated accordingly.

Summary

In this chapter, we got a clear understanding of what microservices are, their benefits, and how they evolved from SoA. We now have a set of principles that we could use to create them, and an overview of how Domain-Driven Design will allow us to evolve our applications as per our requirements. Following these designs, we could have a clean architecture that will help our microservices' life cycle, from development to scaling or monitoring. We should be familiar with the benefits of the reactive systems and the cloud computing model, that will allow us to deliver microservices to the next level of industry standards.

But next, we need to start from the basics, so in the next chapter, we will focus on how we can get started on microservices with Kotlin using Spring Boot 2.0, meanwhile, we will learn the tools that we will use to create them.

2
Getting Started with Spring Boot 2.0

Spring is the most popular Java Framework, according to RedMonk's latest reports, and Spring Boot is becoming the starting point for Java Developers interested in microservices.

More details on the RedMonk report can be found here: `http://redmonk.com/fryan/2017/06/22/language-framework-popularity-a-look-at-java-june-2017/`.

In this chapter, we will be developing our first microservice with Kotlin using Spring Boot 2.0 and getting a deep dive into the Spring Boot application structure and how the component scan works. We will get a basic overview of how we could use Maven and IntelliJ IDEA to develop, build, and package our microservices and how to configure and run, and then learn about:

- SpringBoot 2.0
- Spring Initializr
- Maven
- IntelliJ IDEA
- The component scan
- Spring Application Context
- Spring Configuration
- SpEL

Creating a Spring Boot application

When we decide to create a microservice, we may have a clear view of what we want to do, but deciding how we are going to do it may be more complex than anticipated. In this section, we will guide you through the required initial steps. First, we may need to set up a set of tools, which we will use later for managing our projects' files and dependencies to edit our code.

Then, we will take advantage of using Spring Initializr, a service provided by Spring to easily create new Spring Boot applications. Since Spring Initializr generates a project for a chosen build system, in our case Maven, we will learn how to use it effectively. Finally, we may need an IDE that allows us to help in our developer tasks, from debugging to refactoring, IntelliJ IDEA will be our choice for this.

Setting up

In this section, we will install the tools that we will use for building our microservices. They are:

- JDK 8
- Maven 3.5
- IntelliJ IDEA CE 2017.2

Mac OS X users may skip these steps and just use Homebrew (`https://brew.sh/`) to install all the tools required, running just the following commands:

```
/usr/bin/ruby -e "$(curl -fsSL
https://raw.githubusercontent.com/Homebrew/install/master/install)"
brew install caskroom/cask/brew-cask
brew tap caskroom/versions
brew cask install java8
brew install maven
brew cask install intellij-idea-ce
```

Installing JDK 8

First, we need to have installed JDK 8; we are going to use Java SE Development Kit 8u144 or higher, available on `http://www.oracle.com/technetwork/java/javase/downloads/index.html`. Choose Java Platform (JDK) and then the right version for your operating system.

Complete the standard installation. Next, we need to establish JAVA_HOME and PATH variables in the right folders.

UNIX/Mac OS X

Add this to your ~/.bash_profile:

```
export JAVA_HOME=jdk-install-dir
export PATH=$JAVA_HOME/bin:$PATH
```

Windows

From the **File Browser** Window, right-click **This PC** and select **Properties.** Near computer name click on **change settings**, on the Advanced tab, select **Environment Variables** and then add JAVA_HOME to point to where the JDK software is located, for example, C:\Program Files\Java\jdk1.8.0_144.

Testing the installation

Now we can type in our command line:

```
java -version
```

The output should be something like the following:

```
java version "1.8.0_144"
Java(TM) SE Runtime Environment (build 1.8.0_144-b01)
Java HotSpot(TM) 64-Bit Server VM (build 25.144-b01, mixed mode)
```

Installing Maven 3.5

To install Apache Maven, we will use version 3.5.0 or higher, download through https://maven.apache.org/download.cgi.

Unix /MacOS X

Extract the content of the zip or tar.gz using the following command:

```
unzip apache-maven-3.5.0-bin.zip
```

Alternatively, you can use the following:

```
tar xzvf apache-maven-3.5.0-bin.tar.gz
```

Add this to your `~/.bash_profile`:

```
export PATH=/maven-install-dir/bin:$PATH
```

Windows

Extract the content of the zip with your preferred extracting tool.

Now we need to add Maven binaries to the path; so, from the **File Browser** window, right-click **This PC** and select **Properties.** Near computer name, click on **change settings**, on the **Advanced** tab, select **Environment Variables**, and then locate the **PATH** variable and click on **Edit** and then on the browser to choose the directory where Maven was uncompressed and select the binary folder, for example, `c:\maven-install-dir\bin`.

Testing the installation

In order to verify if the installation was successful, we could run the following on the command line:

```
mvn -version
```

Something like this will be displayed:

```
Apache Maven 3.5.0 (ff8f5e7444045639af65f6095c62210b5713f426;
2017-04-03T20:39:06+01:00)
```

Installing IntelliJ IDEA CE 2017.2

Download the right version for your operating system of the IntelliJ IDEA Community Edition. We are going to use 2017.2.2 available at `https://www.jetbrains.com/idea/download/`.

 IntelliJ IDEA is developed by JetBrains which is the company behind the creation of Kotlin. It will work very effectively with our microservices, however other IDEs such as Eclipse, could work as well. The Community Edition is under Apache 2.0 license and could be used to create any kind of application, including commercial and corporate software, more details are in `http://www.jetbrains.org/display/IJOS/FAQ#FAQ-CommunityEdition`.

Follow the default installation steps, and when you're finished, open **IntelliJ IDEA** CE then from the **Welcome** window, click on the **Configure** button at the bottom right of the screen and then **Project Defaults | Project Structure**.

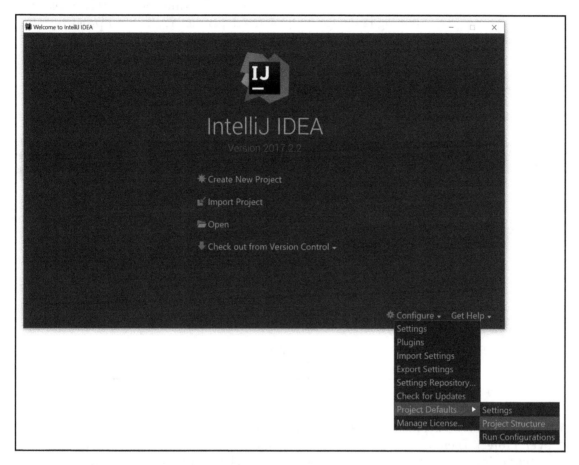

IntelliJ IDEA Welcome Window

In the new window, click on the left-hand side **Project** and in the **Project SDK** option on the right-hand side, click on **new**, then choose **JDK** and browse on your jdk-install-dir.
With this final step, everything should be set up to start creating microservices; for this, we will use Spring Initializr.

Using Spring Initializr

Spring Initializr is a web tool provided by the Spring Framework to create skeletons for Spring Boot applications; this tool allows us to create different kinds of projects for selecting the build system, programming language, or even the dependencies that our project initially has.

Understanding basic usage

First, navigate in your browser to `https://start.spring.io/`:

Spring Initializr Web Tool

We need to choose the project type for the build system that will be used, in our case a **Maven Project**. Then, we must choose our programming language, this will be **Kotlin**, and then the Spring Boot version that will be used, this will be **Spring Boot 2.0.0 M7**.

For the project metadata, we will set up **Group** as `com.microservices` and **Artifact** as `chapter2`.

Now, we need to specify the spring dependencies that we require; in the search box we will type **Web** and select it when it is shown on the list.

Finally, we can click on the **Generate Project** to get a zip file with the contents of the project; the file will be named `chapter2.zip`.

Reviewing the generated project files

If we unzip the file, we will see several files:

```
[.mvn]
  [wrapper]
    maven-wrapper.jar
    maven-wrapper.properties
[src]
  [main]
    [kotlin]
      [com]
        [microservices]
          [chapter2]
            Chapter2Application.kt
    [resources]
      [static]
      [templates]
      application.properties
  [test]
    [kotlin]
      [com]
        [microservices]
          [chapter2]
            Chapter2ApplicationTests.kt
.gitignore
mvnw
mvnw.cmd
pom.xml
```

Maven Files

We will see that the project has a folder named `.mwn` that contains a JAR and properties, a `mwn` and `mwn.cmd` files, this is a **Maven wrapper**: `https://github.com/takari/maven-wrapper`.

Spring uses this wrapper bundling, a Maven version with the project, to ensure that whenever your build your app it uses the same Maven version and is unaffected by any other available Maven version on the system. The `.cmd` file is a windows batch file which invokes the wrapper and the file without extension is the Linux/Mac OS X shell script for the same purpose. We can see that we have created a `pom.xml` with the Maven project definition, an XML file that includes the project structure, dependencies, and how to build the different stages of the project. We will review this file in detail in the next section of this chapter.

Source files

We can see that Spring Initializr has created some source files: one for our main application and another for a default test. These are placed under `src/main/kotlin` and `src/test/kotlin`, respectively.

Resource files

There is a folder to be used for placing resource files, either application properties or static web content. The default `application.properties` is empty and there is no static content, so there are no files inside. We can see a template folder, as Spring could use Thymeleaf for creating server-side html pages, but we are not going to need it in our microservices so this can be deleted.

Gitignore

Spring Initializr has `include` as well as a default `.gitignore` file that has been configured to work effectively with the most popular IDEs.

Understanding advanced usage

Spring Initializr allows for advanced usage; we can click on the **switch to the full version** at the bottom of the page. In this version, we can use some more options. We can customize the project description, the default package name, the packaging of our application that could be JAR or WAR, and the version of Java to use, from 1.7 to 1.8. At the bottom, we can now see all the different dependencies that we could include, classified by category.

 Spring Initializr can also be hosted in your own infrastructure and customized to include your project templates, and provide an API that could be used to generate a project through HTTP requests. See more details at `https://github.com/spring-io/initializr`.

Using Maven

Maven is our chosen build system and we are going to use it whenever we need to compile or package our application; even when we use IntelliJ, it will internally run Maven to build our application. So, we first need to understand some basic Maven concepts.

Life cycle phases

If we've followed the previous section, we have a Maven project already, so we can go to our terminal and from the project folder. Just execute the following command:

```
mvn compile
```

Alternatively, if we use the wrapper, most likely we should use the following:

```
mvnw compile
```

The first time that we run this command, if the application dependencies are not in our system, they will be downloaded and then the application will compile. The next time we launch the same command, if the software has changed it will compile, if not it will inform us that nothing has changed.

What we have set as a parameter when we were invoking Maven, compile, is a Maven life cycle phase. There are many standard phases, let's look at the one that we are going to use:

- **clean**: This will remove files generated at build-time in a project's directory, we should use this when we want to do a build from scratch.
- **validate**: This will validate that our POM file is valid and correct, run it when we want to validate that changes in our POM are working, before building or compiling the whole project.
- **compile**: This will compile our project, but not the tests, it will validate the project first. It will do nothing if the source files have no changes. All phases could be invoked combining them, for example, for a `clean` compilation we could just run:

    ```
    mvnw clean compile
    ```

- **test**: This will run the unit tests on our project, it will compile the project, and compile the tests if they have changed, then run our tests and output the results. If compiling does nothing and there is no change in the tests, this phase will do nothing.
- **package**: This will package our project, ready to be deployed, or installed, before it launches the tests. If they don't pass, the package will fail; so, we can only package if our test passes.

 As you can see, the phases are executed sequentially, running package will run all the previous phases.

Introduction to Maven goals

Maven supports the concept of plugins, a plugin will be attached to a certain phase using a goal, and when that phase is executed the goal is run, if the goal fails the phase fails.

For example, in a Kotlin project a Kotlin plugin will set a goal named `compile` that is attached to the compile phase, so when we run the compile phase, it will compile the Kotlin source code.

We could run a goal from a plugin directly using the format `mvn plugin:goal`, for example in our application we could do the following:

```
mvnw kotlin:compile
```

This will compile our Kotlin code, however if other plugins have attached goals to the compile phase they will not run since we are not executing the phase, just a goal.

Spring Boot provides a plugin to run the application using Maven, which is under the `spring-boot` plugin and the goal name is run, so we could do the following:

```
mvnw spring-boot:run
```

After some seconds, our application will run and we should see this message, among others:

```
Tomcat started on port(s): 8080 (http)
Started Chapter2ApplicationKt in 1.999 seconds (JVM running for 6.747)
```

Currently, if we navigate to `http://localhost:8080`, we can see only an error page as we haven't added anything to our microservice yet. We can stop our application at any time by pressing *Ctrl* + C, but first, we need to understand further what `pom.xml` is.

Understanding the POM file

Maven, when executed, will search for a file named `pom.xml` in the current directory, and if found, it will be used for going through the life cycle phases. This file is usually referred to as a **POM** (**Project Object Model**), the file that defined our project.

The POM that we generate with Spring Initializr contains several tags that specify our project structure, dependencies, and goals for the different life cycle phases. Let's review them individually.

Project definition

At the beginning, the POM file is defined with the group name, project, artifact and version, and other settings such as the packaging method, JAR in our example, and the name and description of the project.

Maven parent

Under the parent tag, we can see a reference to a parent Maven project. This project contains references to the different sprint components, and third-party libraries as well, through a **Bill Of Materials (BOM)** file.

A BOM file indicates the versions that have been certified for a particular project but does not include them. This is a way to indicate what known versions this project works with. We will include the dependencies required as part of the POM project and it will use the versions provided by the BOM by default, so we can omit which versions to choose, however, we could specify different versions if we like to.

 When we are more familiar with the different projects that we like to make and the dependencies versions that we need, it is a good idea to create our own parent project that has exactly what we require.

Project properties

Under the properties tag, it will define the Kotlin compiler version as 1.1.4 and configure it to do incremental builds; we will use Java 8 and the file encoding is set to UTF-8.

Dependencies

For each of the Spring dependencies that we chose in the Spring Initializr, a starter will be listed in the `dependencies` tag. As we only chose web only, one spring dependency is shown, we don't specify which version since the BOM loaded in the parent has already set the default version to be included.

Then, we can see the inclusion of the Kotlin libraries required for our project, referring to the version specified in the Maven properties.

Finally, Spring Boot Test is included in the scope set to test life cycle and is only available in that phase.

Build

The build definition is composed of several elements under the `build` tag; for example, the source and test folders for our project, so the compiler can find them.

The different Maven plugins will be configured within the `plugins` tag.

Mainly, we can see two plugins included, `spring-boot Maven` plugin, as no version is specified it will be determined by the default version on the BOM, and the `Kotlin Maven` plugin to build our Kotlin code. When we compile, we can see a dependency for the compiler plugin is included called all-open, that is required by Spring.

In Kotlin, all classes and members are final by default. This plugin allows that when we use some specific annotations those member are open, so they can be modified, this is required by the `@Autowired` annotation that will be discussed further in this chapter.

Repositories

This final section of the POM Spring Initializr defines the repositories where we find the different dependencies that we require. The spring repositories will not only act as mirrors from the central Maven repository but also include snapshot and milestone versions of the Spring components.

In a Maven project, it will automatically look at dependencies from the central Maven repository, known as Maven Central, if you like to have different repositories it must be specified explicitly. Almost all major software packages are available from Maven Central `https://search.maven.org/`; however, some developers prefer to use JCenter instead `https://bintray.com/bintray/jcenter`.

Now we have more understanding of the POM file and using Maven, but we prefer to use IDEs for most of our work, let's understand how we can use IntelliJ IDEA.

Using IntelliJ IDEA

There is a wide range of IDEs for developing Java applications but currently the major players in the industry are Eclipse and IntelliJ. It is certain that there is a small margin of users with other IDEs as NetBeans, but according to the Java 2017 survey by Baeldung, 45.8% of users are now using IntelliJ, considering that Android Studio is based on IntelliJ IDEA and that JetBrains is the creator of IntelliJ and the Kotlin Language, we consider this an easy starting point for creating microservices in Kotlin.

 For more interesting facts on the Java 2017 survey, check the Baeldung website: `http://www.baeldung.com/java-in-2017`.

Let's start with our generated project in the previous section and add some functionality to it. Meanwhile, to get to know the tool, if you haven't installed and setup IntelliJ, you can go back to the beginning of this chapter to learn how.

Opening our Maven project

In order to open our just created project, follow these steps:

1. Open IntelliJ IDEA
2. In the **Welcome** window, click on the **Open** button
3. Choose the directory that contains the file generated with Spring Initializr; you need to select the folder that contains the POM

4. Click on the **OK** button

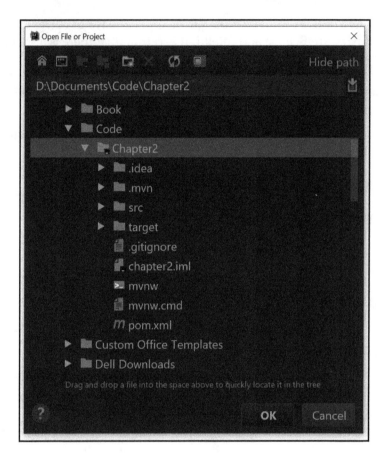

open window

Our project should be imported without any errors and, on the left-hand side of the screen, we should see the project files.

 Sometimes IntelliJ provides suggestions with a popup dialog box at the bottom-right of the screen with tips and suggestions, check what is said as it is usually very helpful.

If we follow the installation step at the beginning of the chapter, IntelliJ should have set the JDK for this project automatically, if not we can always select on the menu **File** | **Project Structure**. Then selecting on the left-hand side of the screen **Project**, then we can verify which JDK we have, or change it, in the right side in the **Project SDK** section.

The **Welcome Window** provides an option to **Import Project** instead to **Open**, but there is no need to use it since IntelliJ works perfectly, opening Maven projects directly without importing.

Executing life cycle phases and goals

IntelliJ provides a Maven project window; if it's not displayed, we can open it selecting on the menu: **View** | **Tool Windows** | **Maven Projects**.

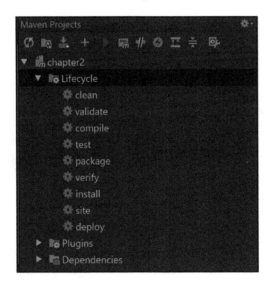

Maven projects window

In this window, we can invoke Maven commands; for example, we can execute the compile life cycle phase by double-clicking on the corresponding option in the Maven project window. This is equivalent to entering this on the command line:

```
mvnw compile
```

Do it so it will open the **Run** window on the bottom-center of the screen where we can see the results of that phase. In that new window, we have a vertical button bar with more options, the top left with the green **play** button will rerun our last command, we can press *Ctrl* + *F5* (*command* + *r* on Mac) to do it through a key binding.

At the top side of the Maven project's windows, we can see another horizontal bar that has additional options, the first one will refresh the Maven project and that should be done if we modify the POM, for example, to add new dependencies.

There are additional options that you can explore, but first, let's take a look at the one looking like a document with a blue **m** on top, that is used to execute a Maven goal. This will open a new window to type Maven goals or life cycle phases to be invoked.

This window has an autocomplete feature, so it will understand our Maven goals and phases, helping us to type our command faster. We could, for example, do a clean compilation typing in the window `clean compile`, this is equivalent to entering on the command line:

```
mvnw clean compile
```

Using this window, we can also directly invoke goals from the Maven plugins defined on the POM. We can, for example, expand the **Plugins** sections on the Maven project's window, then expand `spring-boot` and then double-click on `spring-boot:run`, this will run our microservice. This is equivalent to typing the following in the command line:

```
mvnw spring-boot:run
```

As before, the **Run** window will display the results. Since this command does not immediately end, we will see on the **Run** window a button that allows us to stop process, that effectively will stop our microservice, and we can also rerun this command if we need to, as before with using the **Rerun** button.

While this command is running, if we execute another command in the Maven window a new tab in the **Run** window will appear. We can switch them by pressing on the tab name, and each of them will show a different log and have different buttons to stop or rerun that particular command.

Modifying our microservice

Now, let's navigate in our code so we can edit it for adding some changes.

1. In the **Project** window that is on the top-left side of the screen, expand **src** | **main** | **Kotlin** to view our source files
2. Then we can open our packages until we see our application: `Chapter2Application.kt`

   ```
   package com.microservices.chapter2

   import org.springframework.boot.autoconfigure.SpringBootApplication
   import org.springframework.boot.runApplication

   @SpringBootApplication
   ```

```
class Chapter2Application

fun main(args: Array<String>) {
    runApplication<Chapter2Application>(*args)
}
```

This code will create and run a Spring Boot application, that will launch a microservice listening on `port 8080`.

We can see that, in the gutter area of the **Edit** Window, there is a Kotlin symbol in the same line that our main function is. If we click on it, we can run this function and it will launch our microservice and a **Run** window will appear that allows us to view the log, stop, or restart the process.

Now, let's modify the example code:

```
package com.microservices.chapter2

import org.springframework.boot.autoconfigure.SpringBootApplication
import org.springframework.boot.runApplication
import org.springframework.stereotype.Controller
import org.springframework.web.bind.annotation.RequestMapping
import org.springframework.web.bind.annotation.RequestMethod
import org.springframework.web.bind.annotation.ResponseBody

@SpringBootApplication
class Chapter2Application

@Controller
class FirstController {
  @RequestMapping(value = "/user", method =
arrayOf(RequestMethod.GET))
  @ResponseBody
  fun hello() = "hello world"
}

fun main(args: Array<String>) {
    runApplication<Chapter2Application>(*args)
}
```

If we run the application now and go to the browser to the URL `http://localhost:8080/user/`, we will see the following:

```
hello world
```

This small change adds a controller, basically a class that will handle requests to our microservice, and then we add a mapping for a particular path, in this example /user, then it will output **hello world** to any request.

Now, let's create a new class, in the project window, right-click on our package, and then choose **New | Kotlin File / Class.**

Create files in the project window

A new window will appear asking us for the name, let's type ExampleService and choose **Class** in the **Kind** dropdown.

naming the new file

Then, we will add this code:

```kotlin
package com.microservices.chapter2

import org.springframework.stereotype.Service

@Service
class ExampleService {
  fun getHello(name : String) = "hello $name"
}
```

Finally, we can modify our controller to use this newly created service:

```kotlin
package com.microservices.chapter2

import org.springframework.boot.autoconfigure.SpringBootApplication
import org.springframework.boot.runApplication
import org.springframework.stereotype.Controller
```

```
import org.springframework.web.bind.annotation.PathVariable
import org.springframework.web.bind.annotation.RequestMapping
import org.springframework.web.bind.annotation.RequestMethod
import org.springframework.web.bind.annotation.ResponseBody

@SpringBootApplication
class Chapter2Application

@Controller
class FirstController(val exampleService: ExampleService) {
  @RequestMapping(value = "/user/{name}", method =
arrayOf(RequestMethod.GET))
  @ResponseBody
  fun hello(@PathVariable name: String) =
exampleService.getHello(name)
}

fun main(args: Array<String>) {
    runApplication<Chapter2Application>(*args)
}
```

We set an `exampleService` instance as an attribute of our controller; then, to create our output, we will get the name of the user that we greet as a path variable and we will call the service to get the result.

Executing the service and going to the URL `http://localhost:8080/user/Kotlin`, will output the following:

```
hello Kotlin
```

We will get more understanding of many of the elements in `Chapter 3`, *Creating RESTful services.*

Debugging

IntelliJ IDEA provides a very powerful but simple to use the debugger that we can use to develop our microservices. If we go back to our `ExampleService` class, we can click on the gutter in the same line that our `getHello` method is and we can create a breakpoint, this will be visualized as a red dot on the gutter. Alternatively, we can use the keybinding *Ctrl + F8* in Windows, *command + F8* on a Mac.

Now, we can go back to the application class, click on the **Kotlin** icon but choose to **debug** instead of **run**. If we request again the URL `http://localhost:8080/user/Kotlin`, the debugger should stop the application and show our breakpoint.

When the application is stopped, we can see in the middle-bottom side of the screen, the **Debugger** window:

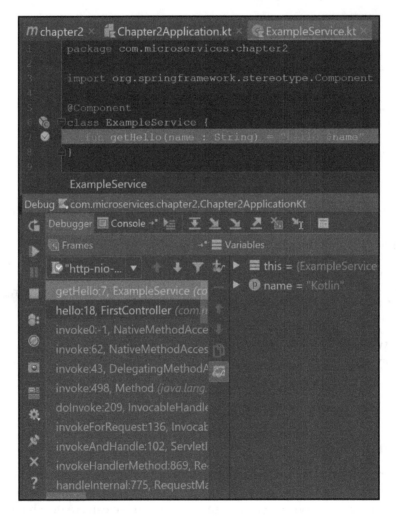

Debugger window

In this window on the left-hand side, we can see a section named **Frames** that allows us to navigate through the stack trace to the point where we were stopped.

On the right-hand side, we can see the variables and their value in the current scope of the debugger. Right-clicking on this allows us to define watches that will monitor values using expressions, or inspect objects to see all attributes and methods for existing values.
On the top, near the tabs, we have a vertical bar that contains buttons to navigate through the execution of the debugger, for example, to step in and out of functions calls, or continue running to the current cursor.

We can invoke the debugger from Maven phases and goals, right-click on the **Maven Projects Windows** to a phase or goal and choose **Debug**.

Tips and Tricks

They are several key bindings and tools that we can use to improve our products using IntelliJ, let's review some of them.

 IntelliJ provides a full range of key bindings for most of the tasks, please have a look at them at this link: `https://resources.jetbrains.com/storage/products/intellij-idea/docs/IntelliJIDEA_ReferenceCard.pdf`.

Execute an action: *Shift + Ctrl + A* on Windows, *shift + command + a* on MacOS. This will allow us to execute any action in the tool, for example, **Run**, **View** Maven projects, **Save** the file, and so on.

Search everywhere: Double *Shift*. This will have a window that allows us to search for everything, from file names to actions, and so on. The search is quite powerful, for example, if we want to open our class, `ExampleService` we can just type **ES** in capitals.

Paste from history: *Shift + Ctrl + V* on Windows, *shift + command + v* on Mac OS, it will display a window with a history on our clipboard.

Iterations and quick-fixes: *Alt + Enter*. This is probably the most powerful tool; many times, we can see a light bulb on the editor, using this key binding where it is will fold options for this, from removing unused imports, to simplify lines of code. Try to experiment with it.

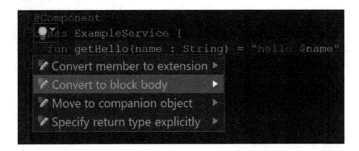

Some quick-fix options

Rename: *Shift + F6*. This will rename anything, from a class name to a file, or even a package, and will also change the code that was using that name; for example, if we rename a function, every call to that function will be renamed.

Refactor this: *Shift + Ctrl + Alt + T* on Windows, *control + T* on MacOS, is a really nice feature to use in any piece of code, from extracting a method to moving a class, changing parameters and functions, and many more.

Many more tricks can be found in this video, it is really long but worth every minute, `https://youtu.be/eq3KiAH4IBI`.

Spring Boot application structure

Microservices, if exposed as web services, either JSON or XML, need to have the corresponding HTTP server capabilities. As well as managing resources and connections to databases, they may consume other services, or even publish data through messages queues.

If you have worked with these kinds of applications before, you may remember how complex they were in order to configure and set up with probably dozens of XML files and properties and in many cases a lot of boilerplate code that initialized many of these systems.

Spring, through Spring Boot, provides a framework that will drastically reduce the boilerplate code and autoconfigure most of the system that we need to use.

Let's review the different components that we will use to create microservices.

Creating an application object

The `@SpringBootApplication` annotation provides a convenient way to bootstrap a Spring application that can be started from a `main()` method. In many situations, you can just delegate to the static `runApplication` method:

```
@SpringBootApplication
class Chapter2Application

fun main(args: Array<String>) {
    runApplication<Chapter2Application>(*args)
}
```

You can see that we have used the `@SpringBootApplication` annotation for marking a class that we will use as our application context. We will learn more about the Spring Application Context shortly.

When a Spring Boot application starts it will autoconfigure all the required systems; if it is a web app, it will start a web application.

 Spring Boot provides an embedded Tomcat server that will start when our application starts. This is a fully functional server, so it's not required to deploy our software in any application server. However, Spring allows us to do it. We will discuss more on this in the section: *Packing and running a Spring Boot application.*

The application will also configure and run any other system that we need, such as a connection pool to a database or a queue.

Defining Spring application context

Every Spring application requires a context, a place where every component is registered. We could think about it like a central directory of object instances created by our application. When we use the Spring Framework and create something, for example, a connection pool, it gets registered in our context or when we create our own components they will be registered as well. So, if in another part of the application we require that component, instead of creating it again we can just access it. However, this provides more advanced features. If we want, for example, to register a controller that handles HTTP requests, as we do in our example, we could just do it anywhere in our classes. Later, the application could use the component scan to find what controllers we have and wire them to web interfaces, without requiring any configuration. Let's understand the component scan better in the following section.

Understanding the component scan

Let's go back to our example that we created previously:

```
package com.microservices.chapter2

import org.springframework.beans.factory.annotation.Autowired
import org.springframework.boot.autoconfigure.SpringBootApplication
import org.springframework.boot.runApplication
import org.springframework.stereotype.Controller
import org.springframework.web.bind.annotation.PathVariable
import org.springframework.web.bind.annotation.RequestMapping
import org.springframework.web.bind.annotation.RequestMethod
import org.springframework.web.bind.annotation.ResponseBody

@SpringBootApplication
class Chapter2Application

@Controller
class FirstController(val exampleService: ExampleService) {
  @RequestMapping(value = "/user/{name}", method =
arrayOf(RequestMethod.GET))
  @ResponseBody
  fun hello(@PathVariable name: String) = exampleService.getHello(name)
}

fun main(args: Array<String>) {
    runApplication<Chapter2Application>(*args)
}
```

We add a controller class, then when our application starts we can see in the log:

```
RequestMappingHandlerMapping : Mapped "{[/user/{name}],methods=[GET]}" onto
public java.lang.String
com.microservices.chapter2.FirstController.hello(java.lang.String)
```

How has the application found our controller and wired into a request mapping?

When the Spring Boot application starts, it will scan all the classes and packages underneath the application context class recursively, and if any class is annotated as a component it will create an instance of it and add it to the Spring Boot application context. This feature is named as the component scan.

 Spring Components instances are named **beans**, so basically we can say that our context is a collection of beans.

Later on, when the Spring Boot application starts, if it's a web application, it will get any class annotated with `@Controller` that is on the context and create a mapping that will get the request coming to our microservice to that class.

Using components

The component scan, while scanning all our packages, needs to understand if any of the classes it found should be added to the spring context as a bean, in order to know which classes need to be added, it will check if the class is annotated with the annotation `@Component`.

 In IntelliJ, we can navigate to a class holding control and click on a class name, for example, if we go to our example, hold control, and click on the `@Controller`.

To visualize this, we can just view the source code of the `@Controller` annotation:

```
@Target({ElementType.TYPE})
@Retention(RetentionPolicy.RUNTIME)
@Documented
@Component
public @interface Controller {
    String value() default "";
}
```

The @Controller annotation uses the @Component annotation, so the component scan will create a bean in the context that will be available to the Spring Framework for any class annotated with @Controller.

Many other Spring classes as well are components, such as @Service that we have used before.

Autowiring

Part of our application may use other parts, for example, a component uses another. If we look at our example, we can see that we created a service named ExampleService and that our Controller uses it as part of the constructor. When the component scan finds our controller, because is annotated with @Controller, it will discover that our class has a constructor that receives parameters.

The constructor parameter is a class that is already in the Spring context since it is as annotated with @Service, so the component scan will get the bean on the context and sends it as a parameter to the constructor of our controller. But sometimes, we may just have this as a parameter within our class, not as a parameter in the constructor, so we can use the @Autowired annotation instead:

```
package com.microservices.chapter2

import org.springframework.beans.factory.annotation.Autowired
import org.springframework.boot.autoconfigure.SpringBootApplication
import org.springframework.boot.runApplication
import org.springframework.stereotype.Controller
import org.springframework.web.bind.annotation.PathVariable
import org.springframework.web.bind.annotation.RequestMapping
import org.springframework.web.bind.annotation.RequestMethod
import org.springframework.web.bind.annotation.ResponseBody

@Controller
class FirstController {
  @Autowired
  lateinit var service: ExampleService

  @RequestMapping(value = "/user/{name}", method =
arrayOf(RequestMethod.GET))
  @ResponseBody
  fun hello(@PathVariable name: String) = service.getHello(name)
}
```

In Kotlin, when we declare something as `lateinit` we just say that this property will be initialized after the constructor. The `@Authowired` will take care of this in this example.

This will have the same results as declaring the service in the constructor, sometimes we may choose this option, especially when we start to have a lot of components and we're not wanting to have all of then passed as parameters in the constructor of the class.

This is called dependency injection and is part of Spring **Inversion of Control** (**IoC**) that allows more advanced users; for example, we could create an interface for our service:

```
package com.microservices.chapter2

interface ServiceInterface {
    fun getHello(name : String) : String
}
```

Then, we could modify the service to use that interface:

```
package com.microservices.chapter2

import org.springframework.stereotype.Service

@Service
class ExampleService : ServiceInterface {
 override fun getHello(name : String) = "hello $name"
}
```

Finally, we could change our controller to be autowired to our interface, `ServiceInterface`, not to the `ExampleService` class:

```
@Controller
class FirstController {

    @Autowired
    lateinit var service: ServiceInterface

    @RequestMapping(value = "/user/{name}", method =
arrayOf(RequestMethod.GET))
    @ResponseBody
    fun hello(@PathVariable name: String) = service.getHello(name)
}
```

What are the benefits of this?

- Hiding implementation details, since we are not directly showing how our service works.
- Decoupling, because tomorrow we can change our service and a new implementation will be used without affecting the consumers of the service.
- Easily handling changes. Spring allows us through Spring Configuration to change which services we use, without changing our code.

We will see more on this in the final section of this chapter.

Packaging and running a Spring Boot application

Now that we know something more about building microservices within Spring Boot, we need to package and run our service. This will teach us how to package a Spring Boot application.

Then, we will analyze the difference between packaging, using JARs or WARs.

Finally, we learn how to run the package applications, and how to creating self-executables JARs.

Packaging

We can package the application using the Maven lifecycle phase **package**, either using the IntelliJ Maven projects window or from the command line.

 We can open a command line to the project folder from IntelliJ using the terminal window from the menu—**View** | **Tool Windows** | **Terminal** or using the *Alt + F12* keybinding.

```
mvnw package
```

Running this from our example project will create a file named chapter2-0.0.1-SNAPSHOT.jar under the target folder.

This command will create a JAR that contains all dependencies required by the application that we are packaging, in our case all the Spring components and third-party libraries that our microservice uses, this is commonly called a Fatjar and allows us to distribute or archive our microservice into a single binary.

Making JARs not WARs

Spring Initializr builds JARs by default, but we can change it to produce WARs instead, if we need to deploy the application in an application server, for example, an external Tomcat server, however, we don't recommend it.

If we go back to our microservices' principles, we should remember that we need to provide a loosely coupled microservice, so if we deploy it in an application server we are coupling our application to it. If tomorrow that server changes, it will affect us.

Spring Boot provides a fully working Tomcat server that starts in seconds and is fully configured for our needs. This allows that everything that is required for our application is under the application control.

 We need to remember to keep updating the version of Spring Boot that we use. The Spring team is constantly doing releases, allowing us to keep up to date with the latest Tomcat versions.

This will benefit our infrastructure as well, as our microservices can run in any box that just has Java JRE on it, no other software or system is required. This makes them a perfect candidate for Cloud-Native microservices that could spawn quickly in any created box or container.

Running Spring Boot applications

Now that we have our microservices packaged, we need to run them, for example from our command line. To run our example, we can just enter the following:

```
java -jar target/chapter2-0.0.1-SNAPSHOT.jar
```

This will launch the application and finally show something like the following:

```
Tomcat started on port(s): 8080 (http)
Started Chapter2ApplicationKt in 2.274 seconds (JVM running for 2.619)
```

We can press *Ctrl + C* to stop it at any time.

This is exactly the same when we execute the goal run on the Spring Boot Maven plugin, but we are not using Maven, we don't need Maven for running our JARs, neither a JDK, just a **JRE (Java Runtime Environment)**.

Creating executable JARs

In a UNIX system, when we need to run a JAR as a process, either `init.d` or `systemd`, we can't just run the JAR itself, we may need to create a shell script to launch our application calling the Java command line, too. Spring, if configured to do so, will create a special script at the beginning of the JAR file that will allow it to be used as an executable.

We need to modify our POM to add this feature, under the `build/plugins` tags:

```
<build>
....
 <plugins>
  <plugin>
   <groupId>org.springframework.boot</groupId>
   <artifactId>spring-boot-maven-plugin</artifactId>
   <configuration>
    <executable>true</executable>
   </configuration>
  </plugin>
....
</build>
```

Now we can directly invoke our JAR as a script, for example from the command line:

```
./target/chapter2-0.0.1-SNAPSHOT.jar
```

This will execute our JAR directly. This allows any UNIX system to execute that script when the JAR is invoked. This is a feature that we may take advantage of to simplify how we start microservices in UNIX systems.

Configuring our application

When we create a Spring Boot application, we may need to use configuration values, things that we want to externalize from the application code itself, or that we may want to change without affecting the main code.

First, we will make some changes in our service and review the different methods to configure the application. Then, we will understand what Spring Expression Language is, and how we can use application profiles. Finally, we will apply our knowledge of configuration to create some conditional beans.

Setting configuration values

There is a time in any application that we may need to have a configurable value, something that we can define outside our main code and that can easily change, let's get an understanding through an example, modifying our service class:

```
package com.microservices.chapter2

import org.springframework.beans.factory.annotation.Value
import org.springframework.stereotype.Service

@Service
class ExampleService : ServiceInterface {
  @Value(value = "\${service.message.text}")
  private lateinit var text: String

  override fun getHello(name : String) = "$text $name"
}
```

In this change, we have introduced a new variable that has a configurable value using the @Value annotation. This will be filled with the configuration value provided by the expression ${service.message} this is a Spring Expression Language query, later on in this section, we will understand that concept further.

 You may notice that we have escaped the $ character using \$, this is because the Kotlin compiler will understand a $ in a string as an inline string, but actually here it is part of a literal string used by Spring.

If we try to run our microservice now, it will not start and will get an error instead:

```
Could not resolve placeholder 'service.message.text' in value
"${service.message.text}"
```

This is because we have defined a configuration value but we haven't provided any configuration to the application. There are several ways to configure a Spring application, but we will review the three that we are going to use to develop microservices:

- Properties
- Yaml
- Command line arguments

Using properties

We can define configuration values using the properties file. Spring Initializr has already created an `application.properties` in the `resources` folder of our project, we can edit it to add this:

```
SERVICE.MESSAGE.TEXT="hello"
```

 You may notice that the label of this **properties file is in uppercase** but the value is referenced in lower case, this is because when we query the configuration we ignore case, and in properties files, it is more standard to have labels in capital letters.

Then, if we run our application it will work as expected, however, the properties file is just a plain text file that may look too complex for multi-level configurations.

Using Yaml

First, we will rename our `application.properties` into `application.yml`, then we can change it to the following:

```
service:
  message:
    text: "hello"
```

This looks better for more complex configurations and will be our preferred method in the rest of the book.

 In this example, the labels in the **yaml file are in lowercase**. This is because, even when able to ignore case as before, it is more standard in yaml files to be either in lowercase or camel case.

Using command-line arguments

Finally, Spring allows us to overwrite configuration variables with command-line arguments. For example, we can run from the command line, as follows:

```
java -jar target/chapter2-0.0.1-SNAPSHOT.jar --service.message.text="other hello"
```

> This can be quite handy in certain conditions; for example, we could overwrite Spring default values, to start a microservice in debug we could run with --debug=true

Understanding Spring Expression Language

We saw in our initial usage of the @Value annotation that we refer to it through an expression ${service.message.default}, this is a query in **Spring Expression Language (SpEL)**.

But Spring provides a range of different kind of expressions that we can use:

- Arithmetic, +, -, *, /, %, ^, div, mod
- Relational, <, >, ==, !=, <=, >=, lt, gt, eq, ne, le, ge
- Logical,& and, or, not, | |, !
- Conditional, as Elvis operators
- Regular Expressions

```
//this should be 7
@Value(value = "#{4+3}")
private lateinit var result1 : Number

//this should be one.value / another.value
@Value(value = "#{ \${one.value} div \${another.value} }")
private lateinit var result2 : Number

//this should be one.value == another.value
@Value(value = "#{ \${one.value} eq \${another.value} }")
private lateinit var result3 : Comparable<Boolean>

//this should be one.value another.value
@Value(value = "#{ \${one.value} and \${another.value} }")
private lateinit var result4 : Comparable<Boolean>
```

```
//this will make that if the variable is not in the config the
value is hello
@Value(value = "\${service.message.simple:hello}")
private lateinit var result5 : String

//will set true if some.value is alphanumeric
@Value("#{ '\${some.value}' matches '[a-zA-Z\\s]+' }")
private lateinit var result6 : Comparable<Boolean>
```

Using profiles

Now that we understand how we can configure our application, we can use the beneficial concept of application profiles. Spring allows us to create profiles within our configuration and we can define the values of our configuration for the different profiles. Later on, we can change the profile that the application uses, and effectively change our configuration values.

Defining profile values

Let's modify our `application.yml` to have some profiles defined:

```
spring:
  profiles:
    active: "development"

service:
  message:
    text: "hello"
---
spring:
  profiles: "development"
service:
  message:
    text: "hi"
---
spring:
  profiles: "production"
service:
  message:
    text: "welcome"
```

First, using `spring.profile.active`, we define what is the current profile for our application, `development`. Then, we define the values for our configuration by default.

After the first `---`, representing a new section in our configuration, we define the values that change from the default values on the development profile. We change the `service.message.simple` to be `hi`. In the next section of our yaml, we define the values for the production profile and we change the value for `service.message.simple` to be `welcome`.

Executing with profiles

If we run our application as usual with the following command:

```
java -jar target/chapter2-0.0.1-SNAPSHOT.jar
```

When we navigate to `http://localhost:8080/user/Kotlin`, we should see the following:

```
hi Kotlin
```

Since the default profile is developing the variable for `service.message.simple` get the value for that profile that is `hi`.

If we like to run the application with a different profile, we can just run it like this:

```
java -jar target/chapter2-0.0.1-SNAPSHOT.jar --
spring.profiles.active="production"
```

When we navigate back to `http://localhost:8080/user/Kotlin`, we should see the following:

```
welcome Kotlin
```

Using profiles, we can change our values for different needs, sometimes it may be needed because of the different environments that the application runs on, but another usage could be because we want our tests to use a dummy database instead of the real one; so, we change the connection details per profile.

Creating conditional beans

In our example microservice, we define a service and the component scan creates a bean for it automatically. Later on, when our controller needs an instance of the bean, it gets injected through the `@Autowired` mechanism.

However, sometimes things get a bit more complex and deciding which bean is injected may require some of our configurations, so let's understand how we could do this.

Creating beans explicitly

Let's go back to our service and remove the `@Service` annotation. If we try to run the application now we get an error:

```
Field exampleService in com.microservices.chapter2.FirstController required
a bean of type 'com.microservices.chapter2.ServiceInterface' that could not
be found.
```

Our controller requires a bean that does not exist, since this class is no longer a component, the component scan will not create a bean for it. We can modify our application class, that holds our Spring application context, to create the bean defining a function that returns a new instance.

```
package com.microservices.chapter2

import org.springframework.beans.factory.annotation.Autowired
import org.springframework.boot.autoconfigure.SpringBootApplication
import org.springframework.boot.runApplication
import org.springframework.context.annotation.Bean
import org.springframework.stereotype.Controller
import org.springframework.web.bind.annotation.PathVariable
import org.springframework.web.bind.annotation.RequestMapping
import org.springframework.web.bind.annotation.RequestMethod
import org.springframework.web.bind.annotation.ResponseBody

@SpringBootApplication
class Chapter2Application{
  @Bean
  fun exampleService() : ServiceInterface = ExampleService()
}
```

Note that we have defined the function to return the interface, not the concrete class, so as to not expose the implementation as a bean, just the contract.

If we run the application now, it should be working since we explicitly created the bean that the controller required, so the `@Autowired` will be able to inject the right bean.

Defining an additional bean

Let's create another service class; I'm going to name it `AdvanceService`:

```
package com.microservices.chapter2

import org.springframework.beans.factory.annotation.Value

class AdvanceService : ServiceInterface {
  @Value(value = "\${service.message.text}")
  private lateinit var text: String
  private var count = 1

  override fun getHello(name: String) : String {
    count++
    return "$text $name ($count)"
  }
}
```

We could add it to the application context as before:

```
@SpringBootApplication
class Chapter2Application{
  @Bean
  fun exampleService() : ServiceInterface = ExampleService()

  @Bean
  fun advanceService() : ServiceInterface = AdvanceService()
}
```

However, if we run the application now, we get a new error:

```
field service in com.microservices.chapter2.FirstController required a
single bean, but 2 were found:
  - exampleService: defined by method 'exampleService' in
com.microservices.chapter2.Chapter2Application
  - advanceService: defined by method 'advanceService' in
com.microservices.chapter2.Chapter2Application
```

This is because Spring finds two beans of the desired type by the controller and cannot decide which one to choose.

Defining beans with conditionals

We can modify our application class to load the bean base on a value using SpEL:

```
package com.microservices.chapter2

import org.springframework.beans.factory.annotation.Autowired
import org.springframework.boot.autoconfigure.SpringBootApplication
import org.springframework.boot.autoconfigure.condition.ConditionalOnExpression
import org.springframework.boot.runApplication
import org.springframework.context.annotation.Bean
import org.springframework.stereotype.Controller
import org.springframework.web.bind.annotation.PathVariable
import org.springframework.web.bind.annotation.RequestMapping
import org.springframework.web.bind.annotation.RequestMethod
import org.springframework.web.bind.annotation.ResponseBody

@SpringBootApplication
class Chapter2Application{
  @Bean
  @ConditionalOnExpression("#{'\${service.type}'=='simple'}")
  fun exampleService() : ServiceInterface = ExampleService()

  @Bean
  @ConditionalOnExpression("#{'\${service.type}'=='advance'}")
  fun advanceService() : ServiceInterface = AdvanceService()
}
```

Then, we can modify our configuration to define which service bean will be enabled:

```
spring:
  profiles:
    active: "development"

service:
  message:
    type: "simple"
    text: "hello"
---
spring:
  profiles: "development"
service:
```

```
  message:
    text: "hi"
---
spring:
  profiles: "production"
service:
  message:
    type: "advance"
    text: "welcome"
```

Then we can run the application again, and everything should work as initially.

Running different configurations

Since our application is now configured, we can use the command line to run multiple variants of the beans and their configuration.

For example, running the advance service:

```
java -jar target/chapter2-0.0.1-SNAPSHOT.jar --
service.message.type="advance"
```

When we visit our microservice URL `http://localhost:8080/user/Kotlin`, we should see the numbers increase per request:

```
hi Kotlin (1)
```

Now, if we run in our production profile, without specifying the service type:

```
java -jar target/chapter2-0.0.1-SNAPSHOT.jar --
spring.profiles.active="production"
```

We should get as output, the number should increase with new requests:

```
welcome Kotlin (1)
```

This customization will allow us to not only change what values our microservices get from the configuration, even what components we use for certain functionalities, without changing our code.

We could archive similar functionality with several other conditional beans that Spring provides. Take a look at the spring documentation: `https://docs.spring.io/spring-boot/docs/2.0.0.BUILD-SNAPSHOT/reference/htmlsingle/#boot-features-condition-annotations`

Summary

Now we have a set of tools that we understand and will boost our productivity when creating microservices. When we create new microservices, instead of starting from scratch, we have to learn how to use Spring Initializr and how to customize it for our needs. We understand now what the component scan is and how by using components we can decouple our microservices implementation and we are ready to configure our microservices using the flexible Spring Configuration.

Now it's time to create more advanced microservices. For starters, we will do a deep dive into creating RESTFul APIs in the next chapter. There, we will learn how we can handle requests, and produce responses, or even handle errors, and how we can use HTTP verbs and status to produce our ubiquitous language for the users of our API.

3
Creating RESTful Services

RESTful APIs are present in most modern applications we use every day, from reading Twitter messages or visiting Facebook pages to reading our emails or doing a Google search. With a lightweight communication protocol and an emphasis on resources, states, and verbs, they have become a natural language for the interchange of information through the HTTP protocol.

In this chapter, we will understand how we can create our own RESTful APIs using Kotlin and the Spring framework. We will learn how we can receive parameters, and how HTTP verbs and status will make our APIs define their ubiquitous language. We spoke about a ubiquitous language in our *Domain-Driven Design* section in Chapter 1, *Understanding Microservices*.

Furthermore, we will learn how to handle JSON requests and responses in our APIs. And finally, we will review how Spring allows us to handle errors in our microservices.

In this chapter, you will learn about:

- RestController
- Request Mapping
- Path Variable
- RequestParam
- Response Entity and Response Body
- Controller Advice

Understanding RestController

Any RESTful API needs to answer requests coming from their client; these requests are handled in Spring by a controller object. In this section, we will understand what a controller actually is and how the `RestController` will help us to create our first component in a RESTful API.

What is a controller

Each request coming to a RESTful API is a stateless message that mainly will:

- Ask for a resource
- Update a resource
- Create a resource
- Delete a resource

Those requests will use JSON as the mechanism to interchange information.

 JavaScript Object Notation (JSON) is a human-readable data format to transmit objects. It is a language-independent data format, but it was derived from JavaScript. Most programming languages include code to generate and parse JSON-format data.

Requests in a Spring web application are handled by a controller, a specialized component whose mission is to handle requests from a client and send responses back. Controllers can be used for a variety of communication protocols, but since we are going to do a RESTful API, we will use a `RestController`.

`RestController` will specify that our controller will handle the request and output a body; this will help us create our responses.

Creating a RestController

For creating our controller, we will start generating a new Spring Boot Application using Spring Initializr, visiting the website: `https://start.spring.io/`.

We learned how we could use Spring Initializr in `Chapter 2`, *Getting Started with Spring Boot 2.0*. You can look at the section Using Spring Initializr to find out more information.

To create a new project, we will choose **Maven project** with **Kotlin** and **Spring Boot 2.0.0 M7**. in Spring Initializr. For the project metadata, we will set a **Group** `com.microservices`, and **Artifact** `chapter3`, and as **Dependencies**, we will include **Web**.

Now, we will unzip the generated project and open it with IntelliJ IDEA. In the **Project** window, we will right-click in our package, **com.microservices**, and we will choose in the drop-down menu, **Kotlin File/Class**. In the new dialog, we will choose to create a class named `CustomerController`, and we will write the following code:

```
package com.microservices.chapter3

import org.springframework.web.bind.annotation.RequestMapping
import org.springframework.web.bind.annotation.RequestMethod
import org.springframework.web.bind.annotation.ResponseBody
import org.springframework.web.bind.annotation.RestController

@RestController
class CustomerController {
  @RequestMapping(value = "/customer", method = arrayOf(RequestMethod.GET))
  fun getCustomer() = "hello from a controller"
}
```

If we insert in our browser the URL `http://localhost:8080/customer`, we will get a message saying `"hello from a controller"`.

Since RESTful services are about returning resources, let's create a class that represents a resource, for example, a customer creating a class named `Customer`:

```
package com.microservices.chapter3

data class Customer(var id: Int = 0, var name: String = "")
```

A data class is a convenient class in Kotlin that allows us to define a class that will have some attributes, attributes that cannot change after creation using `val`, or attributes that can change using `var`.

Kotlin will provide `equals()`, `hashCode()`, `toString()` automatically for those classes, or even the copy or the assignment operator.

Data Classes are a very useful replacement of the traditional POJO classes, Plain Old Java Objects. And they can reduce drastically the amount of boilerplate code that we need in our classes. To learn more about them, you can look at the entry in the Kotlin documentation: `https://kotlinlang.org/docs/reference/data-classes.html`.

Then, we can modify our controller as:

```
@RestController
class CustomerController {
  @RequestMapping(value = "/customer", method = arrayOf(RequestMethod.GET))
  fun getCustomer() = Customer(1, "Kotlin")
}
```

If we go back to our URL `http://localhost:8080/customer`, we will now get a JSON response:

```
{"id":1,"name":"Kotlin"}
```

Understanding our controller

In our example, we have created a controller using the Spring annotation `@RestController`. This controller will be picked up by the component scan, at the application startup and will be added to our Spring context as a bean, as we understood in `Chapter 2`, *Getting Started with Spring Boot 2.0*.

In this controller, we have set a mapping using `@RequestMapping`, for the URL `/customer`, to accept `GET` requests. Since it is a `RestController`, the response will output as a JSON Object.

This mapping will be autoconfigured by Spring Boot and wired into our web application. If we check our application log when we start the microservice, we can see, among other messages:

```
s.w.s.m.m.a.RequestMappingHandlerMapping : Mapped
"{[/customer],methods=[GET]}" onto public
com.microservices.chapter3.Customer
com.microservices.chapter3.CustomerController.getCustomer()
```

When everything is up and running for each request to the mapped URL, our method will be executed and a new instance of the `Customer` object will be created and converted to JSON to be sent back as a response to the request.

If you just look at the lines of code, we can just write a few of them and we have a fully functional REST service. This is one of the reasons why many developers use Spring and Spring Boot; they will get very productive. Try to fully utilize the benefits of Spring for maximizing your productivity as well.

Path and request parameters

Now that we have an understanding of how we can return data in a controller, we should learn how we can ask for a particular resource so we can filter the information and return it as a response. In RESTful APIs, when an application invokes our services for a particular resource, it will query through the URL path, the desired information to be returned.

For example, if an application invokes our API with the URL /customer/1, it is indicating that the resource that has been queried is a particular customer 1 in this example.

But RESTful APIs also allow us to extend a request further providing additional information through parameters.

An application could invoke our API using the URL /customers, indicating the need to receive the customer list. But that URL could provide an additional parameter to specify a filter, for example, to search customers by name giving the URL /customers**?nameFilter="lin"**.

We should never filter the resource that's been requested through request parameters. In RESTful APIs, this is always done through path variables.

Creating a map of customers

But before exploring how we can answer a path request, we need to have a set of customers that we could use, so we could filter them in our new requests.

First, let's modify our application to create a bean that represents our customers:

```
package com.microservices.chapter3

import org.springframework.boot.autoconfigure.SpringBootApplication
import org.springframework.boot.runApplication
import org.springframework.context.annotation.Bean
```

```kotlin
import java.util.concurrent.ConcurrentHashMap

@SpringBootApplication
class Chapter3Application {
  companion object {
    val initialCustomers = arrayOf(Customer(1, "Kotlin"),
        Customer(2, "Spring"),
        Customer(3, "Microservice"))
  }

  @Bean
  fun customers() = ConcurrentHashMap<Int,
Customer>(initialCustomers.associateBy(Customer::id))
}
```

This code creates a hashmap and adds it to the Spring Context as a bean; we chose to use a concurrent version since we don't want to modify this map as we may end up with a synchronization problem, such as when different requests access the same element on the map. Now that our bean is ready, we can autowire it into our controller:

```kotlin
package com.microservices.chapter3

import org.springframework.beans.factory.annotation.Autowired
import org.springframework.web.bind.annotation.RequestMapping
import org.springframework.web.bind.annotation.RequestMethod
import org.springframework.web.bind.annotation.RestController
import java.util.concurrent.ConcurrentHashMap

@RestController
class CustomerController {
  @Autowired
  lateinit var customers : ConcurrentHashMap<Int, Customer>

  @RequestMapping(value = "/customer/", method =
arrayOf(RequestMethod.GET))
  fun getCustomer() = customers[2]
}
```

The @Autowired annotation will get our bean into our controller, so it can use it to answer requests. In this example, we will just return the customer with id 2.

 Beans, the Spring Context, and the @Autowired annotation were reviewed in Chapter 2, *Getting Started with Spring Boot 2.0* .

If we go back to our URL `http://localhost:8080/customer`, we will now get a JSON response:

```
{"id":2,"name":"Spring"}
```

Getting path variables

In Spring, we can get values coming into the URL using the annotation `@PathVariable`. Let's modify our controller to illustrate how:

```
package com.microservices.chapter3

import org.springframework.beans.factory.annotation.Autowired
import org.springframework.web.bind.annotation.PathVariable
import org.springframework.web.bind.annotation.RequestMapping
import org.springframework.web.bind.annotation.RequestMethod
import org.springframework.web.bind.annotation.RestController
import java.util.concurrent.ConcurrentHashMap

@RestController
class CustomerController {
  @Autowired
  lateinit var customers : ConcurrentHashMap<Int, Customer>

  @RequestMapping(value = "/customer/{id}", method =
arrayOf(RequestMethod.GET))
  fun getCustomer(@PathVariable id : Int) = customers[id]
}
```

If we go back to our URL `http://localhost:8080/customer/2`, we will now get this JSON response:

```
{"id":2,"name":"Spring"}
```

Understanding path variables

Spring has mapped our new URL to receive a parameter. We have specified that its name will be an `id` using curly braces on the URL, `/customer/{id}` in our example.
Then, we will create an argument for our method `getCustomer` that is named exactly `id`, and we have annotated this method with the annotation `@PathVariable` and will specify its type to be an `Int`.

When Spring is autoconfiguring our controller, we will understand this annotation and will map the value pass in the URL to the value required to our method, and it will convert it to the right data type specified. This is a very powerful feature that allows us to easily do mapping on path variables in our methods without requiring any kind of configuration.

Defining request parameters

Now, we can improve our mapping by adding request variables that we can use to further understand the request, but first, let's create a new method in our controller to return a list of customers:

```
@RequestMapping(value = "/customers", method = arrayOf(RequestMethod.GET))
fun getCustomers() = customers.map(Map.Entry<Int,
Customer>::value).toList()
```

If we invoke this new URL http://localhost:8080/customers, in our microservice, we will get this result:

```
[{"id":1,"name":"Kotlin"},{"id":2,"name":"Spring"},{"id":3,"name":"Microser
vice"}]
```

We have just transformed our map of customers into a list, and outputted in a new method. But now if we need to filter our customer list, for example, by some part of the customer name, we can modify our new method:

```
@RequestMapping(value = "/customers", method = arrayOf(RequestMethod.GET))
fun getCustomers(@RequestParam(required = false, defaultValue = "")
nameFilter: String) =
    customers.filter {
      it.value.name.contains(nameFilter, true)
    }.map(Map.Entry<Int, Customer>::value).toList()
```

Now, when we request this new URL http://localhost:8080/customers?nameFilter=in, we should get the following response:

```
[{"id":1,"name":"Kotlin"},{"id":2,"name":"Spring"}]
```

However, if we request the previous URL without the param, we will get the same output as before.

String.contains a powerful function. We use it to filter if the name of a customer contains a certain letter and the second parameter of the String.contains function is to set that we want to ignore upper/lower case differences.

Understanding request parameters

In RequestMapping, we do not define parameters using the URL as we did in path variables. We declared them as parameters in our functions and annotated with the @RequestParam annotation. In the annotation, we can specify if the parameter is a required parameter, and if it has a default value, so if it is not present, that value will get injected in our mapping method.

The default value must always be a string, and Spring will convert it back to any other type automatically. We can define as many parameters as we like, and they will be separated with and in the URL. With this last addition, we can start to create more flexible APIs that will handle those parameters to tweak our functionality.

Be cautious about how many parameters we use, and what they are for. If you are starting to make an API behave really differently because of something in the parameters, it could be an indication that a different API may be required.

HTTP verbs and statuses

In RESTful APIs, we use standard HTTP verbs to indicate what we need to do with a particular resource. These verbs define what the client needs to do, but we need to answer in our microservice what response we give back.

For example, when a client asks for a specific customer using the URL http://localhost:8080/customer/1 with the HTTP verb GET, we can answer back with a status **200 OK**, or with a **404 NOT FOUND,** if we don't find the customer.

This two-way communication becomes part of a conversation between the client and the API and will form our ubiquitous language.

Standard HTTP verbs and statuses

In RESTful APIs, HTTP verbs and statuses are very flexible, and our application can decide how to use them, but there are a set of standard and well-known patterns to combine them.

Single resources

Considering that we are using an API that provides a resource through a URL, for example `/customer`, we can use:

URL	VERB	STATUS	MEANING
/customer/1	GET	**200 OK**	We asked for a specific customer, and got back the result
/customer/1	GET	**404 NOT FOUND**	We asked for a specific customer, but they could not be found
/customer	POST	**201 CREATED**	We asked to create a new customer, and it was created
/customer	POST	**400 BAD REQUEST**	We asked to create a new customer, but the data was not correct
/customer/1	PUT	**202 ACCEPTED**	We asked to update a customer, and it was updated correctly
/customer/1	PUT	**404 NOT FOUND**	We asked to update a customer, but the customer was not found
/customer/1	DELETE	**200 OK**	We asked to delete a customer, and we did it correctly
/customer/1	DELETE	**404 NOT FOUND**	We asked to delete a customer, but it could not be found

Collections

If we are using an API to provide a collection of resources, for example, a list of customers giving the URL/customers, we can use:

URL	VERB	STATUS	MEANING
`/customers/`	GET	**200 OK**	We asked for a list of customers and got back the result
`/customers/`	GET	**204 NO CONTENT**	We asked for a list of customers, and there was none
`/customers/?name=son`	GET	**200 OK**	We asked for a list of customers filtering the results
`/customers/?name=son`	GET	**204 NO CONTENT**	The filtering of customers returned no results
`/customers/?name=#`	GET	**400 BAD REQUEST**	The filtering for customers was incorrect

Generic errors

Sometimes APIs can return just generic errors, in many cases, regardless of the verb used; the more common ones are:

STATUS	MEANING
400 BAD REQUEST	We could not answer the request because it is incorrect
401 UNAUTHORIZED	We don't have the credentials for that operation
403 FORBIDDEN	We may have the credentials but we are not allowed to do that operation
422 UNPROCESSABLE ENTITY	We could not process the request; it may be correct, but it is not valid for this operation
500 INTERNAL SERVER ERROR	We have not been able to process the request

A 500 error is really something critical in our application, sometimes it means that it could not even recover from it, such as losing connection to a database or another system. We should never return any 5xx range error with a functional meaning, use 4xx ranges instead.

Handling HTTP verbs

Spring allows us to define the HTTP verbs that our controller method will handle. We do this using the parameter method in our `@RequestMapping`.

For example, in our controller:

```
@RequestMapping(value = "/customer/{id}", method =
arrayOf(RequestMethod.GET))
fun getCustomer(@PathVariable id: Int) = customers[id]
```

This parameter is actually an array, it can be changed, if required, to accept more than one method. For example, as:

```
@RequestMapping(value = "/customer/{id}", method =
arrayOf(RequestMethod.GET, RequestMethod.POST))
fun getCustomer(@PathVariable id: Int) = customers[id]
```

With this change, we set that we will accept either HTTP GET or HTTP POST in this method, however, we recommend you keep one method per function in your controller. If we follow our recommendation, GET will get a resource, and a POST will create a resource, then our method will try to do two different things, and for that, we should have two different methods.

We should always remember the single responsibility principle when designing our method. A method should have only one reason to change.

We already defined how we can handle our HTTP GET in our previous examples. let's review how we can handle other HTTP verbs.

Handling HTTP POST

We will use HTTP POST when we try to create a resource, so if we try to add new customers, we will post a new resource to our customer URL /customer/. We can do this simply with this code:

```
package com.microservices.chapter3

import org.springframework.beans.factory.annotation.Autowired
import org.springframework.web.bind.annotation.*
import java.util.concurrent.ConcurrentHashMap

@RestController
class CustomerController {
  @Autowired
  lateinit var customers : ConcurrentHashMap<Int, Customer>

  @RequestMapping(value = "/customers", method =
arrayOf(RequestMethod.GET))
  fun getCustomers() = customers.map(Map.Entry<Int,
Customer>::value).toList()

  @RequestMapping(value = "/customer/{id}", method =
arrayOf(RequestMethod.GET))
  fun getCustomer(@PathVariable id : Int) = customers[id]

  @RequestMapping(value = "/customer/", method =
arrayOf(RequestMethod.POST))
  fun createCustomer(@RequestBody customer: Customer) {
    customers[customer.id] = customer
  }
}
```

Here, we have used the annotation @RequestBody to specify that we are sending a object. Since this is within a @RESTController, the expected object should be in JSON format. For this example, we can use:

```
{
 "id": 4,
 "name": "New Customer"
}
```

We can simply test this request using cURL:

```
curl -X POST \
 http://localhost:8080/customer/ \
 -H 'content-type: application/json' \
 -d '{
 "id": 4,
 "name": "New Customer"
}'
```

One important thing to consider in that command is that we have set the content-type header to be application/json and this is because we need to in order for Spring to understand that it is a JSON body that we are sending. After executing the command, we can now do a request to a list of customers at the URL http://localhost:8080/customers, to get the following output:

```
[{"id":1,"name":"Kotlin"},{"id":2,"name":"Spring"},{"id":3,"name":"Microser
vice"},{"id":4,"name":"New Customer"}]
```

One thing that we should remember in this example is that the id of the customer is sent in the object and is not present in the URL, and this follows our recommendations of URLs and verbs at the beginning of this section.

Handling HTTP DELETE

When we use the HTTP DELETE, we are asking our service to delete a given resource, and we will do it in the form of /customer/id. This specifies which resource needs to be deleted among all of them:

```
@RequestMapping(value = "/customer/{id}", method =
arrayOf(RequestMethod.DELETE))
fun deleteCustomer(@PathVariable id: Int) = customers.remove(id)
```

For this operation, we have just set the corresponding HTTP verb in the method, and as a path variable, the id of the resource to be deleted. Then, we simply remove it from our customer map. We don't need to have any customer as a body parameter since with the id, we could just remove our resource.

We could test this operation sending a simple request using cURL:

```
curl -X DELETE http://localhost:8080/customer/4
```

After executing the command, we can now do a request to a list of customers at the URL `http://localhost:8080/customers`, to get the output:

```
[{"id":1,"name":"Kotlin"},{"id":2,"name":"Spring"},{"id":3,"name":"Microser
vice"}]
```

Handling HTTP PUT

When we use the `HTTP PUT`, we are asking our service to update a given resource, and we will do it in the form of `/customer/id`.This specifies which resource needs to be updated among all of them. But we need to send a customer as `JSON` body as well so we get exactly what we need to update. In RESTful APIs, the concept is that resources are held in the client and updated back to the server when required. Then, this object represents a state of the object which was queried.

But before implementation, we may need to consider one thing. What happens if the resource that we request to update changes the `id`, is it a valid scenario? It depends on how we have defined our API to work, and it could be actually something that we like to do, so let's implement it in that particular scenario:

```
@RequestMapping(value = "/customer/{id}", method =
arrayOf(RequestMethod.PUT))
fun updateCustomer(@PathVariable id: Int, @RequestBody customer: Customer)
{
  customers.remove(id)
  customers[customer.id] = customer
}
```

For the implementation of this method, we have just chosen to do what our delete and create does. If we execute this `cURL` request:

```
curl -X PUT \
 http://localhost:8080/customer/2 \
 -H 'cache-control: no-cache' \
 -H 'content-type: application/json' \
 -d '{
 "id": 4,
 "name": "Update Customer"
}'
```

After executing the command, we can now do a request to a list of customers at the URL `http://localhost:8080/customers`, to get an output:

```
[{"id":1,"name":"Kotlin"},{"id":2,"name":"Spring"},{"id":4,"name":"Update
Customer"}]
```

Using verb and mapping annotations

We have used `@RequestMapping` in our example, giving the method as a parameter to the annotation, and that is okay but maybe it is too much code for such a simple thing; Spring provides helpers to reduce this declaration:

```
@GetMapping(value = "/customer/{id}")
fun getCustomer(@PathVariable id : Int) = customers[id]
```

For a `GET` request, we could use `@GetMapping`, and we don't need to specify the method; there are equivalent annotations for `POST`, `PUT`, and `DELETE`, `@PostMapping`, `@PutMapping`, and `@DeleteMapping` respectively.

Now with this final change, we complete our verbs code, but we can see some level of duplication in our `PUT` verb which doesn't look right, so we probably need to explore concepts about how we can implement this better.

Implementing a service layer

We have been handling several different HTTP verbs in our implementation, and this is okay, but in doing so, we create some duplication in our code that we may need to remove. For example, updating our customer was combining what our delete and create do.

But there is another thing that we haven't noticed. In a way, we are coupling our API handling, our controller, too, however, our model is stored, making the customer bean a part of our controller that has created that coupling.

Right now, our customers' list is a map, tomorrow, we may want to store it in a database, or handle in a different way, affecting our controller for that to not look right. We are going to use the service pattern for handling this problem.

Creating a service interface

First, we will create a service interface. We could do this in IntelliJ by right-clicking in our package and selecting a new Kotlin **File | Class** and then choosing **Interface** in the drop-down. We will be naming it `CustomerService`.

We will define the methods that our service will need:

```
package com.microservices.chapter3

interface CustomerService {
    fun getCustomer(id: Int) : Customer?
    fun createCustomer(customer: Customer)
    fun deleteCustomer(id: Int)
    fun updateCustomer(id: Int, customer: Customer)
    fun searchCustomers(nameFilter: String): List<Customer>
}
```

These operations don't expose how customers are stored/saved or searched, they are purely the interface that we like to have and are not exposing anything internal on the implementation.

> We have set the type of `getCustomer` as customer. That implies that this value could be null. Kotlin null-safety is a nice feature when sometimes, like this, we may return a null value when we don't find a customer. But, of course, we could use Java Optional Objects for archiving similar results.

Creating an implementation

Now, in IntelliJ, we can set the cursor on the `CustomerService` word and click *Alt + Enter* to show the actions, then we can choose to implement the interface. A new window will show asking for a name. It will have already populated `CustomerServiceImpl`, so we leave it as it is and click **OK**.

Now, we will see the methods of the interface that we like to implement. We can choose the first one and then press *Shift* and the last one to select them all. A new class will appear with this code:

```
package com.microservices.chapter3

class CustomerServiceImpl : CustomerService {
    override fun getCustomer(id: Int) : Customer? {
        TODO("not implemented")
    }
```

```kotlin
  override fun createCustomer(customer: Customer) {
    TODO("not implemented")
  }

  override fun deleteCustomer(id: Int) {
    TODO("not implemented")
  }

  override fun updateCustomer(id: Int, customer: Customer) {
    TODO("not implemented")
  }

  override fun searchCustomers(nameFilter: String): List<Customer> {
    TODO("not implemented")
  }
}
```

But before implementing the methods, we need to have our customers in that class. Let's add a map and initialization as we do in the past on our bean:

```kotlin
package com.microservices.chapter3

import java.util.concurrent.ConcurrentHashMap

class CustomerServiceImpl : CustomerService {
  companion object {
    val initialCustomers = arrayOf(Customer(1, "Kotlin"),
        Customer(2, "Spring"),
        Customer(3, "Microservice"))
  }
  val customers = ConcurrentHashMap<Int,
Customer>(initialCustomers.associateBy(Customer::id))

  override fun getCustomer(id: Int) : Customer? {
    TODO("not implemented")
  }

  override fun createCustomer(customer: Customer) {
    TODO("not implemented")
  }

  override fun deleteCustomer(id: Int) {
    TODO("not implemented")
  }

  override fun updateCustomer(id: Int, customer: Customer) {
    TODO("not implemented")
  }
```

```
override fun searchCustomers(nameFilter: String): List<Customer> {
  TODO("not implemented")
}
}
```

Then, we could easily implement our methods:

```
class CustomerServiceImpl : CustomerService {
  companion object {
    val initialCustomers = arrayOf(Customer(1, "Kotlin"),
        Customer(2, "Spring"),
        Customer(3, "Microservice"))
  }

  val customers = ConcurrentHashMap<Int,
Customer>(initialCustomers.associateBy(Customer::id))

  override fun getCustomer(id: Int) = customers[id]

  override fun deleteCustomer(id: Int) {
    customers.remove(id)
  }

  override fun createCustomer(customer: Customer) {
    customers[customer.id] = customer
  }

  override fun updateCustomer(id: Int, customer: Customer) {
    deleteCustomer(id)
    createCustomer(customer)
  }

  override fun searchCustomers(nameFilter: String): List<Customer> =
      customers.filter {
        it.value.name.contains(nameFilter, true)
      }.map(Map.Entry<Int, Customer>::value).toList()
}
```

Binding the right bean

Now, that we have this service, we may change our Spring Context to create a bean for this service and remove the original customer bean. We just need to change our `Chapter3Application.kt` to remove the bean and just leave it as a simple class:

```
package com.microservices.chapter3

import org.springframework.boot.autoconfigure.SpringBootApplication
import org.springframework.boot.runApplication

@SpringBootApplication
class Chapter3Application

fun main(args: Array<String>) {
    runApplication<Chapter3Application>(*args)
}
```

Then we will annotate our service implementation with the `@Component` annotation:

```
package com.microservices.chapter3

import org.springframework.stereotype.Component
import java.util.concurrent.ConcurrentHashMap

@Component
class CustomerServiceImpl : CustomerService
........
}
```

But then, we need to change the bean that we use in our controller to become the service:

```
package com.microservices.chapter3

import org.springframework.beans.factory.annotation.Autowired
import org.springframework.web.bind.annotation.*

@RestController
class CustomerController {
  @Autowired
  private lateinit var customerService: CustomerService
........

}
```

This will make the component scan to wire a bean implement to that interface; since our implementation is annotated with @Component, it will wire this implementation. If tomorrow, we change our implementation, then the controller will get the new implementation without being affected.

Using the service

Now, we can modify the controller itself to use the new service:

```
package com.microservices.chapter3

import org.springframework.beans.factory.annotation.Autowired
import org.springframework.web.bind.annotation.*

@RestController
class CustomerController {
  @Autowired
  private lateinit var customerService: CustomerService

  @GetMapping(value = "/customer/{id}")
  fun getCustomer(@PathVariable id: Int) = customerService.getCustomer(id)

  @PostMapping(value = "/customer/")
  fun createCustomer(@RequestBody customer: Customer) {
    customerService.createCustomer(customer)
  }

  @DeleteMapping(value = "/customer/{id}")
  fun deleteCustomer(@PathVariable id: Int) {
    customerService.deleteCustomer(id)
  }

  @PutMapping(value = "/customer/{id}")
  fun updateCustomer(@PathVariable id: Int, @RequestBody customer:
Customer) {
    customerService.updateCustomer(id, customer)
  }


  @GetMapping(value = "/customers")
  fun getCustomers(@RequestParam(required = false, defaultValue = "")
nameFilter: String) =
      customerService.searchCustomers(nameFilter)
}
```

If we run our cURL request again, nothing should change and everything will work as before, but this finally changes our controller and it is totally decoupled from the implementation of our customer service, providing greater flexibility for the future.

> Try to think of ways to decouple elements from your software using patterns like this. It will make it easier to maintain and evolve your application.

Handling HTTP statuses

We now handle different kinds of verbs in a precise manner, but we need to be as precise when we respond back to the consumers of our APIs service. For this, we can use HTTP status, as we described at the beginning of this section.

Using ResponseEntity

So far, Spring has handled our response status, every method that we have created will answer with a **200 OK**, but we need to modify our responses so we can give a range of different statuses, as we described at the beginning of this section. Spring provides a generic class named ResponseEntity for this, and we can use it to specify our status when we answer back in our controller.

To understand better, we can modify one of our methods:

```
package com.microservices.chapter3

import org.springframework.beans.factory.annotation.Autowired
import org.springframework.http.HttpStatus
import org.springframework.http.ResponseEntity
import org.springframework.web.bind.annotation.*

@RestController
class CustomerController {
  @Autowired
  private lateinit var customerService: CustomerService

  @GetMapping(value = "/customer/{id}")
  fun getCustomer(@PathVariable id: Int) =
      ResponseEntity(customerService.getCustomer(id), HttpStatus.OK)
.......
}
```

This is actually what the @GetMapping is doing by default, but now we can modify the status to the right value according to what we like to do.

Let's update our methods to use answers with the right response.

Answering a GET request

According to our definition, initially, when we get a GET request for a resource we should answer with the resource and a **200 OK** or with **404 NOT FOUND** if the resource is not found.

So, we can modify our method:

```
@GetMapping(value = "/customer/{id}")
fun getCustomer(@PathVariable id: Int): ResponseEntity<Customer?> {
  val customer = customerService.getCustomer(id)
  val status = if (customer == null) HttpStatus.NOT_FOUND else
HttpStatus.OK
  return ResponseEntity(customer, status)
}
```

First, we get the customer; if the customer is not found, the service will return null, so we can set our status to **404 NOT FOUND** or **200 OK**.

Answering a POST request

When we define how to answer POST requests, we specify that instead of returning a **200 OK,** we should answer a simply **201 CREATED**, and we really don't need to specify a body for our request since we are not returning any object back.

We can modify our method as:

```
@PostMapping(value = "/customer/")
fun createCustomer(@RequestBody customer: Customer): ResponseEntity<Unit> {
  customerService.createCustomer(customer)
  return ResponseEntity(Unit, HttpStatus.CREATED)
}
```

In this scenario, we are set to use a ResponseEntity using Unit, the equivalent in Kotlin of a void type, since we are not going to output anybody.

Answering a DELETE request

In our initial definition, we said that if we are going to delete a resource that is not found, we should answer with **404 NOT FOUND**, and if we delete it, we should answer a **200 OK**, regardless of whether we should need to send a body back to the client.

So, our method will look like this:

```
@DeleteMapping(value = "/customer/{id}")
fun deleteCustomer(@PathVariable id: Int): ResponseEntity<Unit> {
  var status = HttpStatus.NOT_FOUND
  if (customerService.getCustomer(id) != null) {
    customerService.deleteCustomer(id)
    status = HttpStatus.OK
  }
  return ResponseEntity(Unit, status)
}
```

First, we will set that we have not found the customer, and we will check with our service if it actually exists. If so, we delete and set the status to **200 OK**, to finally return Unit, since we don't require a body, and the desired status.

We could debate if that logic should be in our CustomerService or the controller, but it it is the controller which actually has a requirement to answer differently to delete a customer that does not exist, so we keep that logic there.

Answering an UPDATE request

Much like the DELETE request, when we update a customer, we should take care if the resource exists, and again we will not need to return anybody for this request; however, if we modified the resource, we should return a **202 ACCEPTED**.

Let's modify the update method:

```
@PutMapping(value = "/customer/{id}")
fun updateCustomer(@PathVariable id: Int, @RequestBody customer: Customer):
ResponseEntity<Unit> {
  var status = HttpStatus.NOT_FOUND
  if (customerService.getCustomer(id) != null) {
    customerService.updateCustomer(id, customer)
    status = HttpStatus.ACCEPTED
  }
  return ResponseEntity(Unit, status)
}
```

With this method, we have to complete our status responses, but there is one thing more that we could clear up.

Empty responses

In all our methods, we are set to return a JSON response, and this is because we use a RESTController. However, it is interesting to understand that if we are going to return an object, and the returning object is null, the body will be empty, so there will be no content in our response, just status. That is what is happening when we call our get service with a non-existent ID; an empty response is returned.

In the method that we declared before that returns Unit, an empty JSON object will be returned instead. If we invoke them, we will get just { }; that is what we get when we call our delete, or update methods with a non-existent ID, an empty object is returned.

But we could change the code to return no content even for the Unit methods. If we need to, just modifying them like this:

```
@PostMapping(value = "/customer/")
fun createCustomer(@RequestBody customer: Customer): ResponseEntity<Unit?>
{
    customerService.createCustomer(customer)
    return ResponseEntity(null, HttpStatus.CREATED)
}
```

But, what should we return? An empty object or an empty response? It is up to us to decide what is better for our API, but we prefer to have empty responses than empty objects since it will be less confusing to the user of the API to get simply no content than an empty object.

> In Rest API methods, it is a good practice to always return a value, in operations like those described before we could return a simple JSON that says that everything was ok, something like { "result" : "ok" }. This will prevent consumers misunderstanding the response, however, the consumer should always trust the HttpStatus regardless of the response body.

Working with JSON

So far, our APIs have been working using JSON, from return JSON objects as results, to accepting JSON objects in the body of the request. But we need to understand how this works and how we can create and use more complicated JSON objects. In this section, we will review the different mechanisms that Spring provides to handle our JSON requests and responses.

Understanding serialization

In our examples, we have created the Customer class and we have seen that returning an object of that class in our controller, either directly or through a response entity, it will get converted into JSON. This mechanism is known as serialization, converting an object into a representation, in our case, a JSON object.

Spring is used for archiving this Jackson, a widely known library to handle JSON objects in Java. You could find more information about that library on their website: https://github.com/FasterXML/jackson.

When we output a Java object, Spring will use internally an ObjectMapper, a class provided by Jackson, to create the JSON representation. This object mapper will go through the provided object and using a Java Reflection API, will discover any public properties and create the representation.

Using simple objects

For example, let's create a simple class named SimpleObject, with this structure:

```
package com.microservices.chapter3

class SimpleObject {
  public val name = "hello"
  private val place = "world"
}
```

Now, let's create a new controller for testing this, we will name it JsonExamplesController; it will be a RestController that has one GetMapping:

```
package com.microservices.chapter3

import org.springframework.web.bind.annotation.GetMapping
import org.springframework.web.bind.annotation.RestController
```

```
@RestController
class JsonExamplesController {
  @GetMapping(value = "/json")
  fun getJson() = SimpleObject()
}
```

Then, if we execute our microservice and do a request to this URL
`http://localhost:8080/json`, we should get:

```
{"name":"hello"}
```

We can see that the value place has not been created in the JSON, but if we modify our class
to be like:

```
package com.microservices.chapter3

class SimpleObject {
  public val name = "hello"
  private val place = "world"
  public fun getPlace() = place
}
```

Then, if we request again the URL `http://localhost:8080/json`, we should get:

```
{"name":"hello","place":"world"}
```

What is happening now is that the `ObjectMapper` is finding a public method name
`getPlace`, and any public method that is named get and then an uppercase letter will get
serialized into the JSON object as an attribute with the name after they get. So, `getPlace`
will serialize the value of that function into an attribute named `place`.

In fact, if we modify the class like this:

```
class SimpleObject {
  public val name = "hello"
  private val zone = "world"
  public fun getPlace() = zone
}
```

We will get exactly the same result since the `ObjectMapper` is serializing the method, not
the attribute. But we can archive even the same result more simply using Kotlin `data`
`classes`:

```
data class SimpleObject(var name: String = "hello", var place: String =
"world")
```

A `data class` which Kotlin compiles into a JVM class will generate better methods than the `ObjectMapper` will use, so we will get serialized as the previous examples. But some more features, such as providing a constructor for the object that we could benefit if we modify our controller:

```
package com.microservices.chapter3

import org.springframework.web.bind.annotation.GetMapping
import org.springframework.web.bind.annotation.RestController

@RestController
class JsonExamplesController {
  @GetMapping(value = "/json")
  fun getJson() = SimpleObject("hi", "kotlin")
}
```

Then, if we request again the URL `http://localhost:8080/json`, we should get:

```
{"name":"hi","place":"kotlin"}
```

Working with complex objects

Serialization works for complex objects as well. For example, we can create a new class named `ComplexObject`:

```
package com.microservices.chapter3

data class ComplexObject(var object1 : SimpleObject? = null)
```

Then, modify our controller to use it:

```
package com.microservices.chapter3

import org.springframework.web.bind.annotation.GetMapping
import org.springframework.web.bind.annotation.RestController

@RestController
class JsonExamplesController {
  @GetMapping(value = "/json")
  fun getJson() = ComplexObject(object1 = SimpleObject("more", "complex"))
}
```

Then, if we request again the URL `http://localhost:8080/json`, we should get:

```
{"object1":{"name":"more","place":"complex"}}
```

Since our `ComplexObject` is a data class, it will have a `getObject` method. When we deserialize, the `ObjectMapper` will also deserialize the value or that object as an attribute named `object1`.

We can create as many levels as we need, and use nested classes if we need to.

Adding telephones to our customers

Now that we understand serialization a bit more, we can modify our customer class to create an inner class.

You can delete the previously created `SimpleObject` and `JSonExamplesController` since we are going to use our API services to explain further these concepts:

```
package com.microservices.chapter3

data class Customer(var id: Int = 0, var name: String = "", var telephone:
Telephone) {
  data class Telephone(var countryCode: String = "", var telephoneNumber:
String = "")
}
```

If we now run our code, we get a compilation error since in our service. We have an initial set of customers that don't have a telephone, let's just add some to them:

```
package com.microservices.chapter3

import com.microservices.chapter3.Customer.Telephone
import org.springframework.stereotype.Component
import java.util.concurrent.ConcurrentHashMap

@Component
class CustomerServiceImpl : CustomerService {
  companion object {
    val initialCustomers = arrayOf(Customer(1, "Kotlin", Telephone("+44",
"7123456789")),
        Customer(2, "Spring", Telephone("+44", "7123456789")),
        Customer(3, "Microservice", Telephone("+44", "7123456789")))
  }
  . . . . . . . . . . . .
}
```

In this change, we can write `Customer.Telephone`, when we invoke the constructor, since we need to refer to the inner class inside `Customer`, but we could just write `Telephone` if we do a static import at the beginning of the class: `import com.microservices.chapter3.Customer.Telephone`

If we do a request to our get customer URL `http://localhost:8080/customers`, we should now get:

```
[
    {
        "id": 1,
        "name": "Kotlin",
        "telephone": {
            "countryCode": "+44",
            "telephoneNumber": "7123456789"
        }
    },
    {
        "id": 2,
        "name": "Spring",
        "telephone": {
            "countryCode": "+44",
            "telephoneNumber": "7123456789"
        }
    },
    {
        "id": 3,
        "name": "Microservice",
        "telephone": {
            "countryCode": "+44",
            "telephoneNumber": "7123456789"
        }
    }
]
```

Our customer list gets serialized correctly and we see a telephone number for each customer.

Handling null values

We have learned how to handle complex objects, but how can we handle them when things are optional? Let's consider that in the previous example, we can set it so that the customer's telephone is something that we may have, but is optional.

First, we need to modify our Customer class, to make the telephone nullable:

```
package com.microservices.chapter3

data class Customer(var id: Int = 0, var name: String = "", var telephone:
Telephone? = null) {
  data class Telephone(var countryCode: String = "", var telephoneNumber:
String = "")
}
```

We have set a default value of the telephone as null, so let's modify our service:

```
package com.microservices.chapter3

import com.microservices.chapter3.Customer.Telephone
import org.springframework.stereotype.Component
import java.util.concurrent.ConcurrentHashMap

@Component
class CustomerServiceImpl : CustomerService {
  companion object {
    val initialCustomers = arrayOf(Customer(1, "Kotlin"),
        Customer(2, "Spring"),
        Customer(3, "Microservice", Telephone("+44", "7123456789")))
  }
..............
}
```

Now, if we send another request to our get customer URL
http://localhost:8080/customers, we should get:

```
[
    {
        "id": 1,
        "name": "Kotlin",
        "telephone": null
    },
    {
        "id": 2,
        "name": "Spring",
        "telephone": null
```

```
        },
        {
            "id": 3,
            "name": "Microservice",
            "telephone": {
                "countryCode": "+44",
                "telephoneNumber": "7123456789"
            }
        }
    ]
```

Now, we get the object serialized with a null value, but it may not be what we are looking for; we don't want to serialize an optional field.

We could achieve this using a `Jackson` annotation in our data class:

```
package com.microservices.chapter3

import com.fasterxml.jackson.annotation.JsonInclude
import com.fasterxml.jackson.annotation.JsonInclude.Include

@JsonInclude(Include.NON_NULL)
data class Customer(var id: Int = 0, var name: String = "", var telephone:
Telephone? = null) {
    data class Telephone(var countryCode: String = "", var telephoneNumber:
String = "")
}
```

With a final request to our get customer URL `http://localhost:8080/customers`, we should now get:

```
    [
        {
            "id": 1,
            "name": "Kotlin",
        },
        {
            "id": 2,
            "name": "Spring",
        },
        {
            "id": 3,
            "name": "Microservice",
            "telephone": {
                "countryCode": "+44",
                "telephoneNumber": "7123456789"
            }
```

```
    }
]
```

The `@JsonInclude` annotation is indicating in our class that we will only serialize non- null values, and we could include in any data class that we need to, however, we could configure Spring globally to not serialize null objects setting this value in our Spring Configuration, so editing our `application.yaml`:

```
spring.jackson.default-property-inclusion: NON_NULL
```

With this value, we do not need to set the annotation in our data class object anymore.

 We review Spring Configuration works in more detail in our `Chapter 2`, *Getting Started with Spring Boot 2.0*. You could look at it to understand the different ways that we could change our Spring Configuration.

Understanding deserialization

When we send a request to our API, we can send a `JSON` object, and if we have set our `@RequestMapper`, or variant, to have a body, we can convert it into an object. This is called deserialization. Spring uses Jackson as well for deserialization of `JSON` objects into JVM classes, as well as using the `ObjectMapper` class as it was doing for serialization.

Let's understand how this works.

From a request into an object

When we define our `POST` method to create customers, we define it in the following way:

```
@PostMapping(value = "/customer/")
fun createCustomer(@RequestBody customer: Customer): ResponseEntity<Unit?>
{
  customerService.createCustomer(customer)
  return ResponseEntity(null, HttpStatus.CREATED)
}
```

Then, when a request is sent, for example as this cURL request:

```
curl -X POST \
 http://localhost:8080/customer/ \
 -H 'content-type: application/json' \
 -d '{
 "id": 4,
 "name": "New Customer"
}'
```

Spring will get the body of the request and use the ObjectMapper to construct a JVM object of the specified class. The object mapper using reflection will find all the public attributes or setter methods for each property in the JSON object, and either changes them or invoke them.

For example, for our Customer class, it will find a setId function and will pass it the value of the attribute id in the object. This is because data classes will generate setters for each attribute.

Deserializing complex objects

This is how it works when a complex object is sent, for example, with this request:

```
curl -X POST \
  http://localhost:8080/customer/ \
  -H 'content-type: application/json' \
  -d ' {
        "id": 4,
        "name": "New Customer",
        "telephone": {
            "countryCode": "+44",
            "telephoneNumber": "7123456789"
        }
    }'
```

When the ObjectMapper explores the class that we ask to deserialize from JSON into a java object, it will explore as well any other class that it uses. JSON, when it is analyzing the Customer class and finding the attribute telephone, will get the Telephone class and explore the getters and setters for this class as well.

So, when reading the JSON and finding the attribute telephone, it will use the `Telephone` class to create the required object and then assign the value using the setter that the `Customer` class provides.

In a way, we can define the process in something like this pseudocode which is reading the JSON:

```
Reading class Customer
Create a Customer Object
Attribute "id" found in JSON
searching for a setter for id
calling Customer::setId with the value 4
Attribute "name" found in JSON
searching for a setter for name
calling Customer::setName with the value "New Customer"
Attribute "telephone" found in JSON
searching for a setter for telephone
Reading class Telephone
Creating a Telephone Object
Attribute "countryCode" found in JSON
searching for a setter for countryCode
calling Telephone::setCountryCode with the value "+44"
Attribute "telephoneNumber" found in JSON
searching for a setter for telephoneNumber
calling Telephone::telephoneNumber with the value "7123456789"
calling Customer::setTelephone with the object telephone created
end
```

This pseudocode may not be exactly correct, and the implementation of `Jackson` may vary for this, but conceptually, it should be similar.

Validating objects

When we send a JSON object, only the value of the properties that could be set will be handled; if the JSON object has additional data, it will be ignored. And without specifying more, even if we don't send a value that actually is needed in our request, the object will be deserialized somehow.

For example, let's send this request to our API:

```
curl -X POST \
  http://localhost:8080/customer/ \
  -H 'content-type: application/json' \
  -d '{
  "id": 4,
```

```
    "customerName": "New Customer"
  }'
```

We will get a **400 BAD REQUEST** error in our API. This will happen as well if we send a JSON that could not be handled and will not create an object. For example, with this request, that has a missing bracket:

```
curl -X POST \
  http://localhost:8080/customer/ \
  -H 'content-type: application/json' \
  -d '{
  "id": 4,
  "name": "New Customer"
}'
```

Spring will automatically generate another **400 BAD REQUEST** response.

If both cases, we will get some JSON response back as well, something like:

```
{
    "timestamp": 1505233267030,
    "status": 400,
    "error": "Bad Request",
    "message": "JSON parse error: Unexpected end-of-input within/between
Object entries; nested exception is
com.fasterxml.jackson.core.JsonParseException: Unexpected end-of-input
within/between Object entries\n at [Source: (PushbackInputStream); line: 8,
column: 169]",
    "path": "/customer/"
}
```

We will learn how to handle those errors, and customize their messages in the final section of this chapter.

Handling errors

Any software needs to handle errors, either triggered by the business rules that are defined or just to handle extraordinary circumstances that may appear. In RESTful APIs, we use status codes to tell our consumers when an error has occurred, but within our code, we need to handle those scenarios and ensure that they are handled gracefully. During this section, we will review some of the techniques that we could use to handle these situations.

Using controller advice

In our last example, we got an exception when our JSON was not formatted correctly. That exception was `JsonParseException`, and was not handled in any part of our code so Spring was automatically handling it for us and returning an error message.

But we may want to handle the exception yourself so we could customize the error, and the body of the message is returned. For doing so, Spring provides a mechanism to handle any exception that was not caught in our application code using the `ControllerAdvice` and `ExceptionHandler` annotations.

First, lets create a new Kotlin class and name it `ErrorHandler`:

```
package com.microservices.chapter3

import com.fasterxml.jackson.core.JsonParseException
import org.springframework.http.HttpStatus
import org.springframework.http.ResponseEntity
import org.springframework.web.bind.annotation.ControllerAdvice
import org.springframework.web.bind.annotation.ExceptionHandler
import javax.servlet.http.HttpServletRequest

@ControllerAdvice
class ErrorHandler {
  @ExceptionHandler(JsonParseException::class)
  fun JsonParseExceptionHandler(servletRequest: HttpServletRequest,
                                exception: Exception):
ResponseEntity<String> {
    return ResponseEntity("JSON Error", HttpStatus.BAD_REQUEST)
  }
}
```

This class is annotated with `@ControllerAdvice` and will be added to the Spring Context through the context scan. Then, it's declaring a method annotated with the `@ExceptionHandler` annotation that indicates as well what kind of exception we will handle referring the class of the exception. When the `JsonParseException` is thrown and there is not a catch clause that handles it, Spring will search for any exception handler available for that class and will send the error to it.

If we POST our wrong JSON request to the URL `http://localhost:8080/customer/`:

```
{
    "id": 8,
    "customerName": "New Customer",
    "telephone": {
```

```
        "countryCode": "+44",
        "telephoneNumber": "7123456789"
    }
```

We will get a **400 BAD REQUEST** with an error in the response body:

JSON Error

However, we are to create a RESTful API, so we need to answer using JSON. So, let's create a new simple data class that will hold our error response:

```
package com.microservices.chapter3

data class ErrorResponse(val error: String, val message: String)
```

Now, we can modify our error handler to use this new class:

```
package com.microservices.chapter3

import com.fasterxml.jackson.core.JsonParseException
import org.springframework.http.HttpStatus
import org.springframework.http.ResponseEntity
import org.springframework.web.bind.annotation.ControllerAdvice
import org.springframework.web.bind.annotation.ExceptionHandler
import javax.servlet.http.HttpServletRequest

@ControllerAdvice
class ErrorHandler {
  @ExceptionHandler(JsonParseException::class)
  fun JsonParseExceptionHandler(servletRequest: HttpServletRequest,
                                exception: Exception):
ResponseEntity<ErrorResponse> {
     return ResponseEntity(ErrorResponse("JSON Error", exception.message ?:
"invalid json"),
        HttpStatus.BAD_REQUEST)
  }
}
```

If we repeat our wrong request, we will get now the same **400 BAD REQUEST**, but with a JSON result:

```
{
    "error": "JSON Error",
    "message": "JSON parse error: Unexpected end-of-input: expected close
marker for Object (start marker at [Source: (PushbackInputStream); line: 1,
column: 5]); nested exception is
com.fasterxml.jackson.core.io.JsonEOFException: Unexpected end-of-input:
expected close marker for Object (start marker at [Source:
```

```
(PushbackInputStream); line: 1, column: 5])\n at [Source:
(PushbackInputStream); line: 8, column: 175]"
}
```

Additionally, we could log out the exception in the controller advice so we get a trace of a possible problem to handle.

> In our error handler, we have just got the `JsonParseException`, but if we get any other error, for example, something really critical, we will not have a customized message. For this, it may be a good idea to leave in our controller advice a generic handle for the `Throwable` class and at least provide a message according to our API definition.

Creating business exceptions

We know how to handle generic exceptions, but if we need to respond to our business logic, how could we handle them?

Let's consider that we are requesting a customer that does not exist; so far, our `UserService` will return a `null` customer if asked for a customer that does not exist. Then, we just output a **404 NOT FOUND** status code, and since it is our customer, we will not send a body. But let's handle this using a custom business exception.

First, we will create a new class named `CustomerNotFoundException` that will inherit from `Exception`:

```
package com.microservices.chapter3

class CustomerNotFoundException(message: String) : Exception(message)
```

Then, we could modify our `CustomerController` code to throw this exception:

```
package com.microservices.chapter3

import org.springframework.beans.factory.annotation.Autowired
import org.springframework.http.HttpStatus
import org.springframework.http.ResponseEntity
import org.springframework.web.bind.annotation.*

@RestControllerclass CustomerController {
.....
  @GetMapping(value = "/customer/{id}")
  fun getCustomer(@PathVariable id: Int): ResponseEntity<Customer> {
    val customer = customerService.getCustomer(id) ?:
```

```
        throw CustomerNotFoundException("customer '$id' not found")
      return ResponseEntity(customer, HttpStatus.OK)
  }
.....
}
```

Then, we could add this to our `ErrorHandler` class:

```
@ExceptionHandler(CustomerNotFoundException::class)
fun CustomerNotFoundExceptionHandler(servletRequest: HttpServletRequest,
                                     exception: Exception) :
ResponseEntity<ErrorResponse>{
  return ResponseEntity(ErrorResponse("Customer Not Found",
exception.message!! ),
      HttpStatus.NOT_FOUND)
}
```

If we now invoke the URL `http://localhost:8080/customer/11`, we should get a **404 NOT FOUND** response:

```
{
    "error": "Customer Not Found",
    "message": "customer '11' not found"
}
```

Avoiding the controller advice

The controller advice is a great tool, but sometimes, we may use it just like an equivalent to a `GO-TO` instruction. We lose control of our flow and we let something just happen outside of our main logic.

Controller advice should be used only to handle extraordinary circumstances and we could avoid it by adding our business logic when we need to answer errors.

For example, we could simply modify our controller method like this:

```
@GetMapping(value = "/customer/{id}")
fun getCustomer(@PathVariable id: Int): ResponseEntity<Any> {
  val customer = customerService.getCustomer(id)
  return if (customer != null)
    ResponseEntity(customer, HttpStatus.OK)
  else
    ResponseEntity(ErrorResponse("Customer Not Found", "customer '$id' not
found"), HttpStatus.NOT_FOUND)
}
```

This will output exactly the same result, but we need to avoid to have an exception created, and the controller advice, getting the logic on the error together with our controller.

 One of the more confusing times when we analyze failures in a production application is to encounter a larger number of exceptions raised in the application logs, but actually discover that those are not really exceptional errors, they are just business logic errors. Avoiding to create unnecessary exceptions will help to find the real problems on your application.

Summary

Now, we can effectively write RESTful APIs using the Spring Framework. We learned how to create complex objects using JSON and how we can handle them when creating requests and responses in our API. We know how we can use HTTP verbs and statuses to define the ubiquitous language of our API, to provide a clear communication to the API consumers. And finally, we learned how to handle errors and answer back to the users of our RESTful microservice.

Remember our microservices principles when you build your API, Domain-Driven Design is a perfect way to separate your API service following your domain mapping. But these APIs follow the standard approach of most microservices, using traditional blocking operations. In the next chapter, we will learn how to use non-blocking techniques to produce more responses and scalable microservices, and we will learn how the new Spring component, WebFlux, and the Reactor framework allow us to easily create Reactive microservices.

4
Creating Reactive Microservices

Reactive microservices are the next step in the evolution of microservices. Based on the reactive paradigm, they target delivering more responsive, resilient, and elastic message-driven services that will outperform the more traditional non-reactive architectures.

In this chapter, we will learn how easily we can create them using Spring Framework 5.0, and how we can use reactive programming to create them.

 We learned about the benefits of reactive programming in Chapter 1, *Understanding Microservices*. You can review the section covering reactive programming to understand this topic further.

The reactive microservices that we will create in this chapter will be based on our previously created RESTful API examples, showing how easily we can adapt to this new model.

In this chapter, you will learn about:

- Spring WebFlux
- Router functions
- Mono
- Flux
- Introduction to functional programming
- Reactive error handling

Understanding Spring WebFlux

Spring WebFlux is a new component introduced in Spring Framework 5.0 that allows the creation of reactive microservices using Netty as the new web/application server. WebFlux extensively uses the Reactor Framework to implement the reactive streams pattern. In this section, we will understand how to create Spring WebFlux applications, and how we can use them to migrate our non-reactive microservices into this new technological stack.

Creating a Spring WebFlux application

As before, we will use Spring Initializr to create a new Spring Boot Application, but in this case, a WebFlux application. First, navigate to the Spring Initializr site at `https://start.spring.io/`. We will choose to create a **Maven Project** with **Kotlin** and **Spring Boot 2.0.0 M7**. For the project Metadata, we will set the **Group** as `com.microservices`, **Artifact** as `chapter4`, and as **Dependencies**, we will include **Reactive Web**:

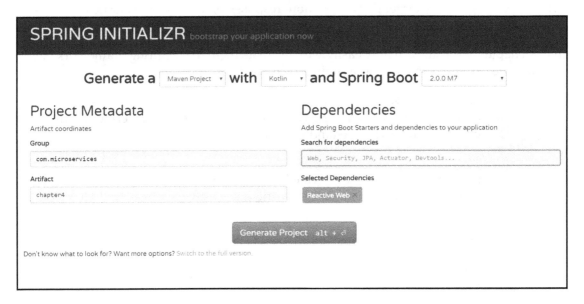

Creating a WebFlux application using Spring Initializr

Then, we will click on the **Generate Project** button to download a zip named `chapter4.zip`; we will uncompress it and open the resulting folder in IntelliJ IDEA. After some time, our project will be ready and we can open the Maven window to see the different life cycle phases, Maven plugins, and their goals.

We cover how to use Spring Initializr, Maven, and IntelliJ IDEA in `Chapter 2`, *Getting Started with Spring Boot 2.0*. You can visit this chapter to understand topics not covered in this section.

If we take a look at our newly created application and open our `Chapter4Application.kt` file, we can see it is a standard Spring Boot application:

```
package com.microservices.chapter4

import org.springframework.boot.autoconfigure.SpringBootApplication
import org.springframework.boot.runApplication

@SpringBootApplication
class Chapter4Application

fun main(args: Array<String>) {
    runApplication<Chapter4Application>(*args)
}
```

Now, we could run our microservice to see some differences from our previously built microservices in other chapters. We can use the Maven window to double-click on the **spring-boot** plugin, **run** goal, or just do so from the command line:

```
mvnw spring-boot:run
```

After some seconds, we will see several log lines, including something like this:

```
INFO 12308 --- [            main] o.s.b.web.embedded.netty.NettyWebServer  :
Netty started on port(s): 8080
```

Our microservice is now ready to handle requests using `Netty`; this is the first change that we need to understand since, in our previous examples, we used Tomcat.

 Interestingly enough, when we choose **Reactive Web** in the dependencies on Spring Initializr, our Maven `pom` will include `spring-boot-starter-webflux` as Dependency. If we choose **Web** as the **Dependency** in Spring Initializr, it will include `spring-boot-starter-web`. We will name this component WebFlux in this chapter for clarity, even though Spring Initializr named it Reactive Web.

Using Netty

Netty was originally developed by JBoss with the idea to create a Client-Server Framework that allows us to perform non-blocking IO operations. To archive this capability, we use a message-driven implementation of the reactor pattern. Nowadays, it is supported by an extensive open source community.

Netty includes support for major algorithm and protocols such as `HTTP`, `SSL/TSL`, or `DNS`, but adds support for modern protocols such as `HTTP/2`, `WebSocket`, or `Google Protocol Buffers`. This is just a summary of some of Netty's capabilities.

 You can find more information on Netty on their website at `https://netty.io/`.

Spring Boot 1.x uses Apache Tomcat as the default application/web server, but Tomcat performs only blocking operations. In order to be able to create reactive services, Spring Boot 2.0 has chosen Netty instead, because of its non-blocking IO capabilities.

When using Spring Boot 2.0, if we include the Spring WebFlux component, when our application starts it will create a new Netty server, but if we use the standard Spring Web, a new Tomcat server will be started instead.

As we discussed in `Chapter 1`, *Understanding Microservices,* one of the desired qualities for any reactive system is to be responsive; event-driven software, such as Netty, will fulfill this requirement among the rest of the Reactive Manifesto.

 We analyze the Reactive Manifesto in `Chapter 1`, *Understanding Microservices*, in the *Reactive microservices* section.

With this technology, our microservices can handle a higher workload and will be more effective than ever before.

 There are other non-blocking IO systems for different technologies such as `NodeJS`, `Nginx`, `Apache Mina`, `Vert.X`, or `Akka`. It will probably be a good idea to learn some of them since reactive systems will be one of the most used technologies in coming years.

Serving static context

As in any Spring Boot application, when we use Netty we can serve static context, but this content will serve reactively with non-blocking IO. Let's first create a new folder in our project under the resource folder; we will name it `public`. Then, right-click on the folder and choose **New** | **HTML File** in the popup menu.

We will edit the file to be like this:

```html
<!DOCTYPE html>
<html lang="en">
<head>
    <meta charset="UTF-8">
    <title>Hello World</title>
</head>
<body>
Reactive Static Content
</body>
</html>
```

If we start our server again with:

mvnw spring-boot:run

When visiting `http://localhost:8080/index.html`, we should get a simple message:

```
Reactive Static Content
```

This content has been served as before, but instead of it being a blocking operation, it is being processed reactively. In a way, we can understand this as if our page was a kind of a file on our system. In a blocking IO approach, when the page is requested on the server, it will read all the page content and start to send it back to the client that requested it. Meanwhile, when this reading is happening, that operation is blocked.

In a non-blocking IO system, our server starts to read the page and sends information as soon as it gets some data, then eventually we will read more data from the file and send back more data to the client, and so on. In fact, it can start sending data from the same page, or other pages, to clients requesting data without needing to block either the reading or sending of the requested page.

This is a real simplification of a much more complex architecture, and if you'd like to learn more, I recommend you read this article: `https://techblog.bozho.net/why-non-blocking/`.

Now, let's add some API endpoints as we did in our previous examples.

Adding a RestController

Using Spring WebFlux, we can create a controller as before, but first, we need our `Customer` class, so let's add it to our project. Create a new class named `Customer`:

```
package com.microservices.chapter4

data class Customer(var id: Int = 0, val name: String = "", val telephone:
Telephone? = null) {
  data class Telephone(var countryCode: String = "", var telephoneNumber:
String = "")
}
```

Now, we can create a simple rest controller; in our case, it will be named `CustomerController`:

```
package com.microservices.chapter4

import org.springframework.web.bind.annotation.GetMapping
import org.springframework.web.bind.annotation.PathVariable
import org.springframework.web.bind.annotation.RestController

@RestController
class CustomerController {
  @GetMapping(value = "/customer/{id}")
  fun getCustomer(@PathVariable id: Int) = Customer(id, "customer $id")
}
```

If we run our server again, after visiting our GET customer URL, `http://localhost:8080/customer/1`, we should get:

```
{"id":1,"name":"customer 1"}
```

> We may get a `telephone` = `null` as a property of our `Customer` object in this new example since we haven't provided a telephone object when we created our customer, but remember that you cannot serialize null values by adding the value `spring.jackson.default-property-inclusion: NON_NULL` to our `application.yml` as we discussed in `Chapter 3`, *Creating RESTful Services*.

But we can use `ResponseEntity` as before to customize our HTTP Status messages, so let's modify our controller for this purpose:

```
package com.microservices.chapter4

import org.springframework.http.HttpStatus
import org.springframework.http.ResponseEntity
import org.springframework.web.bind.annotation.GetMapping
import org.springframework.web.bind.annotation.PathVariable
import org.springframework.web.bind.annotation.RestController

@RestController
class CustomerController {
  @GetMapping(value = "/customer/{id}")
  fun getCustomer(@PathVariable id: Int): ResponseEntity<Customer> {
    return ResponseEntity(Customer(id, "customer $id"), HttpStatus.OK)
  }
}
```

Creating a customer service

We can add a new service to handle our customers, so let's create a `CustomerService` interface:

```
package com.microservices.chapter4

interface CustomerService {
  fun getCustomer(id: Int) : Customer?
  fun searchCustomers(nameFilter: String): List<Customer>
}
```

Then, we can create our service implementing the interface, `CustomerServiceImpl`:

```
package com.microservices.chapter4

import com.microservices.chapter4.Customer.Telephone
import org.springframework.stereotype.Component
import java.util.concurrent.ConcurrentHashMap
```

```
@Component
class CustomerServiceImpl : CustomerService {
  companion object {
    val initialCustomers = arrayOf(Customer(1, "Kotlin"),
        Customer(2, "Spring"),
        Customer(3, "Microservice", Telephone("+44", "7123456789")))
  }

  val customers = ConcurrentHashMap<Int,
Customer>(initialCustomers.associateBy(Customer::id))

  override fun getCustomer(id: Int) = customers[id]

  override fun searchCustomers(nameFilter: String): List<Customer> =
      customers.filter {
        it.value.name.contains(nameFilter, true)
      }.map(Map.Entry<Int, Customer>::value).toList()
}
```

Finally, we can modify our controller to use the service:

```
package com.microservices.chapter4

import org.springframework.beans.factory.annotation.Autowired
import org.springframework.http.HttpStatus
import org.springframework.http.ResponseEntity
import org.springframework.web.bind.annotation.GetMapping
import org.springframework.web.bind.annotation.PathVariable
import org.springframework.web.bind.annotation.RequestParam
import org.springframework.web.bind.annotation.RestController

@RestController
class CustomerController {
  @Autowired
  private lateinit var customerService: CustomerService

  @GetMapping(value = "/customer/{id}")
  fun getCustomer(@PathVariable id: Int): ResponseEntity<Customer?> {
    val customer = customerService.getCustomer(id)
    return ResponseEntity(customer, HttpStatus.OK)
  }

  @GetMapping(value = "/customers")
  fun getCustomers(@RequestParam(required = false, defaultValue = "")
nameFilter: String) =
      customerService.searchCustomers(nameFilter)
}
```

Then, we can create a `GET` request to our customer's URL, `http://localhost:8080/customers`, getting this output, alongside a **200 OK** HTTP status:

```
[
    {
        "id":1,
        "name":"Kotlin"
    },
    {
        "id":2,
        "name":"Spring"
    },
    {
        "id":3,
        "name":"Microservice",
        "telephone":{
            "countryCode":"+44",
            "telephoneNumber":"7123456789"
        }
    }
]
```

 This is quite similar to the service that we create in `Chapter 3`, *Creating RESTful Services*. There, we explained most of the concepts used in this chapter.

Blocking is not reactive

We can see that we can easily convert our more traditional non-reactive microservices to reactive, but this service is not fully reactive yet. Our controller may be, but if the operation performed is a blocking operation, it will do blocking operations as any other non-reactive system would do. So as we have declared, when a client invokes our URL, we will call our service to either get a customer or search for them, and when this operation is completed, we serialize the results as JSON; only then will we return the value to the consumer, as our operation is a blocking operation. We may need to modify our service to become a reactive service.

Creating reactive services

We may have experienced creating non-reactive services, as our `CustomerService` is, but now we need to create our own reactive service. In this section, we will learn how we can transform our services to become reactive.

Understanding subscribers and publishers

First, we need to understand a core component in reactive programming, the subscribe and publish mechanism. Reactive programming is based on the event-model mechanism, in which a set of events are triggered and dispatched to whoever needs them. This abstract concept can easily be understood with how we handle actions from users in almost all UI Frameworks.

Let's think that we want to react to a UI action, for example, pressing a button and then performing an operation such as closing a window. In a normal UI Framework, user actions such as pressing buttons, selecting menus, or scrolling the contents of a window can be considered events. When we choose to listen to those events, what we are defining is a subscriber, an object whose responsibility is to receive an event when it is produced.

On the other hand, we may need to generate events; for example, when we click with our mouse on a button, a new event about the button being clicked needs to be triggered. By doing so we define a publisher, an object whose responsibility is to emit events. Our UI Framework will probably connect things together and when we click the button, the publisher will generate the event, and the subscriber will be notified about it; then, it can react by performing the desired functionality, closing the window.

But events can be chained and combined. In a UI Framework, we may already have a publisher that is sending any mouse click event on the screen, and we may also have a subscriber for those events. Then, when we click on the screen, our publisher emits that generic message and the more generic subscribe will get it and find out that the position of the mouse is actually on a certain button. This generic subscribe will trigger a new event about that button being clicked on, however, is subscribe to that event could process that as an action to perform the desired logic.

Let's visualize this with a bit of pseudocode:

```
Framework Starts
Registering MouseClick as a subscriber for mouse.click events
Registering MouseHandler as a publisher of mouse.click events
Application Starts
Registering Action1 as a subscriber for button1.click event
```

```
Registering Button1Trigger as a publisher for button1.click event
User click on button1
MouseHandler publish a mouse.click event
MouseClick get a mouse.click event
MouseClick finds that is on button1
MouseClick delegate to Button1Trigger
Button1Trigger publish an event of button1.click
Action1 get the button1.click event and close the window
```

This is probably not the most optimal implementation of a UI event system, but it serves to illustrate the concept. In each of these `subscriber` and `publisher` objects, we are not blocking the operation waiting for a result; they are in a way listeners that will be invoked when required. Meanwhile, other actions and events in our UI can happen, even simultaneously, such as pressing a button at the same time that we press a key.

 The publish and subscribe mechanism is not a new concept, and neither is the event-driven system; they have been used for a very long time, from managing our hardware to the more complicated message queue systems. However, with the reactive programming approach, they are more relevant than ever.

Spring uses the Reactor Framework to create reactive microservices. Our controllers can become publishers of results, and Spring will subscribe to produce more events that will send the data back to whoever is using our services. This data will be sent in a reactive stream, as was defined in the reactive streams specification, providing non-blocking back-pressure.

 Reactive Streams and back-pressure were discussed in `Chapter 1`, *Understanding Microservices*, in the *Reactive programming* section. Additionally, you can find more information here: `http://www.reactive-streams.org/`.

Publishing a single object

Reactor provides a way to define a reactive publisher through a class named `Mono`, but that publisher can only send one result.

To create a `Mono`, we can simply do this:

```
val customerMono : Mono<Customer> = Mono.just(Customer(1, "Mono"))
```

But reactor provides a high-level function for Kotlin that we can use to take advantage of more Kotlin characteristics:

```
val customerMono : Mono<Customer> = Customer(1, "Mono").toMono()
```

But since Kotlin has type inference, we can simply write it as:

```
val customerMono = Customer(1, "Mono").toMono()
```

What we should understand is that a `Mono` is not actually the value of the `Customer` instance that we create, it is a promise of what we are going to get. When we declare something as `Mono<Customer>`, we are just indicating that this is a publisher that in future will publish a customer. When someone is subscribed to that publisher, the data will be consumed.

Using Mono in a service

We can now modify our service to return a publisher for a single customer using `Mono`. Let's first change our `CustomerService` interface:

```
package com.microservices.chapter4

import reactor.core.publisher.Mono

interface CustomerService {
  fun getCustomer(id: Int) : Mono<Customer?>
  fun searchCustomers(nameFilter: String): List<Customer>
}
```

Then, we will change our implementation on the `CustomerServiceImpl` class:

```
package com.microservices.chapter4

import com.microservices.chapter4.Customer.Telephone
import org.springframework.stereotype.Component
import reactor.core.publisher.toMono
import java.util.concurrent.ConcurrentHashMap

@Component
class CustomerServiceImpl : CustomerService {
  companion object {
    val initialCustomers = arrayOf(Customer(1, "Kotlin"),
        Customer(2, "Spring"),
        Customer(3, "Microservice", Telephone("+44", "7123456789")))
  }
```

```
    val customers = ConcurrentHashMap<Int,
Customer>(initialCustomers.associateBy(Customer::id))

    override fun getCustomer(id: Int) = customers[id].toMono()

    override fun searchCustomers(nameFilter: String): List<Customer> =
        customers.filter {
           it.value.name.contains(nameFilter, true)
        }.map(Map.Entry<Int, Customer>::value).toList()
}
```

And finally, we will modify our `CustomerController`:

```
package com.microservices.chapter4

import org.springframework.beans.factory.annotation.Autowired
import org.springframework.http.HttpStatus
import org.springframework.http.ResponseEntity
import org.springframework.web.bind.annotation.GetMapping
import org.springframework.web.bind.annotation.PathVariable
import org.springframework.web.bind.annotation.RequestParam
import org.springframework.web.bind.annotation.RestController
import reactor.core.publisher.Mono

@RestController
class CustomerController {
  @Autowired
  private lateinit var customerService: CustomerService

  @GetMapping(value = "/customer/{id}")
  fun getCustomer(@PathVariable id: Int): ResponseEntity<Mono<Customer?>> {
    val customer = customerService.getCustomer(id)
    return ResponseEntity(customer, HttpStatus.OK)
  }

  @GetMapping(value = "/customers")
  fun getCustomers(@RequestParam(required = false, defaultValue = "")
nameFilter: String) =
      customerService.searchCustomers(nameFilter)
}
```

Basically, our controller code has changed, so instead of returning a `ResponseEntity` that contains our customer and the corresponding HTTP status, now we return `Mono`. Spring will understand things and subscribe to our publisher when a new request comes in to return the result reactively.

We can test this—after running our service again, make a request to get the customer API, with a GET request to our URL at `http://localhost:8080/customer/1`, getting this output alongside a **200 OK** HTTP status:

```
{
    "id":1,"name":"Kotlin"
}
```

Publishing multiple objects

Reactor provides a class to create a publisher that will return from 0 to an undetermined number of elements; that class is named `Flux`.

To create a simple `Flux`, we can just do:

```
val customerFlux = Flux.fromIterable(listOf(Customer(1,"one"), Customer(2,
"two")))
```

Or, we can use the adequate Kotlin version:

```
val customerFlux =  listOf(Customer(1,"one"), Customer(2, "two")).toFlux()
```

 `Mono` can be used when we only need to return one result in our publisher, whereas `Flux` can be used for 0 to *N* including 1, but if we are going to return just 1, it is preferable to use `Mono` instead of `Flux` since it is more optimal for that usage.

Using Flux in a service

We can now modify our service to return a publisher for the list of customers through a `Flux`. First, we need to modify our service interface, `CustomerService`:

```
package com.microservices.chapter4

import reactor.core.publisher.Flux
import reactor.core.publisher.Mono

interface CustomerService {
  fun getCustomer(id: Int) : Mono<Customer?>
  fun searchCustomers(nameFilter: String): Flux<Customer>
}
```

Then, we will modify our `CustomerServiceImpl` class:

```
package com.microservices.chapter4

import com.microservices.chapter4.Customer.Telephone
import org.springframework.stereotype.Component
import reactor.core.publisher.toFlux
import reactor.core.publisher.toMono
import java.util.concurrent.ConcurrentHashMap

@Component
class CustomerServiceImpl : CustomerService {
  companion object {
    val initialCustomers = arrayOf(Customer(1, "Kotlin"),
        Customer(2, "Spring"),
        Customer(3, "Microservice", Telephone("+44", "7123456789")))
  }

  val customers = ConcurrentHashMap<Int,
Customer>(initialCustomers.associateBy(Customer::id))

  override fun getCustomer(id: Int) = customers[id].toMono()

  override fun searchCustomers(nameFilter: String) = customers.filter {
    it.value.name.contains(nameFilter, true)
  }.map(Map.Entry<Int, Customer>::value).toFlux()
}
```

We don't need to modify our controller since our `getCustomer` function will infer the return type from the `searchCustomers` method, which now will be a `Flux` instead of a `List`:

```
@GetMapping(value = "/customers")
fun getCustomers(@RequestParam(required = false, defaultValue = "")
nameFilter: String) =
    customerService.searchCustomers(nameFilter)
```

This is one of the benefits of Kotlin type inference; the controller will be unchanged because our method could infer the return type. To find out more, we recommend this section in the Kotlin documentation: https://kotlinlang.org/docs/reference/basic-syntax.html.

Then, we can make a request to the customers API list, giving a `GET` request to our `http://localhost:8080/customers` URL, and getting this output alongside a **200 OK** HTTP status:

```
[
    {
        "id":1,
        "name":"Kotlin"
    },
    {
        "id":2,
        "name":"Spring"
    },
    {
        "id":3,
        "name":"Microservice",
        "telephone":{
            "countryCode":"+44",
            "telephoneNumber":"7123456789"
        }
    }
]
```

Also, like the `Mono` example before this, `Flux` is a promise that will get executed when subscribed to. in this case, when our controller returns the `Flux`, Spring will be subscribed for a new request coming through.

Receiving objects reactively

Now, we understand how to return objects reactively, but how we can accept them? When we create a reactive microservice, Spring can send to our `RequestMapping` a `Mono` publisher that will have the object in the body when we subscribe to it. But we need to make our service accept a `Mono` with a promise of a value, so first let's modify our service interface:

```
package com.microservices.chapter4

import reactor.core.publisher.Flux
import reactor.core.publisher.Mono

interface CustomerService {
  fun getCustomer(id: Int) : Mono<Customer?>
  fun searchCustomers(nameFilter: String): Flux<Customer>
  fun createCustomer(customerMono: Mono<Customer>) : Mono<*>
```

```
}
```

Why have we set the result of our function to be a `Mono`? When we create a reactive microservice, we may need to get data reactively, but we need to respond reactively as well in order for Spring to understand that we need to create a publisher that Spring will be subscribed to. So, Spring will publish the information coming from the request and subscribe our response; when our code answers back with a response, spring will send it to whoever sent the original request.

Let's view how we actually do that with the code in our controller:

```
package com.microservices.chapter4

import org.springframework.beans.factory.annotation.Autowired
import org.springframework.http.HttpStatus
import org.springframework.http.ResponseEntity
import org.springframework.web.bind.annotation.*
import reactor.core.publisher.Mono

@RestController
class CustomerController {
  @Autowired
  private lateinit var customerService: CustomerService

  @GetMapping(value = "/customer/{id}")
  fun getCustomer(@PathVariable id: Int): ResponseEntity<Mono<Customer?>> {
    val customer = customerService.getCustomer(id)
    return ResponseEntity(customer, HttpStatus.OK)
  }

  @GetMapping(value = "/customers")
  fun getCustomers(@RequestParam(required = false, defaultValue = "")
nameFilter: String) =
      customerService.searchCustomers(nameFilter)

  @PostMapping(value = "/customer/")
  fun createCustomer(@RequestBody customerMono: Mono<Customer>) =
      ResponseEntity(customerService.createCustomer(customerMono),
HttpStatus.CREATED)
}
```

So basically, we are indicating that our response will be the result of creating the customer through another publisher that will be created in our service since `createCustomer` returns a `Mono`.

Let's create the implementation of the service in our `CustomerServiceImpl` class:

```
package com.microservices.chapter4

import com.microservices.chapter4.Customer.Telephone
import org.springframework.stereotype.Component
import reactor.core.publisher.Mono
import reactor.core.publisher.toFlux
import reactor.core.publisher.toMono
import java.util.concurrent.ConcurrentHashMap

@Component
class CustomerServiceImpl : CustomerService {
  companion object {
    val initialCustomers = arrayOf(Customer(1, "Kotlin"),
        Customer(2, "Spring"),
        Customer(3, "Microservice", Telephone("+44", "7123456789")))
  }

  val customers = ConcurrentHashMap<Int,
Customer>(initialCustomers.associateBy(Customer::id))

  override fun getCustomer(id: Int) = customers[id].toMono()

  override fun searchCustomers(nameFilter: String) = customers.filter {
    it.value.name.contains(nameFilter, true)
  }.map(Map.Entry<Int, Customer>::value).toFlux()

  override fun createCustomer(customerMono: Mono<Customer>): Mono<*> {
    return customerMono.subscribe {
      customers[it.id] = it
    }.toMono()
  }
}
```

We are returning the result of our subscription in a new `Mono`. Let's `POST` a customer into our API service URL, `http://localhost:8080/customer/`, for example, with this `curl` request:

```
curl -X POST \
  http://localhost:8080/customer/ \
  -H 'content-type: application/json' \
  -d '{
```

```
  "id": 8,
  "name": "New Customer",
  "telephone": {
    "countryCode": "+44",
    "telephoneNumber": "7123456789"
  }
}
'
```

We will get this as an output:

```
{
    "disposed": false,
    "scanAvailable": true
}
```

The reason we get this is that the `subscribe` method returns a Disposable object, and it gets serialized into JSON. But we may not want that; we'd like to have an empty result as the example for our RESTful API.

 We discuss how to handle HTTP verbs and statuses, and serialize responses, in `Chapter 3`, *Creating RESTful Services*; review this chapter if this is strange or new to you.

In order to handle this, we will modify our service as follows:

```
override fun createCustomer(customerMono: Mono<Customer>): Mono<*> =
    customerMono.map {
      customers[it.id] = it
    }
```

If we POST this object with the same `curl` request, we should now get an empty object, {}. This is because we are using a mapper on the received `Mono` and transforming it; since we haven't written an additional object, it will return an empty object.

For example, if we change our service to be like this:

```
override fun createCustomer(customerMono: Mono<Customer>): Mono<*> =
    customerMono.map {
      customers[it.id] = it
      it
    }
```

When we execute our `curl` request again, we will get the same object that we posted:

```
{
    "id": 18,
    "name": "New Customer",
    "telephone": {
        "countryCode": "+44",
        "telephoneNumber": "7123456789"
    }
}
```

But we can change our service to return an empty object explicitly:

```
override fun createCustomer(customerMono: Mono<Customer>): Mono<*> =
    customerMono.map {
        customers[it.id] = it
        Mono.empty<Any>()
    }
```

This will return an empty object as well as a result, along with the corresponding **201 CREATED** HTTP status; we are using a `Mono.Empty` that is a `Mono<Any>` with no value; when converted in the JVM, it will be a `Mono<Object>` since the `<Any>` Kotlin class is converted to object class in the JVM. Now, we understand how we can make our microservices reactive—if we take a closer look at the syntax of our controller, it looks like our non-reactive implementation.

However, if we take a closer look at our service implementation, we can see that using reactive publishers, either `Mono` or `Flux`, looks very much like functional programming. Let's explore this concept further in the next section.

Using functional web programming

So far, we have learned how to create our reactive microservices with an annotation based syntax almost identical to the non-reactive approach. However, Spring Framework 5 provides a mechanism to develop these microservices using functional programming. In this section, we will learn how we can use it to explore a more flexible and modern syntax.

We will use the example already created in the previous section of this chapter, so follow the steps to get started.

Using RouterFunction

As with the annotated base system, first we need to define how our microservice will handle incoming requests, but instead of creating a controller, we will use a `RouterFunction`.

First, we will create a new class named `CustomerRouter`, with a `RouterFunction`:

```
package com.microservices.chapter4

import org.springframework.context.annotation.Bean
import org.springframework.stereotype.Component
import org.springframework.web.reactive.function.server.RouterFunction
import org.springframework.web.reactive.function.server.router

@Component
class CustomerRouter {
  @Bean
  fun customerRoutes(): RouterFunction<*> = router {
    "/functional".nest {
    }
  }
}
```

We are creating a new component, so it will be picked up by the component scan that exposes `Bean`, which creates a `RouterFunction` that is a new bind, allowing us to define routes for our web application, and when we can handle them, in this case, our route will handle any request to the `/functional` path.

 To create this router function, we use the Kotlin DSL that Spring creates for web-flux. To learn more about DSL, you can review this article in the Kotlin documentation: `https://kotlinlang.org/docs/reference/type-safe-builders.html`.

Now, we need to add something to our `RouterFunction` to actually handle that path; let's create something simple:

```
package com.microservices.chapter4

import org.springframework.context.annotation.Bean
import org.springframework.stereotype.Component
import org.springframework.web.reactive.function.server.RouterFunction
import org.springframework.web.reactive.function.server.ServerResponse
import org.springframework.web.reactive.function.server.router
import reactor.core.publisher.toMono
```

```
@Component
class CustomerRouter {
  @Bean
  fun customerRoutes(): RouterFunction<*> = router {
    "/functional".nest {
      "/customer".nest {
        GET("/") {
          ServerResponse.ok().body("hello world".toMono(),
String::class.java)
        }
      }
    }
  }
}
```

What we have defined now is that nested to the /functional route, if we request the /customer route with a GET request, we will send a response with a **200 OK**, HTTP status, and the body will be a simple String saying "hello world".

If we visit http://localhost:8080/functional/customer, we should get this simple message:

```
hello world
```

One interesting fact is that ServerResponse.ok is a ServerResponse.Builder, a method to build a response, that finally will generate a Mono<ServerResponse>. That response will have another Mono inside it with our object, a Mono<String>. So, we will be a publisher for a response from the server that will have a publisher of a promised value, a String in this example.

So, our Mono<ServerResponse> object contains Mono<String>, which will contain a string with our value, which will be "hello world".

Remember that a Mono is not a value, it is the promise that if we subscribe to it, it will get that value when it is ready.

We can simplify this example by removing unnecessary types, such as Kotlin type inference, and a couple of static imports:

```
package com.microservices.chapter4

import org.springframework.context.annotation.Bean
import org.springframework.stereotype.Component
```

```
import org.springframework.web.reactive.function.server.ServerResponse.ok
import org.springframework.web.reactive.function.server.router
import reactor.core.publisher.toMono

@Component
class CustomerRouter {
  @Bean
  fun customerRoutes() = router {
    "/functional".nest {
      "/customer".nest {
        GET("/") {
          ok().body("hello world".toMono(), String::class.java)
        }
      }
    }
  }
}
```

Finally, let's use our Customer class to return a value:

```
package com.microservices.chapter4

import org.springframework.context.annotation.Bean
import org.springframework.stereotype.Component
import org.springframework.web.reactive.function.server.ServerResponse.ok
import org.springframework.web.reactive.function.server.router
import reactor.core.publisher.toMono

@Component
class CustomerRouter {
  @Bean
  fun customerRoutes() = router {
    "/functional".nest {
      "/customer".nest {
        GET("/") {
          ok().body(Customer(1, "functional web").toMono(),
          Customer::class.java)
        }
      }
    }
  }
}
```

The last parameter on the body method indicates the JVM class that will be inside the Mono we send as a response. For this, we will use the Kotlin JVM method, ::class.java.

Now when we visit our URL, `http://localhost:8080/functional/customer`, we should get our customer:

```
{
    "id":1,
    "name":"functional web"
}
```

The body functions that we use have different implementations, but we will look at some more later on in this chapter.

Creating handlers

In our router, we define how we need to act on the HTTP GET request, by creating a lambda that will output our response. That piece of code is usually referred to as a handler. Let's expand the lambda to understand it better:

```
package com.microservices.chapter4

import org.springframework.context.annotation.Bean
import org.springframework.stereotype.Component
import org.springframework.web.reactive.function.server.ServerRequest
import org.springframework.web.reactive.function.server.ServerResponse.ok
import org.springframework.web.reactive.function.server.router
import reactor.core.publisher.toMono

@Component
class CustomerRouter {
  @Bean
  fun customerRoutes() = router {
    "/functional".nest {
      "/customer".nest {
        GET("/") { it: ServerRequest ->
          ok().body(Customer(1, "functional web").toMono(),
          Customer::class.java)
        }
      }
    }
  }
}
```

Our lambda has one parameter that is an object of the `ServerRequest` class. This object will contain all the details of the request that was sent to our handle, including the parameters or even the body of the request. We originally omitted it since our method did not need to handle anything from the request. Having handlers as lambdas can be alright, but we can create a new class for them so we can have a more understandable code.

Let's create a new class that we will call `CustomerHandler`:

```
package com.microservices.chapter4

import org.springframework.stereotype.Component
import org.springframework.web.reactive.function.server.ServerRequest
import org.springframework.web.reactive.function.server.ServerResponse
import org.springframework.web.reactive.function.server.ServerResponse.ok
import reactor.core.publisher.Mono
import reactor.core.publisher.toMono

@Component
class CustomerHandler {
  fun get(severRequest: ServerRequest): Mono<ServerResponse> {
    return ok().body(Customer(1, "functional web").toMono(),
    Customer::class.java)
  }
}
```

But since we are using Kotlin, let's convert this function in an expression body with type inference:

```
package com.microservices.chapter4

import org.springframework.stereotype.Component
import org.springframework.web.reactive.function.server.ServerRequest
import org.springframework.web.reactive.function.server.ServerResponse.ok
import reactor.core.publisher.toMono

@Component
class CustomerHandler {
  fun get(severRequest: ServerRequest) =
      ok().body(Customer(1, "functional web").toMono(),
      Customer::class.java)
}
```

Now, we can wire this class in our router, and use it in our lambda:

```
package com.microservices.chapter4

import org.springframework.beans.factory.annotation.Autowired
import org.springframework.context.annotation.Bean
import org.springframework.stereotype.Component
import org.springframework.web.reactive.function.server.ServerRequest
import org.springframework.web.reactive.function.server.router

@Component
class CustomerRouter {
  @Autowired
  lateinit var customerHandler: CustomerHandler

  @Bean
  fun customerRoutes() = router {
    "/functional".nest {
      "/customer".nest {
        GET("/") { it: ServerRequest ->
          customerHandler.get(it)
        }
      }
    }
  }
}
```

But since our lambda has sent its parameter to our new handler function, we can just do a method reference instead:

```
package com.microservices.chapter4

import org.springframework.beans.factory.annotation.Autowired
import org.springframework.context.annotation.Bean
import org.springframework.stereotype.Component
import org.springframework.web.reactive.function.server.router

@Component
class CustomerRouter {
  @Autowired
  lateinit var customerHandler: CustomerHandler
  @Bean
  fun customerRoutes() = router {
    "/functional".nest {
      "/customer".nest {
        GET("/", customerHandler::get)
      }
    }
```

```
    }
  }
```

Finally, instead of using the `@Autowired` annotation, just inject our handle as part of our `CustomerRouter` constructor:

```
package com.microservices.chapter4

import org.springframework.context.annotation.Bean
import org.springframework.stereotype.Component
import org.springframework.web.reactive.function.server.router

@Component
class CustomerRouter(private val customerHandler: CustomerHandler) {
  @Bean
  fun customerRoutes() = router {
    "/functional".nest {
      "/customer".nest {
        GET("/", customerHandler::get)
      }
    }
  }
}
```

 Any class annotated with `@Component` can declare in the construct the beans that are needed as parameters for the constructor. When the component scan finds the class, it will detect that the constructor can use other beans and inject them. This allows us to avoid using `@Autowired`; we can declare those beans as immutable values with `val`, instead of a mutable `var` as Autowired required.

Using reactive services

Now that we have a handler, we can connect it to our previously created reactive services. Let's first bind them in our handle through the constructor and use it:

```
@Component
class CustomerHandler(val customerService: CustomerService) {
  fun get(serverRequest: ServerRequest) =
      ok().body(customerService.getCustomer(1), Customer::class.java)
}
```

If we try to run this example now, we will get a compilation error and this is because our service method was defined as:

```
fun getCustomer(id: Int): Mono<Customer?>
```

Since `Customer` is nullable, we cannot bind to `Customer::class.java`, so let's modify our service interface:

```
package com.microservices.chapter4

import reactor.core.publisher.Flux
import reactor.core.publisher.Mono

interface CustomerService {
  fun getCustomer(id: Int) : Mono<Customer>
  fun searchCustomers(nameFilter: String): Flux<Customer>
  fun createCustomer(customerMono: Mono<Customer>) : Mono<*>
}
```

But now we need to modify our implementation to not return a null value:

```
package com.microservices.chapter4

import com.microservices.chapter4.Customer.Telephone
import org.springframework.stereotype.Component
import reactor.core.publisher.Mono
import reactor.core.publisher.toFlux
import reactor.core.publisher.toMono
import java.util.concurrent.ConcurrentHashMap

@Component
class CustomerServiceImpl : CustomerService {
  companion object {
    val initialCustomers = arrayOf(Customer(1, "Kotlin"),
        Customer(2, "Spring"),
        Customer(3, "Microservice", Telephone("+44", "7123456789")))
  }

  val customers = ConcurrentHashMap<Int,
Customer>(initialCustomers.associateBy(Customer::id))

  override fun getCustomer(id: Int) = customers[id]?.toMono() ?:
Mono.empty()

  override fun searchCustomers(nameFilter: String) = customers.filter {
    it.value.name.contains(nameFilter, true)
  }.map(Map.Entry<Int, Customer>::value).toFlux()
```

```
override fun createCustomer(customerMono: Mono<Customer>): Mono<*> =
    customerMono.map {
        customers[it.id] = it
        Mono.empty<Any>()
    }
}
```

We modify our implementation and now if our customer is not found, which means it's null, we will return an empty `Mono`. Since we are not returning a nullable object, we don't need to specify our class in the body function, so we can just change our handler:

```
package com.microservices.chapter4

import org.springframework.stereotype.Component
import org.springframework.web.reactive.function.server.ServerRequest
import org.springframework.web.reactive.function.server.ServerResponse.ok
import org.springframework.web.reactive.function.server.body

@Component
class CustomerHandler(val customerService: CustomerService) {
    fun get(serverRequest: ServerRequest) =
        ok().body(customerService.getCustomer(1))
}
```

There's one more step to get the parameters for our `GET` request—the customer that we are querying for; we will pass that parameter as part of our path, as we do in our RESTful APIs examples, in an URL such as `/customer/1`.

 For more details on how to build RESTful APIs, you can review `Chapter 3`, *Creating RESTful Services*.

Let's modify our router to declare that we need one parameter:

```
package com.microservices.chapter4

import org.springframework.context.annotation.Bean
import org.springframework.stereotype.Component
import org.springframework.web.reactive.function.server.router

@Component
class CustomerRouter(private val customerHandler: CustomerHandler) {
    @Bean
    fun customerRoutes() = router {
        "/functional".nest {
```

```
    "/customer".nest {
      GET("/{id}", customerHandler::get)
    }
  }
 }
}
```

This is similar to how we declare routes for `RequestMapping` in our RESTful APIs examples, but we need to get the parameter in our handler, so let's modify it:

```
package com.microservices.chapter4

import org.springframework.stereotype.Component
import org.springframework.web.reactive.function.server.ServerRequest
import org.springframework.web.reactive.function.server.ServerResponse.ok
import org.springframework.web.reactive.function.server.body

@Component
class CustomerHandler(val customerService: CustomerService) {
  fun get(serverRequest: ServerRequest) =
ok().body(customerService.getCustomer(serverRequest.pathVariable("id").toInt()))
}
```

Now if we visit our customer URL, for example, `http://localhost:8080/functional/customer/2`, we will get the following as output with a **200 OK** HTTP status response:

```
{
    "id":2,
    "name":"Spring"
}
```

But what happens if we request a customer that does not exist? For example, with the `http://localhost:8080/functional/customer/9` URL. We will get an empty body, but a **200 OK** HTTP status response. We need to modify our code to return **404 NOT FOUND**, as we already did in our RESTful APIs examples, but first let's change our method to handle the creation of the response through our `Mono`:

```
package com.microservices.chapter4

import org.springframework.stereotype.Component
import org.springframework.web.reactive.function.BodyInserters.fromObject
import org.springframework.web.reactive.function.server.ServerRequest
import org.springframework.web.reactive.function.server.ServerResponse.ok

@Component
```

```
class CustomerHandler(val customerService: CustomerService) {
  fun get(serverRequest: ServerRequest) =
    customerService.getCustomer(serverRequest.pathVariable("id").toInt())
      .flatMap { ok().body(fromObject(it)) }
}
```

Now we are invoking our service, firstly to obtain `Mono`, which we will convert into a response using the `flatMap` method from reactive publishers. This method will subscribe to `Mono` and when it has a value, it will produce a `Mono<ServerResponse>`, using the `ok().body()` method. But the `ok().body()` function requires a `Mono`. In our case, we will create `Mono<Customer>` using the `fromObject` method.

This will produce the following:

- Our method will be subscribed to our `Mono<Customer>` and returned by the `getCustomer` method using `flatMap`
- When that `Mono<Customer>` has a value, we will receive a `Customer` object in `it` parameter
- Then we will convert the value in a new `Mono<Customer>` using the `fromObject` method
- Finally, we will create `Mono<ServerResponse>` with the just-created `Mono<Customer>`

So, our method will return our final `Mono<ServerResponse>`, and when someone subscribes to it, we will get our `Customer` object.

Now, let's add the code for handling the empty `Mono`:

```
package com.microservices.chapter4

import org.springframework.stereotype.Component
import org.springframework.web.reactive.function.BodyInserters.fromObject
import org.springframework.web.reactive.function.server.ServerRequest
import org.springframework.web.reactive.function.server.ServerResponse.notFound
import org.springframework.web.reactive.function.server.ServerResponse.ok

@Component
class CustomerHandler(val customerService: CustomerService) {
  fun get(serverRequest: ServerRequest) =
    customerService.getCustomer(serverRequest.pathVariable("id").toInt())
      .flatMap { ok().body(fromObject(it)) }
      .switchIfEmpty(notFound().build())
}
```

In this step, we have used the original `Mono` to subscribe if the value is empty, and then we will use the `notFound` function to answer with the **404 NOT FOUND** HTTP Status. Since we will not have a body for this answer, we will just use the `build` method to complete our response.

WebFlux provides several `ServerResponse` helper functions to specify the HTTP Status as `ok()`, `notFound()`, `badRequest()`, `deleted()`, or `created()`, but we can use the `status()` function instead:

```
package com.microservices.chapter4

import org.springframework.http.HttpStatus
import org.springframework.stereotype.Component
import org.springframework.web.reactive.function.BodyInserters.fromObject
import org.springframework.web.reactive.function.server.ServerRequest
import org.springframework.web.reactive.function.server.ServerResponse.ok
import org.springframework.web.reactive.function.server.ServerResponse.status

@Component
class CustomerHandler(val customerService: CustomerService) {
  fun get(serverRequest: ServerRequest) =
      customerService.getCustomer(serverRequest.pathVariable("id").toInt())
          .flatMap{ ok().body(fromObject(it)) }
          .switchIfEmpty(status(HttpStatus.NOT_FOUND).build())
}
```

Regardless, we think that we should use the more convenient helper functions, such as `NOT_FOUND`, to make our code more readable.

Handling multiple routes

In our router, we can create multiple paths to handle multiple requests, for example, let's create a new path for querying the customer list:

```
package com.microservices.chapter4

import org.springframework.context.annotation.Bean
import org.springframework.stereotype.Component
import org.springframework.web.reactive.function.server.router

@Component
class CustomerRouter(private val customerHandler: CustomerHandler) {
  @Bean
```

```
fun customerRoutes() = router {
  "/functional".nest {
    "/customer".nest {
      GET("/{id}", customerHandler::get)
    }
    "/customers".nest {
      GET("/", customerHandler::get)
    }
  }
}
```

Now, we have a new router to get the customer list, but this can be done as well to define multiple HTTP verbs to handle:

```
package com.microservices.chapter4

import org.springframework.context.annotation.Bean
import org.springframework.stereotype.Component
import org.springframework.web.reactive.function.server.router

@Component
class CustomerRouter(private val customerHandler: CustomerHandler) {
  @Bean
  fun customerRoutes() = router {
    "/functional".nest {
      "/customer".nest {
        GET("/{id}", customerHandler::get)
        POST("/", customerHandler::get)
      }
      "/customers".nest {
        GET("/", customerHandler::get)
      }
    }
  }
}
```

We have just invoked the existing handler, but we should create new ones. Before this, let's talk about the layers that we have in our application. We need to understand them before creating new ones.

- **Routers**: Handle the paths and verbs that are reactive service will answer
- **Handlers**: Perform the logic to transform a concrete request into a response
- **Services**: Encapsulate the business logic of our domain

Having these separate layers will help us to make changes where we need to add new functionality. Our router can invoke the same handler for different functionality, and our handlers can combine several services. Changing one layer may not trigger changes in another. For example, if we change our domain logic in our service, we may not need to change our routes or handlers.

> In the same way that we need to avoid coupling in our microservice architecture, we should also try to avoid it when we create our layers. Think in those layers and how they interact when creating microservices. Remember to apply the Single Responsibility Principle; a layer should have only one reason to change.

Using query parameters

We will change our /customers route to search for customers, in the same way, that our RESTful APIs examples did.

First, we need to create a new handler in our CustomerHandler class for this search:

```
package com.microservices.chapter4

import org.springframework.http.HttpStatus
import org.springframework.stereotype.Component
import org.springframework.web.reactive.function.BodyInserters.fromObject
import org.springframework.web.reactive.function.server.ServerRequest
import org.springframework.web.reactive.function.server.ServerResponse.ok
import
org.springframework.web.reactive.function.server.ServerResponse.status

@Component
class CustomerHandler(val customerService: CustomerService) {
  fun get(serverRequest: ServerRequest) =
      customerService.getCustomer(serverRequest.pathVariable("id").toInt())
          .flatMap{ ok().body(fromObject(it)) }
          .switchIfEmpty(status(HttpStatus.NOT_FOUND).build())

  fun search(serverRequest: ServerRequest) =
      ok().body(customerService.searchCustomers(""), Customer::class.java)
}
```

When we invoke our service, it will return a Flux of the Customer object, so a publisher with a promise of those values; then, we will add it to the body, creating a Mono<ServerResponse> with a **200 OK** HTTP Status.

Now, let's change our `CustomerRouter` to invoke this new handler:

```
package com.microservices.chapter4

import org.springframework.context.annotation.Bean
import org.springframework.stereotype.Component
import org.springframework.web.reactive.function.server.router

@Component
class CustomerRouter(private val customerHandler: CustomerHandler) {
  @Bean
  fun customerRoutes() = router {
    "/functional".nest {
      "/customer".nest {
        GET("/{id}", customerHandler::get)
        POST("/", customerHandler::get)
      }
      "/customers".nest {
        GET("/", customerHandler::search)
      }
    }
  }
}
```

Now, when we invoke `http://localhost:8080/functional/customers`, we should get our list of customers:

```
[
    {
        "id": 1,
        "name": "Kotlin"
    },
    {
        "id": 2,
        "name": "Spring"
    },
    {
        "id": 3,
        "name": "Microservice",
        "telephone": {
            "countryCode": "+44",
            "telephoneNumber": "7123456789"
        }
    }
]
```

Our Router will send the request to the handler that will invoke the service. This service will return a `Flux` of customers, as before, that we will get into the body of the response.

Now, we just need to handle the query parameter. The query parameters are available through the `queryParam` method of the `ServerRequest` object, but this method returns an `Optional` object since we may or we may not have the parameter that we are searching for in the request.

 The `Optional` class was introduced in Java 8. It allows us to have an object encapsulated within and deals with the concept of not having a valid object in Optional, named as an absent object, which is very similar to `Mono.empty`. One of the advantages of that object is that we don't need to take care of null objects. Kotlin null-safety is a different approach for the same kind of solution.

Finally, let's modify our `search` function to use the `Optional` value:

```
package com.microservices.chapter4

import org.springframework.http.HttpStatus
import org.springframework.stereotype.Component
import org.springframework.web.reactive.function.BodyInserters.fromObject
import org.springframework.web.reactive.function.server.ServerRequest
import org.springframework.web.reactive.function.server.ServerResponse.ok
import
org.springframework.web.reactive.function.server.ServerResponse.status

@Component
class CustomerHandler(val customerService: CustomerService) {
  fun get(serverRequest: ServerRequest) =
      customerService.getCustomer(serverRequest.pathVariable("id").toInt())
          .flatMap{ ok().body(fromObject(it)) }
          .switchIfEmpty(status(HttpStatus.NOT_FOUND).build())

  fun search(serverRequest: ServerRequest) =
ok().body(customerService.searchCustomers(serverRequest.queryParam("nameFil
ter")
          .orElse("")), Customer::class.java)
}
```

Now, we will get the `nameFilter` query parameter from the request. If it is absent, we will send the server an empty String instead. Since our service is filtering by the `receive` parameter, if we send an empty String, it will return all the customers. If we invoke our customers URL, `http://localhost:8080/functional/customers?nameFilter=in`, again, we should get this output:

```
[
    {
        "id": 1,
        "name": "Kotlin"
    },
    {
        "id": 2,
        "name": "Spring"
    }
]
```

Processing a JSON body

When we need to implement other methods, we may need to be able to handle a JSON in the body of the request. A clear example of this is the route to create a customer. As in the example with our RESTful APIs, this should happen when we receive a POST HTTP request on our /customer route.

First, we will need to modify our `CustomerHandler` class to create a new method that we'll name `create`:

```
package com.microservices.chapter4

import org.springframework.http.HttpStatus
import org.springframework.stereotype.Component
import org.springframework.web.reactive.function.BodyInserters.fromObject
import org.springframework.web.reactive.function.server.ServerRequest
import org.springframework.web.reactive.function.server.ServerResponse.ok
import org.springframework.web.reactive.function.server.ServerResponse.status
import org.springframework.web.reactive.function.server.bodyToMono

@Component
class CustomerHandler(val customerService: CustomerService) {
  fun get(serverRequest: ServerRequest) =
      customerService.getCustomer(serverRequest.pathVariable("id").toInt())
          .flatMap { ok().body(fromObject(it)) }
          .switchIfEmpty(status(HttpStatus.NOT_FOUND).build())
```

```
    fun search(serverRequest: ServerRequest) =
ok().body(customerService.searchCustomers(serverRequest.queryParam("nameFil
ter")
            .orElse("")), Customer::class.java)

    fun create(serverRequest: ServerRequest) =
        customerService.createCustomer(serverRequest.bodyToMono()).flatMap {
          status(HttpStatus.CREATED).body(fromObject(it))
        }
    }
}
```

This newly created method will use the `bodyToMono` function from the `ServerRequest` class that provides a Kotlin-rectified function that will create a `Mono` from the body of the request. In this case, it will be `Mono<Customer>`. Then, we can use this when creating a new `ServerResponse`, as we have done before.

Now, we need to modify our `CustomerRouter` class to use this new method:

```
package com.microservices.chapter4

import org.springframework.context.annotation.Bean
import org.springframework.stereotype.Component
import org.springframework.web.reactive.function.server.router

@Component
class CustomerRouter(private val customerHandler: CustomerHandler) {
  @Bean
  fun customerRoutes() = router {
    "/functional".nest {
      "/customer".nest {
        GET("/{id}", customerHandler::get)
        POST("/", customerHandler::create)
      }
      "/customers".nest {
        GET("/", customerHandler::search)
      }
    }
  }
}
```

We can test this new route using the `curl` request:

```
curl -X POST \
  http://localhost:8080/functional/customer/ \
  -H 'content-type: application/json' \
  -d '{
  "id": 18,
```

```
    "name": "New Customer",
    "telephone": {
      "countryCode": "+44",
      "telephoneNumber": "7123456789"
    }
}'
```

Finally, if we now invoke http://localhost:8080/functional/customers, we should get our newly created customer alongside a **200 CREATED** HTTP Status:

```
[
    {
        "id": 1,
        "name": "Kotlin"
    },
    {
        "id": 2,
        "name": "Spring"
    },
    {
        "id": 18,
        "name": "New Customer",
        "telephone": {
            "countryCode": "+44",
            "telephoneNumber": "7123456789"
        }
    },
    {
        "id": 3,
        "name": "Microservice",
        "telephone": {
            "countryCode": "+44",
            "telephoneNumber": "7123456789"
        }
    }
]
```

But why are we now using status() instead of the created() ServerResponse method? The reason is that created() needs the URL of the resource that we just created, following common practices when using the **201 CREATED** HTTP status.

In order to make that change, we need to modify our CustomerService.createCustomer method to return the newly created customer.

Let's modify our `CustomerService` interface first to change the method signature:

```kotlin
package com.microservices.chapter4

import reactor.core.publisher.Flux
import reactor.core.publisher.Mono

interface CustomerService {
    fun getCustomer(id: Int) : Mono<Customer>
    fun searchCustomers(nameFilter: String): Flux<Customer>
    fun createCustomer(customerMono: Mono<Customer>) : Mono<Customer>
}
```

And then modify our implementation to return the created object:

```kotlin
package com.microservices.chapter4

import com.microservices.chapter4.Customer.Telephone
import org.springframework.stereotype.Component
import reactor.core.publisher.Mono
import reactor.core.publisher.toFlux
import reactor.core.publisher.toMono
import java.util.concurrent.ConcurrentHashMap

@Component
class CustomerServiceImpl : CustomerService {
    companion object {
        val initialCustomers = arrayOf(Customer(1, "Kotlin"),
            Customer(2, "Spring"),
            Customer(3, "Microservice", Telephone("+44", "7123456789")))
    }

    val customers = ConcurrentHashMap<Int,
Customer>(initialCustomers.associateBy(Customer::id))

    override fun getCustomer(id: Int) = customers[id]?.toMono() ?:
Mono.empty()

    override fun searchCustomers(nameFilter: String) = customers.filter {
        it.value.name.contains(nameFilter, true)
    }.map(Map.Entry<Int, Customer>::value).toFlux()

    override fun createCustomer(customerMono: Mono<Customer>) =
customerMono.map {
        customers[it.id] = it
        it
    }
}
```

Finally, we can modify our handler to return the location of the created resource:

```
package com.microservices.chapter4

import org.springframework.http.HttpStatus
import org.springframework.stereotype.Component
import org.springframework.web.reactive.function.BodyInserters.fromObject
import org.springframework.web.reactive.function.server.ServerRequest
import org.springframework.web.reactive.function.server.ServerResponse.*
import org.springframework.web.reactive.function.server.bodyToMono
import java.net.URI

@Component
class CustomerHandler(val customerService: CustomerService) {
  fun get(serverRequest: ServerRequest) =
      customerService.getCustomer(serverRequest.pathVariable("id").toInt())
          .flatMap { ok().body(fromObject(it)) }
          .switchIfEmpty(status(HttpStatus.NOT_FOUND).build())

  fun search(serverRequest: ServerRequest) =
  ok().body(customerService.searchCustomers(serverRequest.queryParam("nameFil
  ter")
          .orElse("")), Customer::class.java)

  fun create(serverRequest: ServerRequest) =
      customerService.createCustomer(serverRequest.bodyToMono()).flatMap {
        created(URI.create("/functional/customer/${it.id}")).build()
      }
}
```

If we invoke this as before, we will get the **201 CREATED** response again as an empty body result, but additionally, we get a header with the location of the created resource: `/functional/customer/18`.

Handling reactive errors

As we have done before, any microservice needs to be built for failure, so when we create reactive microservices, we can handle any error gracefully. The Reactor Framework provides mechanisms that we need to understand to handle those errors. In this section, we learn how to use them to make our reactive microservice as good at handling errors as our non-reactive microservices.

Capturing errors on Handlers

When we create handlers, we may encounter errors, and those errors can be handled with one special method in any reactive publisher onErrorResume. Let's modify our create method in the CustomerHandler class to understand how it works:

```
package com.microservices.chapter4

import org.springframework.http.HttpStatus
import org.springframework.stereotype.Component
import org.springframework.web.reactive.function.BodyInserters.fromObject
import org.springframework.web.reactive.function.server.ServerRequest
import org.springframework.web.reactive.function.server.ServerResponse.*
import org.springframework.web.reactive.function.server.bodyToMono
import reactor.core.publisher.onErrorResume
import java.net.URI

@Component
class CustomerHandler(val customerService: CustomerService) {
  fun get(serverRequest: ServerRequest) =
      customerService.getCustomer(serverRequest.pathVariable("id").toInt())
          .flatMap { ok().body(fromObject(it)) }
          .switchIfEmpty(status(HttpStatus.NOT_FOUND).build())

  fun search(serverRequest: ServerRequest) =
ok().body(customerService.searchCustomers(serverRequest.queryParam("nameFil
ter")
          .orElse("")), Customer::class.java)

  fun create(serverRequest: ServerRequest) =
      customerService.createCustomer(serverRequest.bodyToMono()).flatMap {
        created(URI.create("/functional/customer/${it.id}")).build()
      }.onErrorResume(Exception::class) {
        badRequest().body(fromObject("error"))
      }
}
```

Using onErrorResume, we can notify any reactive publisher that if we get an error, we can handle it in our method. We have created a lambda that gives a **400 BAD REQUEST** output response with a simple text.

To test this, we can just perform the following JSON request using `curl`:

```
curl -X POST \
  http://localhost:8080/functional/customer/ \
  -H 'content-type: application/json' \
  -d '{
  "id": 18,
  "name": "New Customer",
  "telephone": {
    "countryCode": "+44",
    "telephoneNumber": "7123456789"
  }
}
bad json'
```

This request will produce just a **400 BAD REQUEST** response with a text that says:

```
error
```

We can create a simple JSON response as we did in our RESTful APIs examples, bringing our `ErrorResponse` class:

```
package com.microservices.chapter4

data class ErrorResponse(val error: String, val message: String)
```

Now, we can just adapt the response to our error:

```
package com.microservices.chapter4

import org.springframework.http.HttpStatus
import org.springframework.stereotype.Component
import org.springframework.web.reactive.function.BodyInserters.fromObject
import org.springframework.web.reactive.function.server.ServerRequest
import org.springframework.web.reactive.function.server.ServerResponse.*
import org.springframework.web.reactive.function.server.bodyToMono
import reactor.core.publisher.onErrorResume
import java.net.URI

@Component
class CustomerHandler(val customerService: CustomerService) {
  fun get(serverRequest: ServerRequest) =
      customerService.getCustomer(serverRequest.pathVariable("id").toInt())
          .flatMap { ok().body(fromObject(it)) }
          .switchIfEmpty(status(HttpStatus.NOT_FOUND).build())

  fun search(serverRequest: ServerRequest) =
ok().body(customerService.searchCustomers(serverRequest.queryParam("nameFil
```

```
ter")
            .orElse("")), Customer::class.java)

    fun create(serverRequest: ServerRequest) =
        customerService.createCustomer(serverRequest.bodyToMono()).flatMap {
            created(URI.create("/functional/customer/${it.id}")).build()
        }.onErrorResume(Exception::class) {
            badRequest().body(fromObject(ErrorResponse("error creating
customer",
                it.message ?: "error")))
        }
}
```

If we repeat the `curl` request again, we should get something like:

```
{
    "error": "error creating customer",
    "message": "JSON decoding error: Unexpected character ('b' (code 98)):
expected a valid value (number, String, array, object, 'true', 'false' or
'null'); nested exception is com.fasterxml.jackson.core.JsonParseException:
Unexpected character ('b' (code 98)): expected a valid value (number,
String, array, object, 'true', 'false' or 'null')\n at [Source: UNKNOWN;
line: 9, column: 2]"
}
```

 The `onErrorResume` method is available on any reactive publisher, so we can use it in our `CustomerService` as well as other layers of the application; we do it so that our handler will not get an error.

Publishing errors

We know how to handle errors, but sometimes we need to produce them. For example, let's try to create an error if we are trying to create a customer that is already created.

For this, we will create a simple `Exception` class, `CustomerExistException`:

```
package com.microservices.chapter4

class CustomerExistException(override val message: String) :
Exception(message)
```

Now we can modify the `create` method in our `CustomerServiceImpl` class to use this new exception:

```
package com.microservices.chapter4

import com.microservices.chapter4.Customer.Telephone
import org.springframework.stereotype.Component
import reactor.core.publisher.Mono
import reactor.core.publisher.toFlux
import reactor.core.publisher.toMono
import java.util.concurrent.ConcurrentHashMap

@Component
class CustomerServiceImpl : CustomerService {
  companion object {
    val initialCustomers = arrayOf(Customer(1, "Kotlin"),
        Customer(2, "Spring"),
        Customer(3, "Microservice", Telephone("+44", "7123456789")))
  }

  val customers = ConcurrentHashMap<Int,
Customer>(initialCustomers.associateBy(Customer::id))

  override fun getCustomer(id: Int) = customers[id]?.toMono() ?:
Mono.empty()

  override fun searchCustomers(nameFilter: String) = customers.filter {
    it.value.name.contains(nameFilter, true)
  }.map(Map.Entry<Int, Customer>::value).toFlux()

  override fun createCustomer(customerMono: Mono<Customer>) =
      customerMono.flatMap {
        if (customers[it.id] == null) {
          customers[it.id] = it
          it.toMono()
        } else {
          Mono.error(CustomerExistException("Customer ${it.id} already
          exist"))
        }
      }
}
```

In this case, we have to check if the customer exists first, and if not, we will just store and return it as a `Mono`, but if not, we will just create a `Mono.error`. In the same way that `Mono.empty` creates a `Mono` that has no value, a `Mono.error` will create a `Mono` that includes an error.

Let's try now to send this `curl` request twice:

```
curl -X POST \
 http://localhost:8080/functional/customer/ \
 -H 'content-type: application/json' \
 -d '{
 "id": 18,
 "name": "New Customer",
 "telephone": {
 "countryCode": "+44",
 "telephoneNumber": "7123456789"
 }
}
'
```

The second time that this request is sent, we should get this output with a **400 BAD REQUEST** response:

```
{
    "error": "error creating customer",
    "message": "Customer 18 already exist"
}
```

With this completed, we are now ready to handle errors effectively in our reactive services.

Summary

In this chapter, we have discovered how to create a reactive microservice to produce high-quality non-blocking IO microservices. We learned more concepts on the reactive programming model and the publisher and subscribe patterns. Now, we have two programming models to choose from when we create reactive microservices, a more traditional annotation-based model, and a new functional-style model. Finally, we have learned how to handle errors to create microservices built for failure.

But any reactive system is as reactive as the backend it uses, so when our microservice needs to inquiry data, for example, from a database, we can do it reactively as we are still keeping the full capabilities on the reactive microservices.

In the next chapter, we will learn how we can use MongoDB reactively when creating reactive microservices. We will learn how we could use Spring Data to perform reactive operations against our databases, and how easily we can use and configure MongoDB in our applications. Then, we will create RESTful APIs with CRUD repositories to deliver fast, non-blocking reactive microservices that are fully integrated with NoSQL databases.

5
Reactive Spring Data

In `Chapter 4`, *Creating Reactive Microservices*, we learned how we can create non-blocking reactive microservices. However, if our microservices need to query data using blocking operations, we will lose the benefits of the reactive programming. Spring Framework 5 and Spring Data provide reactive capabilities for most modern databases.

 We reviewed the main concepts of reactive programming in `Chapter 1`, *Understanding Microservices*, in the *Reactive Microservices* section. You can review this section to get more insight into this new reactive programming model.

In this chapter, we will learn how to use Spring Data to perform reactive operations against our database. But first, we will learn how to use and configure MongoDB in our applications, the NoSQL database chosen for this chapter. Then, we will see how we can easily connect our previously created RESTful APIs with CRUD repositories using the previously created examples. With these final steps, we will be ready to deliver fast, non-blocking reactive microservices that are fully integrated with NoSQL databases.

In this chapter, you will learn about:

- NoSQL
- MongoDB
- Spring Data
- ReactiveCrudRepository
- ReactiveMongoOperations
- ReactiveMongoTemplate

NoSQL databases

You may be familiar with SQL databases since they are probably the most common database model used on millions of applications. But NoSQL databases are widely used in the industry due to their capabilities, and they can be easily integrated into our microservices. In this section, we will learn about them and how we can use MongoDB as a repository for the data required by our microservices.

What is a SQL database?

To understand what a NoSQL database is, we first need to understand what a SQL database is. In a SQL database, the data is organized in a tabular manner. We have different tables representing collections on our database, and each of these tables contain a set of columns that define them; those columns may have attributes such as what kind of data it can store.

In each of those tables, we may have rows that represent entries in each collection. The tables themselves may have other attributes, such as indexes or keys, that allow us to search or point to particular elements on the table. Finally, those tables may contain relationships with other tables that link elements together.

All these tables, columns, and relationships represent our database schema, a solid but rigid definition of our data model. This is a traditional example of a couple of tables representing customers and their telephone numbers.The following is the Customer table:

ID	NAME
1	spring
2	reactive
3	data

This is the Customer_Telephone table:

CUSTOMER_ID	TELEPHONE
2	+447123987654
3	+447123456789

One of the main challenges on a SQL database is scaling since neither these relationships nor the schema can be easily split. For example, in the preceding table, if we need to split the `Customer` table, we may need to split the `Customer_Telephone` table as well, according to how they are related.

For example, customers 2 and 3 have a telephone number, but customer 1 does not. If we need to move the data for each customer to a different database, customers 2 and 3 and their telephone numbers need to move together, so both tables need to move to the same place. This is getting exponentially more complex when more tables, relationships, and dependencies are in place in our database.

What is a NoSQL database?

In a NoSQL database, the information is arranged in a different manner; instead of a tabular representation, the overall idea is to have a lax schema where data contained may change freely.

There are dozens of ways to arrange the data in a NoSQL database, however, document-based is the most common approach. In order to understand this, let's look at an example of a customer collection in a document-oriented database such as MongoDB:

```
{
    "_id" : 1,
    "name" : "spring"
},
{
    "_id" : 2,
    "name" : "data"
},
{
    "_id" : 3,
    "name" : "reactive",
    "telephone" : "+447123456789"
}
```

Each element in the collection is a free set of data that contains different objects with values, and each of these can have a complex structured as required. For example, we can have something like:

```
{
    "_id" : 3,
    "name" : "reactive",
    "telephone" : "+447123456789",
    "address" : [
```

```
        { "home" : "123 super street" } ,
        { "work" : "347 normal street" }
    ]

}
```

In this case, splitting the data is not complicated anymore, but we should make browsing the data more efficient. However, it is not so easy to implement other mechanisms such as keeping relations aligned between different sets of data.

 NoSQL databases are great, but that doesn't mean they're the best solution for any problem. For certain cases, a more traditional database may be better for the task. Try to understand what is what and what you need before choosing one or the other and always remember: **one solution does not fit all situations**.

Installing MongoDB

For the rest of the examples, we are going to require the MongoDB community server, so let's start installing it. First, we need to download the right version for our operating system by visiting https://www.mongodb.com/download-center?jmp=nav#community. It is available for Windows, Linux, and macOS. We can install it wherever we want to get a couple of programs under the bin folder:

- mongod: The database server
- mongo: The client

Starting our database server

First, we will create a directory that we can use to store our data, so under the Mongo bin directory, we will execute the following command:

```
mkdir data
```

Now, we can start our database with this command:

```
mongod -dbpath data
```

This will output several log lines, and at the end, we should see something like:

```
I NETWORK  [thread1] waiting for connections on port 27017
```

This server will run until we press *Ctrl + C*, but for now, let's keep it open.

Connecting with the Mongo client

In another terminal window, in the same Mongo `bin` directory, we can just run:

```
mongo
```

After a couple of seconds, we will see:

```
I CONTROL [initandlisten]
>
```

That is our command interface. We can now just type any command followed by *Enter*. For example, if we execute the `db.version()` command, we will get something like:

```
> db.version()
3.4.9
```

We can close our connection to the database and end the client using the `exit` command:

```
> exit
bye
```

 You can find out what other commands are available by using the `help` command or reading the detailed MongoDB documentation: `https://docs.mongodb.com/manual/`. MongoDB also provides free courses and certification at `https://university.mongodb.com`.

Creating a database

We have now installed a MongoDB server that can handle several databases, but we are going to need one for our examples.

First, let's find out what databases exist using the `show dbs` command:

```
> show dbs
admin 0.000GB
local 0.000GB
```

By default, there are two databases on our server: the admin database and the local database; these are system databases that Mongo requires to function:

- `admin database`: Holds different security and administration information
- `local database`: Stores the data required for this instance of our MongoDB server

Those two databases cannot be deleted, so we need to create our own, but first, we need to inform the client that we are going to use a different database using the `use` command:

```
> use microservices
switched to db microservices
```

 If we close our client now, the database will be not be created; MongoDB will not create it until we insert some data in our database. You can use the `show dbs` command to see that it is not actually there yet.

Now, we can create a collection within our database and use the `db.createCollection` command:

```
> db.createCollection("Customers")
{ "ok" : 1 }
```

This will create a collection that we can use to add documents to it.

 Now that our database exists, we can see it with the `show dbs` command, but even the `db.createCollection` command will not really create our collection until we add data to it. If we use the `show collections` command, it won't display any results yet.

Let's add one customer to our customers collection with the `insert` command:

```
> db.Customers.insertOne( { "name" : "spring" } )
WriteResult({ "nInserted" : 1 })
```

We can even add two customers to one single command:

```
> db.Customers.insertMany( [ { "name" : "reactive" }, { "name" :
"microservices" } ] )
BulkWriteResult({
        "writeErrors" : [ ],
        "writeConcernErrors" : [ ],
        "nInserted" : 2,
        "nUpserted" : 0,
```

```
            "nMatched"  :  0,
            "nModified"  :  0,
            "nRemoved"  :  0,
            "upserted"  :  [ ]
    })
```

Now that our database has a collection that contains data, let's explore some other commands we can use.

Using commands

We can check our data using the `find` command:

```
> db.Customers.find()
{ "_id"  :  ObjectId("59d6adc1ad712390e783617e"),  "name"  :  "spring" }
{ "_id"  :  ObjectId("59d6adcead712390e783617f"),  "name"  :  "reactive" }
{ "_id"  :  ObjectId("59d6adcead712390e7836180"),  "name"  :  "microservices" }
```

 Every document created contains an_id property name, this is because we didn't provide an `id` when we were inserting the data in our collection, so MongoDB autogenerated one.

We can now update one document in our collection using the `update` command:

```
> db.Customers.update({ "_id"  :  ObjectId("59d6adc1ad712390e783617e")} ,
{"name"  :  "super spring"})
WriteResult({ "nMatched"  :  1, "nUpserted"  :  0, "nModified"  :  1 })
```

Or, we can delete one document using the `remove` command:

```
> db.Customers.remove({ "_id"  :  ObjectId("59d6adcead712390e783617f")})
WriteResult({ "nRemoved"  :  1 })
```

Now, we can check our result by executing the `find` command again:

```
> db.Customers.find()
{ "_id"  :  ObjectId("59d6adc1ad712390e783617e"),  "name"  :  "super spring" }
{ "_id"  :  ObjectId("59d6adcead712390e7836180"),  "name"  :  "microservices" }
```

update, remove, or even find can be used as the first parameter for a query where we can create expressions for filtering or finding one or many results:

```
> db.Customers.find( { "name" : "super spring"} )
{ "_id" : ObjectId("59d6adc1ad712390e783617e"), "name" : "super spring" }
```

Collection names in MongoDB are case sensitive; db.Customers.find() or db.customers.find() act in different collections, which are Customers and customers, respectively. If the commands explained here don't work, check the case of the collections in them.

MongoDB allows us to find documents using regular expressions such as:

```
> db.Customers.find({"name" : /.*spring.*/i})
{ "_id" : ObjectId("59d6adc1ad712390e783617e"), "name" : "super spring" }
```

This will list any customer whose name contains spring, ignoring case.

There are a dozen of commands that we can use in a collection. In the client, we can just type db.Customers.help() to list them or we can look to the extensive MongoDB manual at https://docs.mongodb.com/getting-started/shell/.

Now that we have a database that we can use for storing our data, let's look at how we can utilize it in Spring microservices using Spring Data.

Using Spring Data

Spring Data provides a familiar and consistent Spring-based programming model for data access. It makes it easy to use data access technologies, including NoSQL and SQL databases. Since Spring Framework 5, Spring Data provides reactive capabilities based on the Reactor framework.

We learned how to use the Reactor Framework in Chapter 4, *Creating Reactive Microservices*, you may need to review it again in order to fully understand this chapter.

Currently, the Spring Data reactive implementation supports only NoSQL databases and we can choose between MongoDB, Cassandra, or Redis. In this section, we will learn how we can set up a project that uses Spring Data to connect to our MongoDB server.

Setting up the project

For setting up our project we will use Spring Initializr, so let's visit `https://start.spring.io/`:

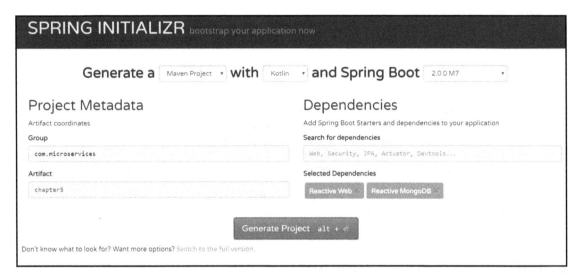

Configuring our project in Spring Initializr

We have chosen to create a **Maven Project** using **Kotlin** and **Spring Boot 2.0.0 M7**; we choose the **Group** to be `com.microservices` and the **Artifact** as `chapter5`. For **Dependencies**, we have set **Reactive Web** and **Reactive MongoDB**.

Now, we can click **Generate Project** to download it as a zip file. After we unzip it, we can open it with IntelliJ IDEA to start working on our project.

After some minutes, our project will be ready and we can Open the Maven window to see the different lifecycle phases as well as the Maven plugins and their goals.

We cover how to use Spring Initializr, Maven, and IntelliJ IDEA in `Chapter 2`, *Getting Started with Spring Boot 2.0*. You can check out this chapter to learn about topics not covered in this section.

Let's run our microservice:

In the Maven window, we double-click the **spring-boot** plugin, **run** goal, or just do the following from the command line:

```
mvnw spring-boot:run
```

After some seconds, we will see several log lines, including something like this:

```
INFO 2712 --- [ main] o.s.b.web.embedded.netty.NettyWebServer : Netty
started on port(s): 8080
INFO 2712 --- [ main] c.e.chapter5.Chapter5ApplicationKt : Started
Chapter5ApplicationKt in 3.018 seconds (JVM running for 6.028)
INFO 2712 --- [localhost:27017] org.mongodb.driver.cluster : Exception in
monitor thread while connecting to server localhost:27017

com.mongodb.MongoSocketOpenException: Exception opening socket
```

Our service is running, but we get an exception in the log because we can't connect to the MongoDB, either because it is not running or because we haven't configured it yet.

Configuring our connection

By default, Spring Data MongoDB will try to connect to a localhost database server in the default MongoDB port 27017. We get that error because our database server was not running. Go to our MongoDB directory, in the bin folder, and run:

```
mongod -dbpath data
```

Remember that data is a folder we created previously; if it was not created, create it before we run the MongoDB server. If we run our microservice again in the log lines, we should see something like:

```
INFO 11440 --- [localhost:27017] org.mongodb.driver.connection : Opened
connection [connectionId{localValue:1, serverValue:1}] to localhost:27017
```

Spring Data Mongo allows us to change the configuration, but first, let's stop our MongoDB server to run it in a different port by pressing *Ctrl* + *C* in the terminal window that is currently running.

Now, we will run it on --port 27700 and launch it with this command:

```
mongod -dbpath data --port 27700
```

To configure in IntelliJ, we'll go to our project window. Expand the elements until you find the `application.properties` file that should be in the `src/resources` folder. Select it with a single click and then press *Shift + F6* to rename it to `application.yml`.

 If we need to connect to our MongoDB server using the mongo client, located in the MongoDB installation path under the `bin` folder, we must specify the port of our server with `mongo --dbport 27700`.

Now, let's add configuration values to our file:

```
spring:
  data:
    mongodb:
      uri: "mongodb://localhost:27700"
      database: "microservices"
```

We just set our connection string to the MongoDB server, providing the host and port that it's running on as well the name of the database that we will use. If the database does not exist, Spring will create it for us.

 Spring allows us to have configuration values in properties or yaml files. As we recommend in `Chapter 2`, *Getting Started with Spring Boot 2.0*, we use yaml as our preferred method.

We can run our microservices again so that everything is up and running. If we look at our terminal windows when the MongoDB server was launched, we will see something like:

```
I NETWORK  [thread1] connection accepted from 127.0.0.1:51499 #2 (1
connection now open)
```

That means that our MongoDB server has got a connection from our microservice, so let's do something with it.

Sending commands to MongoDB

Spring Data provides a class to send commands to our MongoDB reactively, `ReactiveMongoOperations`. Let's try to do that.

First, we need to create the class that we are going to use to initialize our database. We will name it DatabaseInitializer:

```
package com.microservices.chapter5

import org.springframework.stereotype.Component
import javax.annotation.PostConstruct

@Component
class DatabaseInitializer {
  @PostConstruct
  fun initData() {
  }
}
```

We have created a Component Spring and annotated a method with @PostConstruct; this will make a spring to call that particular method after the component is created. Now, we can wire the ReactiveMongoOperations object that the spring has created when we initialized our MongoDB connection, and we can use it to initialize a collection in our database:

```
package com.microservices.chapter5

import org.springframework.beans.factory.annotation.Autowired
import org.springframework.data.mongodb.core.ReactiveMongoOperations
import org.springframework.stereotype.Component
import javax.annotation.PostConstruct

@Component
class DatabaseInitializer {
  @Autowired
  lateinit var mongoOperations: ReactiveMongoOperations

  @PostConstruct
  fun initData() {
    mongoOperations.createCollection("Customers").subscribe {
      println("Customers collections created")
    }
  }
}
```

We have sent a command to the MongoDB server to create a collection in our database. This is a reactive command so we need to `subscribe` to it, then when the collection is created, we can just print a message. But we don't want to create the collection every single time, so let's first check whether we already have the collection:

```
package com.microservices.chapter5

import org.springframework.beans.factory.annotation.Autowired
import org.springframework.data.mongodb.core.ReactiveMongoOperations
import org.springframework.stereotype.Component
import javax.annotation.PostConstruct

@Component
class DatabaseInitializer {

  @Autowired
  lateinit var mongoOperations: ReactiveMongoOperations

  @PostConstruct
  fun initData() {
    mongoOperations.collectionExists("Customers").subscribe {
      if (it != true)
    mongoOperations.createCollection("Customers").subscribe {
        println("Customers collections created")
      } else println("Customers collections already exist")
    }
  }
}
```

We have sent a command to check whether the customer collection exists, then we decided to `subscribe` to the command. We will receive the result of the check in the lambda that we have created as the first parameter with a Boolean value indicating whether the collection exists or not. Then, we can send a command to create the collection. We have to chain a set of `subscribe` to the database commands as `collectionExists` or `createCollection`, in order to create the collection.

If we run our service once, we should see this message in our log:

```
Customers collections created
```

But if we're running it a second time, we will see:

```
Customers collections already exist
```

We can use the MongoDB client to check whether we have successfully created the collection in our database. From the MongoDB installation path, under the `bin` folder, we can just execute this command:

```
mongo --port 27700
> use microservices
switched to db microservices
> show collections
Customers
```

Reactive repositories

We now have a connection to our database and we can send commands, but we need to learn how we can add or modify data in our collection since this Spring provides Reactive repositories.

Creating a repository

First, we need to bring back our `Customer` class that we used in our previous example since we are going to use it now, so let's add it to our project:

```
package com.microservices.chapter5

data class Customer(var id: Int=0, var name: String="", var telephone:
Telephone? = null) {
  data class Telephone(var countryCode: String = "", var telephoneNumber:
String = "")
}
```

But we need to modify it in order to store it in our MongoDB. We will set the name of the collection to store this object using `@Document`:

```
package com.microservices.chapter5

import org.springframework.data.mongodb.core.mapping.Document

@Document(collection = "Customers")
data class Customer(var id: Int=0, var name: String="", var telephone:
Telephone? = null) {
  data class Telephone(var countryCode: String = "", var telephoneNumber:
String = "")
}
```

Then, we need to create our repository. For this, we will add a new interface to our project. Let's name it `CustomerRepository`:

```
package com.microservices.chapter5

import org.springframework.data.repository.reactive.ReactiveCrudRepository

interface CustomerRepository : ReactiveCrudRepository<Customer, Int>
```

This interface inherits from the `ReactiveCrudRepository` interface and we need to specify the class that we are going to store in the repository, `Customer` in our example, and the type of the key used for each entry, `Int` as it is the `id` for our `Customer` class.

 CRUD is a common acronym in databases that stands for: CREATE, READ, UPDATE, and DELETE. These are the usual operations that you perform on any database, regardless of what database are you working on.

Spring will use the interface that performs CRUD operations on a database. In our example, when the microservice starts Spring Boot, it will find that interface and create a component that will implement those operations with reactive commands.

Using the repository

We can modify our `DatabaseInitializer` class to add some initial data to our database using the repository that we just created:

```
package com.microservices.chapter5

import org.springframework.beans.factory.annotation.Autowired
import org.springframework.data.mongodb.core.ReactiveMongoOperations
import org.springframework.stereotype.Component
import javax.annotation.PostConstruct

@Component
class DatabaseInitializer {
    @Autowired
    lateinit var customerRepository: CustomerRepository

    @Autowired
    lateinit var mongoOperations: ReactiveMongoOperations

    @PostConstruct
    fun initData() {
```

```
        mongoOperations.collectionExists("Customers").subscribe {
            if (it != true)
    mongoOperations.createCollection("Customers").subscribe {
            println("Customers collections created")
            } else println("Customers collections already exist")
            customerRepository.save(Customer(1, "spring")).subscribe{
            println("Default customers created")
            }
        }
    }
}
```

Here, we first have an instance of CustomerRepository wiring into our DabaseInitializer class, and just after checking on the existence of collection, regardless of whether or not it exists, we save one customer in our customers collection inside the database. The save operation on our repository is also a reactive operation, so we need to subscribe to it in order to get notified when it is completed.

If we now run our service, we should get this message in the log:

```
Default customers created
```

Our customers will be added to the database collection any time we run the service, and if the record actually exists, they will be updated.

We could use the mongo client to see that our customer is created:

```
> db.Customers.find()
{ "_id" : 1, "name" : "spring", "_class" : "com.example.chapter5.Customer"
}
```

We can see that Spring has sent a special value named _class while creating the object. This is the Class that was originally used to create that object in our collection; in this example, it is:com.example.chapter5.Customer.

This will be used when reading those objects back from the collection into our microservice to understand which class Spring could use to create an instance of that object.

Completing our initialization

We have created our initialization on an object, but let's create a set of them, as we did in previous chapters:

```kotlin
package com.microservices.chapter5

import com.microservices.chapter5.Customer.Telephone
import org.springframework.beans.factory.annotation.Autowired
import org.springframework.data.mongodb.core.ReactiveMongoOperations
import org.springframework.stereotype.Component
import javax.annotation.PostConstruct

@Component
class DatabaseInitializer {
  @Autowired
  lateinit var customerRepository: CustomerRepository

  @Autowired
  lateinit var mongoOperations: ReactiveMongoOperations

  companion object {
    val initialCustomers = listOf(Customer(1, "Kotlin"),
        Customer(2, "Spring"),
        Customer(3, "Microservice", Telephone("+44", "7123456789")))
  }

  @PostConstruct
  fun initData() {
    mongoOperations.collectionExists("Customers").subscribe {
      if (it != true)
mongoOperations.createCollection("Customers").subscribe {
        println("Customers collections created")
      } else println("Customers collections already exist")
      customerRepository.saveAll(initialCustomers).subscribe{
        println("Default customers created")
      }
    }
  }
}
```

We have declared our `initialCustomers` in a `companion object`, a list of the customers that we will initially have in the database, and modified our `PostConstruct` to save it. Finally, since we now use a repository, we don't really need to create a collection since the repository itself will take care of it, so we can simplify our `PostConstruct` code:

```kotlin
package com.microservices.chapter5

import com.microservices.chapter5.Customer.Telephone
import org.springframework.beans.factory.annotation.Autowired
import org.springframework.stereotype.Component
import javax.annotation.PostConstruct

@Component
class DatabaseInitializer {
  @Autowired
  lateinit var customerRepository: CustomerRepository

  companion object {
    val initialCustomers = listOf(Customer(1, "Kotlin"),
        Customer(2, "Spring"),
        Customer(3, "Microservice", Telephone("+44", "7123456789")))
  }

  @PostConstruct
  fun initData() {
    customerRepository.saveAll(initialCustomers).subscribe {
      println("Default customers created")
    }
  }
}
```

If we now use the mongo client to query our database, we can see everything created:

```
> use microservices
switched to db microservices
> db.Customers.find()
{ "_id" : 2, "name" : "Spring", "_class" : "com.example.chapter5.Customer"
}
{ "_id" : 1, "name" : "Kotlin", "_class" : "com.example.chapter5.Customer"
}
{ "_id" : 3, "name" : "Microservice", "telephone" : { "countryCode" :
"+44", "telephoneNumber" : "7123456789" }, "_class
" : "com.example.chapter5.Customer" }
>
```

Using ReactiveMongoTemplate

We have used `ReactiveCrudRepository` to perform CRUD operations in our database, but since we need to perform operations with reactive types, such as Mono or Flux, we need to use `ReactiveMongoTemplate` to handle this reactively.

So, we are going to change `CustomerRepository` to become a class that is annotated with `@Repository`:

```
package com.microservices.chapter5

import org.springframework.data.mongodb.core.ReactiveMongoTemplate
import org.springframework.stereotype.Repository
import reactor.core.publisher.Mono

@Repository
class CustomerRepository(private val template: ReactiveMongoTemplate) {
  fun create(customer: Mono<Customer>) = template.save(customer)
}
```

A class annotated with the repository can receive a `ReactiveMongoTemplate` object in the constructor, which it can use to perform reactive operations, for example, receiving a `Mono<Customer>` to save it on the database. Remember that a `Mono` or `Flux` is a promise of values; when we are saving them, we are indicating to Spring Data to save it to the database when that object has a value.

In the same way, those operations can return `Mono` or `Flux`.

 We review how the publish/subscribe mechanism works in `Chapter 4,` *Creating Reactive Microservices*. You can refresh your familiarity with the information by reading that chapter again.

We can now change our initialization instead of being in separate class to be in this repository, and delete the `DatabaseInitializer` class:

```
package com.microservices.chapter5

import org.springframework.data.mongodb.core.ReactiveMongoTemplate
import org.springframework.stereotype.Repository
import reactor.core.publisher.Mono
import reactor.core.publisher.toMono
import javax.annotation.PostConstruct

@Repository
```

```
class CustomerRepository(private val template: ReactiveMongoTemplate) {
  companion object {
    val initialCustomers = listOf(Customer(1, "Kotlin"),
        Customer(2, "Spring"),
        Customer(3, "Microservice", Customer.Telephone("+44",
"7123456789")))
  }

  @PostConstruct
  fun initializeRepository() =
initialCustomers.map(Customer::toMono).map(this::create).map(Mono<Customer>
::subscribe)

  fun create(customer: Mono<Customer>) = template.save(customer)
}
```

We just map our list into `Mono<Customer>`, then invoke our create a method and `subscribe` to the results.

With this, we are ready to start connecting to our RESTful APIs with CRUD operations.

From CRUD to REST

Now that we have a Repository, we can use it in our microservice to perform the operations that our microservice will expose. So, let's try to modify our previously created reactive RESTful operations into CRUD operations in our database and answer back to whoever invoked it reactively.

 We learned how to create reactive RESTful Microservices in `Chapter 4`, *Creating Reactive Microservices*. We'll use some of the code that was created during that chapter; if you are not familiar with it, you may want to review the content of that chapter.

Bringing back our service

Previously, we have created a service class to hide the implementation details how we persist in our Model, so let's do it again by creating a `CustomerService` interface, for now, just a method to get a `Customer` from an `id`:

```
package com.microservices.chapter5

import reactor.core.publisher.Mono
```

```
interface CustomerService {
  fun getCustomer(id: Int): Mono<Customer>
}
```

Now, we will create the implementation of the service:

```
package com.microservices.chapter5

import reactor.core.publisher.Mono

class CustomerServiceImpl : CustomerService {
  override fun getCustomer(id: Int): Mono<Customer> {
  }
}
```

We now need to add a READ operation to our repository to get a customer:

```
package com.microservices.chapter5

import org.springframework.data.mongodb.core.ReactiveMongoTemplate
import org.springframework.data.mongodb.core.findById
import org.springframework.stereotype.Repository
import reactor.core.publisher.Mono
import reactor.core.publisher.toMono
import javax.annotation.PostConstruct

@Repository
class CustomerRepository(private val template: ReactiveMongoTemplate) {
  companion object {
    val initialCustomers = listOf(Customer(1, "Kotlin"),
        Customer(2, "Spring"),
        Customer(3, "Microservice", Customer.Telephone("+44",
"7123456789")))
  }

  @PostConstruct
  fun initializeRepository() =
initialCustomers.map(Customer::toMono).map(this::create).map(Mono<Customer>
::subscribe)

  fun create(customer: Mono<Customer>) = template.save(customer)
  fun findById(id: Int) = template.findById<Customer>(id)
}
```

Finally, let's add the repository to our service so we can actually get the value from the database:

```
package com.microservices.chapter5

import org.springframework.beans.factory.annotation.Autowired
import org.springframework.stereotype.Service

@Service
class CustomerServiceImpl : CustomerService {
  @Autowired
  lateinit var customerRepository: CustomerRepository

  override fun getCustomer(id: Int) = customerRepository.findById(id)
}
```

Since we will create a RESTful microservice in order to handle if we have a telephone or not, in our Customer class, we use a null value, then we need to remember to configure jackson to not serialize null objects, just adding to our application.yml:

```
spring.jackson.default-property-inclusion: NON_NULL
```

Mapping GET to READ

Now, we need to create our route to handle an HTTP GET request with a READ operation on the service. Let's first create our CustomerHandler class:

```
package com.microservices.chapter5

import org.springframework.http.HttpStatus
import org.springframework.stereotype.Component
import org.springframework.web.reactive.function.BodyInserters.fromObject
import org.springframework.web.reactive.function.server.ServerRequest
import org.springframework.web.reactive.function.server.ServerResponse.ok
import
org.springframework.web.reactive.function.server.ServerResponse.status

@Component
class CustomerHandler(val customerService: CustomerService) {
  fun get(serverRequest: ServerRequest) =
      customerService.getCustomer(serverRequest.pathVariable("id").toInt())
          .flatMap { ok().body(fromObject(it)) }
          .switchIfEmpty(status(HttpStatus.NOT_FOUND).build())
}
```

Now, let's create our `CustomerRouter` for sending the HTTP `GET` request to our `CustomerHandler`:

```
package com.microservices.chapter5

import org.springframework.context.annotation.Bean
import org.springframework.stereotype.Component
import org.springframework.web.reactive.function.server.router

@Component
class CustomerRouter(private val customerHandler: CustomerHandler) {
  @Bean
  fun customerRoutes() = router {
    "/customer".nest {
      GET("/{id}", customerHandler::get)
    }
  }
}
```

So far, this is identical to the example of our previous chapter, and this is because our service is the only thing that actually changes.

> This is a great feature that we need to consider—if tomorrow we need to change our service to persist the data in a different way, we don't need to change our routers classes or our handlers classes, just our service implementation, and this is the kind of decoupling that we need to have in our software.

Now, we can just simply make a request to `http://localhost:8080/customer/1` to get a **200 OK** status and our customer:

```
{
    "id": 1,
    "name": "Kotlin"
}
```

If we use an URL for a customer that does not exist, for example, `http://localhost:8080/customer/5`, we get **404 NOT FOUND**. Since our repository will not find the data, it will return a `Mono.empty` and we already handle that in our handler using `switchIfEmpty`.

Mapping POST to CREATE

We already have a create method in our repository, so let's modify our service to use it, but first, we need to modify our `CustomerService` interface:

```
package com.microservices.chapter5

import reactor.core.publisher.Mono

interface CustomerService {
  fun getCustomer(id: Int): Mono<Customer>
  fun createCustomer(customer: Mono<Customer>) : Mono<Customer>
}
```

Then, let's implement it in our `CustomerServiceImpl` class by using our repository:

```
package com.microservices.chapter5

import org.springframework.beans.factory.annotation.Autowired
import org.springframework.stereotype.Service
import reactor.core.publisher.Mono

@Service
class CustomerServiceImpl : CustomerService {
  @Autowired
  lateinit var customerRepository: CustomerRepository

  override fun getCustomer(id: Int) = customerRepository.findById(id)
  override fun createCustomer(customer: Mono<Customer>) =
customerRepository.create(customer)
}
```

Now, let's add the appropriate method in our `CustomerHandler` class, as we do originally:

```
package com.microservices.chapter5

import org.springframework.http.HttpStatus
import org.springframework.stereotype.Component
import org.springframework.web.reactive.function.BodyInserters.fromObject
import org.springframework.web.reactive.function.server.ServerRequest
import org.springframework.web.reactive.function.server.ServerResponse.*
import org.springframework.web.reactive.function.server.bodyToMono
import java.net.URI

@Component
class CustomerHandler(val customerService: CustomerService) {
  fun get(serverRequest: ServerRequest) =
```

```
        customerService.getCustomer(serverRequest.pathVariable("id").toInt())
            .flatMap { ok().body(fromObject(it)) }
            .switchIfEmpty(status(HttpStatus.NOT_FOUND).build())
    fun create(serverRequest: ServerRequest) =
        customerService.createCustomer(serverRequest.bodyToMono()).flatMap {
            created(URI.create("/customer/${it.id}")).build()
        }
}
```

Finally, we need to add in the mapping to our `CustomerRouter` to handle the HTTP POST request:

```
package com.microservices.chapter5

import org.springframework.context.annotation.Bean
import org.springframework.stereotype.Component
import org.springframework.web.reactive.function.server.router

@Component
class CustomerRouter(private val customerHandler: CustomerHandler) {
  @Bean
  fun customerRoutes() = router {
    "/customer".nest {
      GET("/{id}", customerHandler::get)
      POST("/", customerHandler::create)
    }
  }
}
```

We can try sending a POST request using this `curl` command, which will get a **200 OK** response:

```
curl -X POST \
  http://localhost:8080/customer/ \
  -H 'content-type: application/json' \
  -d '{
  "id": 18,
  "name": "New Customer",
  "telephone": {
    "countryCode": "+44",
    "telephoneNumber": "7123456789"
  }
}
'
```

If we now use the mongo client, we can see that the data is created:

```
> use microservices
switched to db microservices
> db.Customers.find()
{ "_id" : 1, "name" : "Kotlin", "_class" : "com.example.chapter5.Customer"
}
{ "_id" : 2, "name" : "Spring", "_class" : "com.example.chapter5.Customer"
}
{ "_id" : 3, "name" : "Microservice", "telephone" : { "countryCode" :
"+44", "telephoneNumber" : "7123456789" }, "_class" :
"com.example.chapter5.Customer" }
{ "_id" : 18, "name" : "New Customer", "telephone" : { "countryCode" :
"+44", "telephoneNumber" : "7123456789" }, "_class" :
"com.example.chapter5.Customer" }
>
```

Mapping DELETE

In order to handle an HTTP DELETE request with a DELETE operation, we first need to add a new method to our CustomerRepository class:

```
package com.microservices.chapter5

import org.springframework.data.mongodb.core.ReactiveMongoTemplate
import org.springframework.data.mongodb.core.findById
import org.springframework.data.mongodb.core.query.Criteria.where
import org.springframework.data.mongodb.core.query.Query
import org.springframework.data.mongodb.core.query.isEqualTo
import org.springframework.data.mongodb.core.remove
import org.springframework.stereotype.Repository
import reactor.core.publisher.Mono
import reactor.core.publisher.toMono
import javax.annotation.PostConstruct

@Repository
class CustomerRepository(private val template: ReactiveMongoTemplate) {
  companion object {
    val initialCustomers = listOf(Customer(1, "Kotlin"),
        Customer(2, "Spring"),
        Customer(3, "Microservice", Customer.Telephone("+44",
"7123456789")))
  }

  @PostConstruct
  fun initializeRepository() =
```

```
initialCustomers.map(Customer::toMono).map(this::create).map(Mono<Customer>
::subscribe)

    fun create(customer: Mono<Customer>) = template.save(customer)
    fun findById(id: Int) = template.findById<Customer>(id)
    fun deleteById(id: Int) =
template.remove<Customer>(Query(where("_id").isEqualTo(id)))
}
```

To implement this function, we will use a `Query` object, a class that allows us to search for entries in `MongoDB` reactively. We will try to find customers with an `id` equal to the `id` passed to our `deleteById` function. Since this is a reactive operation, we are telling Spring Data that we are subscribed to `Query`, and when completed, to remove the found object. The removed function will return a `Mongo<DeleteResult>` object that will inform us of the result of the operation when it is completed.

Now, we need to modify our `CustomerService` interface to create a new operation for deleting a customer:

```
package com.microservices.chapter5

import reactor.core.publisher.Mono

interface CustomerService {
    fun getCustomer(id: Int): Mono<Customer>
    fun createCustomer(customer: Mono<Customer>) : Mono<Customer>
    fun deleteCustomer(id: Int): Mono<Boolean>
}
```

The idea is that this function returns `Mono<Boolean>` with the result of the operation, but let's implement it in our `CustomerServiceImpl` class:

```
package com.microservices.chapter5

import org.springframework.beans.factory.annotation.Autowired
import org.springframework.stereotype.Service
import reactor.core.publisher.Mono

@Service
class CustomerServiceImpl : CustomerService {
    @Autowired
    lateinit var customerRepository: CustomerRepository

    override fun getCustomer(id: Int) = customerRepository.findById(id)
    override fun createCustomer(customer: Mono<Customer>) =
customerRepository.create(customer)
```

```
    override fun deleteCustomer(id: Int) =
customerRepository.deleteById(id).map { it.deletedCount > 0 }
    }
```

The new function that we just created will call to our repository to delete the Customer with the given id, and it will map the result of the operation, the Mongo<DeleteResult> object, into a Mongo<Boolean>.

The DeleteResult object contains an attribute with the count of objects deleted in the collection. We expect that if an object is greater than 0, it is deleted.

 The reason that we have chosen to return a Mongo<Boolean> instead of a Mongo<DeleteResult> in our service is to hide that our implementation depends on a MongoDB object. This will allow us to change the implementation to a different repository without affecting who uses our service, and with this we still have our software components decoupled.

We need to add a new method to our CustomerHandler class in order to use the new method on the service:

```
package com.microservices.chapter5

import org.springframework.http.HttpStatus
import org.springframework.stereotype.Component
import org.springframework.web.reactive.function.BodyInserters.fromObject
import org.springframework.web.reactive.function.server.ServerRequest
import org.springframework.web.reactive.function.server.ServerResponse.*
import org.springframework.web.reactive.function.server.bodyToMono
import java.net.URI

@Component
class CustomerHandler(val customerService: CustomerService) {
  fun get(serverRequest: ServerRequest) =
      customerService.getCustomer(serverRequest.pathVariable("id").toInt())
          .flatMap { ok().body(fromObject(it)) }
          .switchIfEmpty(status(HttpStatus.NOT_FOUND).build())

  fun create(serverRequest: ServerRequest) =
      customerService.createCustomer(serverRequest.bodyToMono()).flatMap {
        created(URI.create("/customer/${it.id}")).build()
      }

  fun delete(serverRequest: ServerRequest) =
customerService.deleteCustomer(serverRequest.pathVariable("id").toInt())
          .flatMap {
            if (it) ok().build()
```

```
        else status(HttpStatus.NOT_FOUND).build()
    }
}
```

In our handler, we just invoke the service of getting the `Boolean` value inside our `Mono<Boolean>` using `flatMap`. If we have deleted any record, the valued received will be true, and our function will return a **200 OK** status, if not a **404 NOT FOUND**.

Finally, we need to modify our `CustomerRouter` to invoke the new handler method when we get an HTTP `DELETE` request:

```
package com.microservices.chapter5

import org.springframework.context.annotation.Bean
import org.springframework.stereotype.Component
import org.springframework.web.reactive.function.server.router

@Component
class CustomerRouter(private val customerHandler: CustomerHandler) {
  @Bean
  fun customerRoutes() = router {
    "/customer".nest {
      GET("/{id}", customerHandler::get)
      POST("/", customerHandler::create)
      DELETE("/{id}", customerHandler::delete)
    }
  }
}
```

Now, we can send a simple curl request to delete a customer from our database to get a **200 OK**:

```
curl -X DELETE http://localhost:8080/customer/1
```

If we launch the same curl request, we should get a **404 NOT FOUND** response.

Finding Customers

So far, we have used simple MongoDB commands to obtain data. If we need to implement something more complex, such as searching for customers, we need to perform more advanced queries.

First, we will need a new method in our `CustomerRepository` class:

```
package com.microservices.chapter5

import org.springframework.data.mongodb.core.ReactiveMongoTemplate
import org.springframework.data.mongodb.core.find
import org.springframework.data.mongodb.core.findById
import org.springframework.data.mongodb.core.query.Criteria.where
import org.springframework.data.mongodb.core.query.Query
import org.springframework.data.mongodb.core.query.isEqualTo
import org.springframework.data.mongodb.core.remove
import org.springframework.stereotype.Repository
import reactor.core.publisher.Mono
import reactor.core.publisher.toMono
import javax.annotation.PostConstruct

@Repository
class CustomerRepository(private val template: ReactiveMongoTemplate) {
  companion object {
    val initialCustomers = listOf(Customer(1, "Kotlin"),
        Customer(2, "Spring"),
        Customer(3, "Microservice", Customer.Telephone("+44",
"7123456789")))
  }

  @PostConstruct
  fun initializeRepository() =
initialCustomers.map(Customer::toMono).map(this::create).map(Mono<Customer>
::subscribe)

  fun create(customer: Mono<Customer>) = template.save(customer)
  fun findById(id: Int) = template.findById<Customer>(id)
  fun deleteById(id: Int) =
template.remove<Customer>(Query(where("_id").isEqualTo(id)))
  fun findCustomer(nameFilter: String) = template.find<Customer>(
      Query(where("name").regex(".*$nameFilter.*", "i")))
}
```

We will search our repository for a `Customer` matching a regular expression; in this example, we will find any customer whose name contains the filter that we are searching for.

We will add a new operation to our `CustomerService` interface:

```
package com.microservices.chapter5

import reactor.core.publisher.Flux
```

```
import reactor.core.publisher.Mono

interface CustomerService {
  fun getCustomer(id: Int): Mono<Customer>
  fun createCustomer(customer: Mono<Customer>) : Mono<Customer>
  fun deleteCustomer(id: Int): Mono<Boolean>
  fun searchCustomers(nameFilter: String): Flux<Customer>
}
```

Then, we need to implement by calling to our repository method:

```
package com.microservices.chapter5

import org.springframework.beans.factory.annotation.Autowired
import org.springframework.stereotype.Service
import reactor.core.publisher.Mono

@Service
class CustomerServiceImpl : CustomerService {
  @Autowired
  lateinit var customerRepository: CustomerRepository

  override fun getCustomer(id: Int) = customerRepository.findById(id)
  override fun createCustomer(customer: Mono<Customer>) =
customerRepository.create(customer)
  override fun deleteCustomer(id: Int) =
customerRepository.deleteById(id).map { it.deletedCount > 0 }
  override fun searchCustomers(nameFilter: String) =
customerRepository.findCustomer(nameFilter)
}
```

Now, let's update our `CustomerHandler` to invoke the new method on the service:

```
package com.microservices.chapter5

import org.springframework.http.HttpStatus
import org.springframework.stereotype.Component
import org.springframework.web.reactive.function.BodyInserters.fromObject
import org.springframework.web.reactive.function.server.ServerRequest
import org.springframework.web.reactive.function.server.ServerResponse.*
import org.springframework.web.reactive.function.server.bodyToMono
import java.net.URI

@Component
class CustomerHandler(val customerService: CustomerService) {
  fun get(serverRequest: ServerRequest) =
      customerService.getCustomer(serverRequest.pathVariable("id").toInt())
          .flatMap { ok().body(fromObject(it)) }
```

```
            .switchIfEmpty(status(HttpStatus.NOT_FOUND).build())

    fun create(serverRequest: ServerRequest) =
        customerService.createCustomer(serverRequest.bodyToMono()).flatMap {
            created(URI.create("/customer/${it.id}")).build()
        }

    fun delete(serverRequest: ServerRequest) =
customerService.deleteCustomer(serverRequest.pathVariable("id").toInt())
            .flatMap {
                if (it) ok().build()
                else status(HttpStatus.NOT_FOUND).build()
            }

    fun search(serverRequest: ServerRequest) =
    ok().body(customerService.searchCustomers(serverRequest.queryParam("nameFil
    ter")
            .orElse("")), Customer::class.java)
}
```

Finally, we will update `CustomerRouter` to handle a new GET request to the `/customers` path:

```
package com.microservices.chapter5

import org.springframework.context.annotation.Bean
import org.springframework.stereotype.Component
import org.springframework.web.reactive.function.server.router

@Component
class CustomerRouter(private val customerHandler: CustomerHandler) {
  @Bean
  fun customerRoutes() = router {
    "/customer".nest {
      GET("/{id}", customerHandler::get)
      POST("/", customerHandler::create)
      DELETE("/{id}", customerHandler::delete)
    }
    "/customers".nest {
      GET("/", customerHandler::search)
    }
  }
}
```

With this final change, we can now get all of our customers in the database using `http://localhost:8080/customers`, or we can filter them using the parameter as `http://localhost:8080/customers?nameFilter=in`.

Summary

In this chapter, we have learned how we can use Spring Data to persist the model of our microservices reactively. We gained an understanding of what a NoSQL database is and what kind of operations we can perform when we implement our RESTful non-blocking microservices.

In the next chapter, we will learn how to create Cloud Native microservices and what benefits they can add to our applications. We will learn how Spring Cloud provides a vendor-independent approach for creating Cloud-Native applications, and how easily we can use it in our microservices.

6
Creating Cloud-Native Microservices

Creating microservices that are able to work natively in a cloud infrastructure is something that we should look forward to when we design a microservices architecture that follows our microservices principles. We reviewed the microservices principles and cloud architecture in Chapter 1, *Understanding Microservices*. You may need to look at that chapter to get a better understanding of some of the topics in this chapter.

In this chapter, we will learn about Cloud-Native microservices, and how Spring Cloud allows us to easily create them using a vendor-independent approach. To understand more about Spring Cloud, we will discuss how it works and how we can use it to create our microservices. Finally, we will cover the most important components that Spring Cloud provides.

In this chapter, we will cover:

- Understanding Spring Cloud
- Configuration server
- Service discovery
- Gateway

Understanding Spring Cloud

Modern microservices architecture focuses on deploying microservices into a cloud. This will enable a more optimal model for our products since we can grow or shrink the infrastructure as per our needs; however, the landscape of cloud providers has grown drastically, and many platforms need to tide our microservices to a particular vendor. Spring Cloud allows a vendor-agnostic approach that permits us to deploy our services in any cloud and take the full benefits of cloud computing, converting our microservices into Cloud-Native microservices.

In this section, we will be introduced to the main topics in this chapter.

What is a Cloud-Native application?

The cloud has very interesting capabilities, as we discussed in `Chapter 1`, *Understanding Microservices*, in the *Cloud-Native Microservices* section. Applications that will be deployed in a cloud need to use cloud capabilities in order to work effectively.

For example, in a cloud we should be able to scale our application; we can start three instances of a service if we need to increase the capacity of the application. We can increase the number of instances from three to five, but when we do this, we need to do it in a timely manner so that new instances are ready to work right away, therefore the application needs to be built with the ability to start quickly.

In the same way, an application that is on a cloud may consume other services from the platform and should go through the platform capabilities. If we are invoking one service from another, since the instances are created or destroyed dynamically, we can't just have a static set of URLs to access them. Our application should query the cloud to find the services and their instances.

Since we don't know when an instance will be created or destroyed, it is not so easy to synchronize data between the ones that are running, neither guarantee that different requests for a client or customer will always hit the same instance. Hence, we can not guarantee affinity in the same way that a traditional architecture can.

We highlight this because we believe that a cloud application needs to be aware that it is running on a cloud, since the actions that will be performed need to be understood in the context that is used; the same things that work outside a cloud may not work in a cloud. For this, we need to create cloud-aware microservices.

However, we can try to make an application that is not cloud-aware work in a cloud. For our previous example, when instances are created or destroyed, we can map them using a routing system external to the cloud, so our application can still use it, without using the cloud capabilities to discover services.

> We never recommend making things that are not cloud-aware to run in a cloud. If we are in a cloud, it is to fully utilize its benefits. If not, it's probably better that we choose a more traditional architecture.

When we create a cloud-aware microservice that is used natively in the cloud where it's running, we are creating a Cloud-Native microservice. Spring Cloud allows us to easily create Cloud-Native microservices.

Spring Cloud architecture

Spring Cloud provides a framework to easily create Cloud-Native microservices with the benefit of having a vendor-agnostic approach, while the same components can be used seamlessly in a range of cloud providers. But before using it, we need to understand how the architecture of their components works.

There are some key components in this architecture, but before understanding them, we will review the architectural patterns that will be used to build our Cloud-Native microservices:

- Configuration server
- Service discovery
- Gateway
- Circuit breaker

Configuration server

Configuring our microservices is usually a complex topic, as we learned in Chapter 2, *Getting Started with Spring Boot 2.0*. We can use Spring configuration to simplify this, but it is still a complicated process.

We can't just statically set the microservices configuration in our application code, since it can change when our cloud changes. We need a mechanism that allows our services to request their configuration.

A **Configuration Server** provides the capability to be queried about configurations, so when a microservice starts, it can retrieve all the values that need to be configured, such as URL, database connections, password, and anything that can be configured, from the **Configuration Server**:

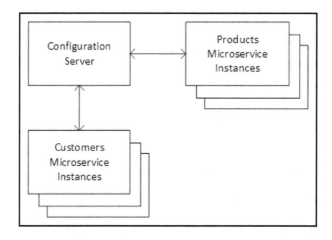

Configuration Server

For example, let's imagine that we have a **Configuration Server** ready and two microservices that use it; the **Products Microservice Instances** and the **Customers Microservice Instances**. When new instances are created, they can retrieve their configuration from the config server.

This allows us to easily create those service instances since all configuration required by our microservice will be provided by the **Configuration Server**. This speeds the creation of the new instance since they don't require any more configuration than the one provided by the **Configuration Server**.

Service discovery

In a cloud, we may need to connect to other services, but we don't actually know where this service is and how many instances are available. This requirement can be satisfied using a **Service Discovery Server**. Each instance of any service, when created, will be registered in the Service Discovery server. Thus, an application can ask what instance is available, but the Service Discovery needs to keep an up-to-date view of what is available.

When the microservice is shutting down, it needs to be deregistered from the Discovery Service, so it gets removed from the known instances; however, a microservice could go down drastically (for example, in an application error) without informing the discovery service. This could result in a situation where the discovery service may have registered instances that are actually not working or no longer available. To avoid that situation, discovery services could use the **Heart-beat** mechanism.

A **Heart-beat** is a way for a microservice to tell a Service Discovery that it is available and ready to work. It is like sending a request to the Discovery Server every five minutes to confirm that it is still alive. If the Discovery Server does not receive those Heart-beats from a microservice instance, it will assume the microservice is dead and removes it from the list of known instances of that microservice. Finally, with an updated list of microservice instances, it is possible for a microservice to find, when needed, the instance of any service.

Let's visualize this with an example:

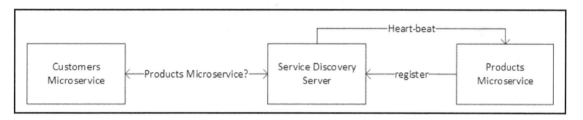

Service Discovery

In this example, we have a **Products Microservice** that is registered in a **Service Discovery Server**, and will periodically notify that it is still up and running via a **Heart-beat**. When another microservice, such as customers in this example, asks for the **Products Microservice**, the **Service Discovery Server** will be able to answer back with the available instances of the **Products Microservice**.

Load Balancer

When we have a microservice that needs to send a request to a different microservice, we can use a Service Discovery to get the list of instances available of the services that we want to use. Then we may need to choose one instance among them to perform our request. Eventually, we may need to perform another request, and in that case, we may want to choose a different instance so our request is distributed evenly to the different instances.

To achieve this, we can use the Load Balancer pattern. To perform, for example, a round-robin iteration on the instance of a microservice to distribute calls to them. So when we perform the first request, it will choose the first instance, for the next request, the second instance, and so on, until there are no more instances and we return back to the first.

On top of that, we may need to add the information from our Service Discovery service, since the instances can be created and destroyed, and then register or unregister from the Service Discovery Server. We may need to check that the list of the instance that we are iterating is up to date and managed correctly. This will make an optimal usage of the instances of our microservices, and split the load among them evenly.

Gateway

When we need to expose our microservices to be used by any application, we may need to use the **Gateway** pattern. In a **Gateway** pattern, we have an entry point to our microservice whose mission is to simplify the access to them; instead, to make the consumer applications use a Discovery Server and a Load Balancer to find our microservice instances, we expose them using a simple route and managing the details for them.

Let's draw an example to explore this topic further:

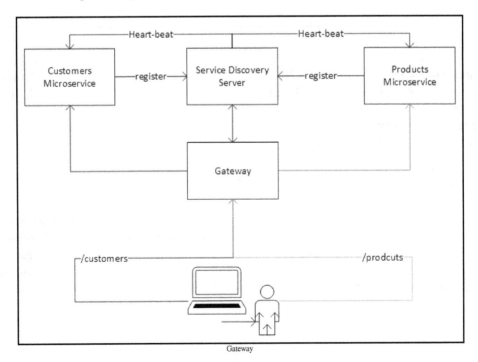

Gateway

We have two microservices registered on our **Service Discovery Server**, **Customers Microservice**, and **Products Microservice**. When an application (for example, a web application) invokes our Gateway using the /products path, our Gateway can:

- Find all the instances of the **Products Microservice** using the Service Discovery Server
- Rotate among them using a Load Balancer
- Invoke the selected instance
- Return the result back to the calling application

And if the web application uses the /customers path, we can send that request to the microservice customers instead. The web application does not need to use the Service Discovery directly, neither the Load Balancer, since this is done by the **Gateway** internally, giving a simple interface to the calling applications.

Since our **Gateway** is an entry point to our microservice, we can use it to add a couple of benefits to our architecture. Our **Gateway** can be used as the entry point for our security, checking the credentials or privileges to access those microservices, and if those security mechanisms need to be changed, we will change them just in a single place—our access point, our Gateway.

Decouple who implements a call, if tomorrow the /products path will be implemented by another microservice, we can change it in our Gateway without affecting the application that uses it.

 The Gateway pattern is a common pattern for enterprise applications that have existed for a very long time, but in today's cloud era, it makes more sense than ever before.

Circuit breaker

In our microservice, we may need to perform operations that can eventually fail. If those operations fail, we need to ensure that we are still able to answer our users, and that other parts of the software work as they should.

Let's imagine that we have three microservices:

- The *Opportunities* microservice will return a list of customers and the offers tied to each of them
- The *Customers* microservices will return just customer information
- The *Offers* microservice will return offers information

The *Opportunities* microservice will call the *Customers* microservices to get the customer information, and for each of the customers, it will call the *Offers* microservice to retrieve the offers tied to them. Let's assume that the *Offers* microservice is not working, and since *Opportunities* uses *Offers* every single time our *Opportunities* microservice is being called, we return an error back to the users of our microservice. In doing so, we may be overstressing the *Offers* microservice that we know is not working, but we continue calling it and getting an error.

In fact, we may even decrement the performance of the *Opportunities* microservice; since waiting for a response from the *Offers* microservice may take a long time, we are leaking a problem from a dependency, *Offers*, into our *Opportunities* microservice. To prevent this from happening, we can encapsulate the operation by calling the *Offers* microservice from the *Opportunities* microservice in a circuit breaker. A circuit breaker can have an open or closed status, telling us if the operation that encapsulates can be used—think of circuit breakers as fuses in an electrical installation.

When the operation fails, we can just close the circuit for a period of time, then if new requests are coming to our *Opportunities* microservice since the circuit is closed, we just return an error without sending a request to the *Offers* microservice. After a certain amount of time, we can check whether the Offers microservice is working again, opening the circuit and allowing to return valid responses again, but in the period of time that the circuit was closed, we were given time for the Offers microservice to recover. But we can find other benefits in this technique.

A circuit breaker allows us to define a fallback mechanism. If we can't answer with the offers since the circuit is closed, we could just return a default set of offers to whoever invokes our *Opportunities* microservice. This will allow our application to still show some information. In most cases, this is much better than just an error without any information at all.

We always need to ensure that a failure in one part of our application does not make other parts, or even the whole application, fail. Circuit breakers are a perfect mechanism for this, even in the worst scenarios.

Spring Cloud Netflix

Netflix is one of the big contributors to open source initiatives. They are a company with a tremendous focus on microservices, so within the Netflix **OSS** (**Open Source Software**), they originally created many components that implement the cloud architecture pattern, and we can easily use them with Spring Cloud since doing so allows us to choose the implementation of the pattern.

Let's review the ones that we are going to use:

- **Eureka**: A Service Discovery service that we can easily use to register or find instances of our microservices.
- **Ribbon**: A configurable software Load Balancer that can be integrated with Eureka to distribute calls within the microservices instances.
- **Hystrix**: A configurable circuit breaker, with a fall-back mechanism, that we can use when creating microservices.
- **Zuul**: A Gateway Server that uses Eureka, Ribbon, and Hystrix to implement the Gateway pattern.

Creating a Spring Cloud microservice

In order to create a Cloud-Native microservice, we will use Spring Initializr as we have been doing in previous chapters.

We can start by visiting `https://start.spring.io/`:

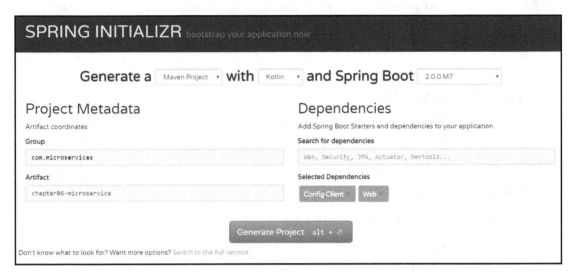

Creating a cloud project in Spring Initializr

We have chosen to create a **Maven Project** using **Kotlin** and **Spring Boot 2.0.0 M7**, we choose the **Group** to be `com.microservices` and the **Artifact** to be `chapter06-microservice`. For **Dependencies**, we have set **Config Client** and **Web**.

Now we can click **Generate Project** to download it as a ZIP file. After we unzip it, we can open it with IntelliJ IDEA to start working on our project.

After a few minutes, our project will be ready and we can open the Maven window to see the different life cycle phases, and Maven plugins and their goals.

We covered how to use Spring Initializr, Maven, and IntelliJ IDEA in `Chapter 2`, *Getting Started with Spring Boot 2.0*. You can visit this chapter to learn about topics not covered in this section.

As a starting dependency, we choose the Config Client, since we know that this is the first Cloud component that our microservice needs to use.

Let's run it to see how our Cloud-Native microservice starts. In the Maven window, just double-click the **spring-boot** plugin, **run** goal, or just do it from the command line in the `microservice` folder:

```
mvnw spring-boot:run
```

After a few seconds, we will see several log lines, including something like this:

```
INFO 13784 --- [              main] c.c.c.ConfigServicePropertySourceLocator :
Fetching config from server at: http://localhost:8888
WARN 13784 --- [ main] c.c.c.ConfigServicePropertySourceLocator : can not
locate PropertySource: I/O error on GET request for
"http://localhost:8888/application/default": Connection refused: connect;
nested exception is java.net.ConnectException: Connection refused: connect
```

Our service is running, but we can't connect to the config server, so by default our microservice will try to find it in `http://localhost:8888`.

In the next section of this chapter, we will discuss how we can create a Configuration Server for a Cloud-Native microservice.

Configuration Server

A Configuration Server allows us to serve any microservice the configuration that it may need, so when a microservice starts, it will require no more configurations than just the one from where the Configuration Service is located.

In order to serve that configuration, we can use a variety of backends, from our machine filesystem or a Git repository that will include our configuration files, to a database.

A single config server can be used to provide configuration for several applications, and at the same time, we can provide a set of configurations that we can share with them.

Finally, a Configuration Server can manage application profiles. This gives us the ability to get different configurations based on how we start our microservice. This flexibility can be employed for a range of uses, from varying the configuration per environment to different configuration modes that application could use.

Let's explore this concept further.

Creating a Configuration Server

We can use Spring Initializr again to create our Configuration Server by visiting `https://start.spring.io/`.

We have chosen to create a **Maven Project** using **Kotlin** and **Spring Boot 2.0.0 M7**, we chose the **Group** to be `com.microservices` and the **Artifact** to be `chapter06-config-server`. For **Dependencies**, we have set **Config Server**.

Now we can click **Generate Project** to download it as a ZIP file. After we unzip it, we can open it with IntelliJ IDEA to start working on our Configuration Server.

We can run it as we ran our microservice before, for example, using the command line in the `config server` folder:

```
mvnw spring-boot:run
```

After a few seconds, we should see the log lines:

```
INFO 1872 --- [ main] o.s.b.w.embedded.tomcat.TomcatWebServer : Tomcat
started on port(s): 8080 (http) with context path ''
INFO 1872 --- [ main] c.m.c.Chapter06ConfigServerApplicationKt : Started
Chapter06ConfigServerApplicationKt in 3.773 seconds (JVM running for 6.848)
```

Our Configuration Server has started on port `8080`, but since our microservice is looking for port `8888`, it won't work, so first let's change it.

We will open our `resources` folder in IntelliJ IDEA using the `main/src/resources` expanding project window.

Now we will click the `application.properties` file and press *Shift + F6* to rename it to `application.yml`, then we will edit it:

```
server:
  port: 8888
```

Now we can run our Configuration Server again, and it will run on port `8888`, let's launch it as before from the `config server` folder:

```
mvnw spring-boot:run
```

Now within the logs line, we should see that we are running on port 8888:

```
INFO 12188 --- [ main] o.s.b.w.embedded.tomcat.TomcatWebServer : Tomcat
started on port(s): 8888 (http) with context path ''
INFO 12188 --- [ main] c.m.c.Chapter06ConfigServerApplicationKt : Started
Chapter06ConfigServerApplicationKt in 3.857 seconds (JVM running for 6.925)
```

But now we need to modify it to actually make it a Configuration Server, so let's open our `Chapter06ConfigServerApplication` class and use the `@EnableConfigServer` annotation:

```
package com.microservices.chapter06configserver


import org.springframework.boot.autoconfigure.SpringBootApplication
import org.springframework.boot.runApplication
import org.springframework.cloud.config.server.EnableConfigServer

@SpringBootApplication
@EnableConfigServer
class Chapter06ConfigServerApplication

fun main(args: Array<String>) {
  runApplication<Chapter06ConfigServerApplication>(*args)
}
```

If we now run our Configuration Server, we will get an error, since we haven't specified where the configuration files are located.

We can configure our config server to the user of a folder within our resources by editing `application.yml`:

```
server:
  port: 8888
spring:
  profiles:
    active: native
  cloud:
    config:
      server:
        native:
          search-locations: classpath:config/
```

First, we have set that we are going to use just the `native` filesystem (not a Git backend or a database) for our configurations activating the native profile, then we indicate that our configurations are on the `/config` location within our classpath.

After running the Configuration Server again, we can request the
`http://localhost:8888/application/default` URL, and the output should look like
this:

```
{
  "name": "application",
  "profiles": [
    "default"
  ],
  "label": null,
  "version": null,
  "state": null,
  "propertySources": []
}
```

Now let's add the default configuration file for applications in the
`/src/main/resources/config/application.yml` path in our configuration server
folder:

```
microservice:
  example:
    greetings: "hello"
```

If we rerun our Configuration Server and request the
`http://localhost:8888/application/default` configuration URL again, we should
now get:

```
{
  "name": "application",
  "profiles": [
    "default"
  ],
  "label": null,
  "version": null,
  "state": null,
  "propertySources": [
    {
      "name": "classpath:config/application.yml",
      "source": {
        "microservice.example.greetings": "hello"
      }
    }
  ]
}
```

When we start the Configuration Server, we may need to do a `mvnw clean` before actually starting it. If not, it will probably not load the new configuration.

We can invoke `clean` and `spring-boot:run` in a single command:

```
mvnw clean spring-boot:run
```

This is because the Configuration Server may have cached our configuration files, and cleaning will remove them.

Getting configurations

Now that we have our Configuration Server running, we can run our microservice, so let's run it again from the microservice folder:

```
mvnw spring-boot:run
```

The log lines should look something like this:

```
INFO 15312 --- [ main] c.c.c.ConfigServicePropertySourceLocator : Fetching
config from server at: http://localhost:8888
INFO 9496 --- [ main] b.c.PropertySourceBootstrapConfiguration : Located
property source: CompositePropertySource {name='configService',
propertySources=[MapPropertySource
{name='classpath:config/application.yml'}]}
```

This means that our microservice has been able to connect to our Configuration Server and retrieve its configuration.

Let's add a simple `RestController` to our microservice so we can check that the configuration is correctly read.

> We learned how to create Controllers in `Chapter 3`, *Creating RESTful Services*, you may need to review that chapter to better understand the following examples.

We will create a new class named `GreetingsController` with this code:

```
package com.microservices.chapter06microservice

import org.springframework.beans.factory.annotation.Value
import org.springframework.web.bind.annotation.GetMapping
import org.springframework.web.bind.annotation.RestController
```

```
@RestController
class GreetingsController {

  @Value("\${microservice.example.greetings}")
  private lateinit var greetings: String

  @GetMapping("/greetings")
  fun greetings() = greetings
}
```

This code will create a simple controller so that when our microservice is invoked using the `http://localhost:8080/greetings` URL, it will return the value configured for `microservice.example.greetings`, which will simply give the following output:

```
hello
```

But this value is configured in our Configuration Server, so let's stop both the microservices and the Configuration Server, and edit the `application.yml` file on the `Configuration Server` folder under the `resources/config/application.yml` file:

```
microservice:
  example:
    greetings: "hello from config server"
```

Now we can restart our first Configuration Server and then our microservice. If we visit the `http://localhost:8080/greetings` URL, we will now get this as the result:

```
hello from config server
```

We have restarted both the Configuration Server and the microservices so that change can take place, but let's understand why:

- We need to restart the Configuration Server so it will able to pick up our configuration changes
- We need to restart the microservice since the configuration is only picked up when it starts
- We must always start the Configuration server first; if we don't, the microservice will not have a configuration

 There is a way that we can do all this without restarting, but it is far more complex than the scope of this book. We recommend looking at the official Configuration Server documentation to explore that topic further: `http://cloud.spring.io/spring-cloud-config/single/spring-cloud-config.html`.

We have set up our configuration within `config/application.yml`. This file is the one holding the configurations for any application requesting the configuration from the configuration server, but most likely, we will have several microservices retrieving the configuration from it, so we need to specify each configuration individually.

To do this, first we will change the configuration file for our microservice; we will rename our `application.properties` into `application.yml`, selecting it in the project window and pressing *Shift + F6*, and then we will edit it to the following:

```
spring:
  application:
    name: "greetings"
```

Here, we have defined our application name, and this will be used when we request the configuration from our configuration server.

Now we will add a new configuration file in the `Configuration Server` folder under the `src/main/resources/config` path, and we will name it `greetings.yml`:

```
microservice:
  example:
    greetings: "hello for the greetings application"
```

If we now restart both the Configuration Server and the microservice when visiting `http://localhost:8080/greetings`, we will get:

```
hello for the greetings application
```

However, let's make a request to our Configuration Server to the `http://localhost:8888/greetings/default` URL to understand how this configuration works. This will produce the following output:

```
{
  "name": "greetings",
  "profiles": [
    "default"
  ],
  "label": null,
  "version": null,
  "state": null,
  "propertySources": [
    {
      "name": "classpath:config/greetings.yml",
      "source": {
        "microservice.example.greetings": "hello for the greetings
application"
```

```
      }
    },
    {
      "name": "classpath:config/application.yml",
      "source": {
        "microservice.example.greetings": "hello from config server"
      }
    }
  ]
}
```

As we can see here, both configurations are available; the default application configuration, and our microservice configuration. The Spring Cloud client is the one combining them when we retrieve a value. This is great because it will allow defining default configuration values for all microservices and individual values that change for specific microservices.

Ciphering data

Sometimes we will have sensitive information in our configuration files, such as passwords, and we may not want them to be visible in plain text. The Spring Configuration Server allows us to cipher the data that we set in our configuration files.

To cipher data in the JVM, you may need to install **Java Cryptography Extension (JCE)** in JAVA_HOME under the lib folder. Java 8 is available for download at http://www.oracle.com/technetwork/java/javase/downloads/jce8-download-2133166.html. Follow the instructions provided in the README.txt file.

First, let's modify our Configuration Server by adding a bootstrap.yml file under main/src/resources in our configuration server folder:

```
encrypt.key: "this_is_a_secret"
spring:
  cloud:
    config:
      server:
        encrypt:
          enabled: false
```

Here, we specify what will be the secret/key that will be used when ciphering data; of course, you should change that value to be something more secure. Then, we tell our Configuration Server not to decrypt the configuration when it is sending it to the client. In that way, our clients need to decrypt it when they receive it.

After restarting our Configuration Server, we can now use a URL to encrypt data. For example, if we want to encrypt a message, we can perform a cURL request as:

```
curl http://localhost:8888/encrypt -d "secret message"
7b310fe9e22a913d6a21dd768a616f9700ba4bde6f1879b4d82a5a09ea8344a4
```

Now we can set the value in our `src/main/resources/config/greetings.yml` file:

```
microservice:
  example:
    greetings:
"{cipher}7b310fe9e22a913d6a21dd768a616f9700ba4bde6f1879b4d82a5a09ea8344a4"
```

If we request the configuration for our microservice using the `http://localhost:8888/greetings/default` URL, we can see that it is a cipher.

Finally, we will modify our microservice to use the same key as our configuration server by adding a `bootstrap.yml` file under the `main/src/resources` folder:

```
encrypt.key: "this_is_a_secret"
```

After restarting the microservice, if we go to our `http://localhost:8080/greetings` greetings URL, we should get:

```
secret message
```

We get our message decrypted as expected, and now we can use this technique to encrypt our more sensitive information.

Now that we have encrypted our value, we can remove the secret that we used to cipher the information from the configuration server, since we don't require it to serve the configuration to our microservice, and keep it only in the one that needs to decipher. In the same way, we can use different secrets for different microservices to improve security.

Using application profiles

The configuration may change for many reasons. In our development environment, we will probably not always have the same configuration as in our production environment, since things such as connections to the external system (for example, databases, or other services) may change between them.

Spring Cloud provides an easy mechanism to change our configuration using profiles. Let's modify our configuration files to be able to handle different profiles.

In our config server directory, we will create a new file under the `main/src/resources/config/greetings-production.yml` path:

```
microservice:
  example:
    greetings: "hello from another profile"
```

This will specify the value of our configuration for another profile, and since we performed a configuration change, we need to restart our configuration server.

Now, if we want to run our microservice with a different profile, we first need to build our microservice as a jar with:

```
mvnw package
```

Then, we can run with a different profile from our microservice folder with this command:

```
java -jar target/chapter06-microservice-0.0.1-SNAPSHOT.jar --
spring.cloud.config.profile=production
```

After restarting the microservice, if we go to our `http://localhost:8080/greetings` greetings URL, we should get:

```
hello from another profile
```

Spring Cloud Configuration is incremental. When our microservice runs, it first gets the configuration from `application.yml`, then the values that need to be overwritten on `greetings.yml`, and finally for the profile that is selected—in our case, the values that change in the `greetings-production.yml`.

The incremental configuration of Spring Cloud allows us to build configuration files for each need, changing only what needs to change at each stage. For example, we may not need to change some details on the configuration per environment, but others will. Try to just update the values that change in each file to keep your configuration simple to maintain.

Service discovery

Service Discovery Servers allow us to dynamically register the instances of our microservices. Having a dynamic list of instances could be used either by applications or other microservices when they need to perform a request. They help us to dynamically manage when instances are starting or stopping to give an accurate view on the scaling of our microservices. Finally, they provide a mechanism to disconnect instances where they are not available using a Heart-beat mechanism.

Spring Cloud provides a vendor-independent approach to Service Discovery. We can use a range of different implementations, such as Hashicorp Consul, Netflix Eureka, or Apache Zookeeper. In this section, we will learn how easily we can integrate with Eureka using Spring Cloud.

Creating a Service Discovery Server

We can use Spring Initializr again to create our Discovery Server by visiting `https://start.spring.io/`.

We have chosen to create a **Maven Project** using Kotlin and **Spring Boot 2.0.0 M7**, we chose the **Group** to be `com.microservices` and the **Artifact** to be `chapter06-discovery-server`. For **Dependencies**, we have set **Eureka Server**. Now we can click **Generate Project** to download it as a ZIP file. After we unzip it, we can open it with IntelliJ IDEA to start working on our Eureka server.

First, we will rename `application.properties` to `application.yml`, selecting it in the project window and pressing *Shift + F6*, and then we will edit it:

```
server:
  port: 8761
spring:
  application:
    name: "discovery-server"
```

We have set our Discovery Server to run on port `8761`. This is the default for a Eureka server, and we have set an application name.

Then we need to modify our application to actually be a Eureka server, so let's edit our `Chapter06DiscoveryServerApplication` class in our Eureka server directory to add the `@EnableEurekaServer` annotation:

```
package com.microservices.chapter06discoveryserver

import org.springframework.boot.autoconfigure.SpringBootApplication
import org.springframework.boot.runApplication
import org.springframework.cloud.netflix.eureka.server.EnableEurekaServer

@SpringBootApplication
@EnableEurekaServer
class Chapter06DiscoveryServerApplication

fun main(args: Array<String>) {
  runApplication<Chapter06DiscoveryServerApplication>(*args)
}
```

Now we can run it from our `Discovery Server` folder with the following command:

```
mvnw spring-boot:run
```

After a few seconds, we should see some messages in the logline, finally telling us that our `Eureka server` is up:

```
INFO 13540 --- [ Thread-11] e.s.EurekaServerInitializerConfiguration :
Started Eureka Server
```

We can explore what is registered in the Service Discovery service using the included dashboard in the `http://localhost:8761/` URL.

Connecting to the Discovery Server

Now that we have a working Discovery Server, we can use it to register our microservices; but first, we need to add the Eureka client, so let's edit `pom.xml` from our microservice to add as a `dependency`:

```
. . . . .
<dependencies>
 <dependency>
  <groupId>org.springframework.cloud</groupId>
  <artifactId>spring-cloud-starter-netflix-eureka-client</artifactId>
```

```
    </dependency>
    .....
    </dependencies>
```

Now we can run our microservice, but remember that our Config Server and Discovery Server should be up and be running before we do that; from our microservice folder, we can just write:

```
mvnw spring-boot:run
```

In the log lines from our microservice, we should now see:

```
INFO 9092 --- [nfoReplicator-0] com.netflix.discovery.DiscoveryClient :
DiscoveryClient_GREETINGS/DESKTOP-2407SAG.home:greetings: registering
service...
INFO 9092 --- [nfoReplicator-0] com.netflix.discovery.DiscoveryClient :
DiscoveryClient_GREETINGS/DESKTOP-2407SAG.home:greetings - registration
status: 204
INFO 9092 --- [ main] o.s.b.w.embedded.tomcat.TomcatWebServer : Tomcat
started on port(s): 8080 (http) with context path ''
INFO 9092 --- [ main] .s.c.n.e.s.EurekaAutoServiceRegistration : Updating
port to 8080
INFO 9092 --- [ main] c.m.c.Chapter06MicroserviceApplicationKt : Started
Chapter06MicroserviceApplicationKt in 5.687 seconds (JVM running for 9.085)
```

This means that our microservice is now registered in the discovery service.

 We do not need to configure where our Discovery Server is, because it is running on the http://localhost:8761 port. By default, our microservice will connect to that URL. We may need to change this in application.yml in the eureka.client.serviceUrl.defaultZone value to the URL of our Eureka server, or in application.yml in our configurations in our config server directory, so all microservices will connect to the same Eureka.

If we now go to our `http://localhost:8761/` Service Discovery dashboard URL, we should see our services registered:

Instances currently registered with Eureka			
Application	**AMIs**	**Availability Zones**	**Status**
DISCOVERY-SERVER	n/a (1)	(1)	**UP** (1) - DESKTOP-2407SAG.home:discovery-server:8761
GREETINGS	n/a (1)	(1)	**UP** (1) - DESKTOP-2407SAG.home:greetings

Instances registered in Eureka

Using Spring Boot actuator

Eureka provides a mechanism to see whether the microservices instances that are registered are still running, every time the microservices send a request to Eureka to say that they are still up and ready to get requests. This is a Heart-beat.

If Eureka does not receive a Heart-beat after some time, it will disconnect that instance, so when it is queried, it will be not available. If the microservice is again starting to send Heart-beats, Eureka will reconnect. By default, the Heart-beat implementation is just to send a regular request letting you know that it's still active.

But Spring provides a better mechanism to know whether a service is up and running, called **Spring Boot actuator**. Spring Boot actuator provides the capability to explore the spring context and check for indicators when everything is OK. For example, if we have a connection pool, an indicator can check whether it is able to connect or not.

Spring Boot actuator will propagate this information in different ways, like the health check URL or through JMX, and can also propagate to Eureka with the Heart-beats. First, we will add Spring Boot actuator to our project by editing the `pom.xml` file of our microservice to add it as a `dependency`:

```
.....
<dependencies>
 <dependency>
   <groupId>org.springframework.boot</groupId>
   <artifactId>spring-boot-starter-actuator</artifactId>
 </dependency>
.....
</dependencies>
```

Now we need to edit the `application.yml` file for our microservice:

```
spring:
  application:
    name: "greetings"
eureka:
  client:
    healthcheck:
      enabled: true
```

We have set up the `Eureka` client to send the `healthcheck` information when performing Heart-beats.

After running our microservice again, we can explore its status in the `http://localhost:8080/actuator/health` URL. This will provide information about the status of our microservice, but more interestingly, this information will be used to notify Eureka in the Heart-beats whether the microservice is still active or not.

> The `/actuator/health` URL is a very interesting feature, but we need to be cautious when it is enabled. We can protect it using different mechanisms, or even change the default path to prevent sensitive information from being exposed. For more information, check the Spring Boot actuator documentation at `https://docs.spring.io/spring-boot/docs/current/reference/html/production-ready-monitoring.html`.

Gateway

A Cloud Gateway allows us to simplify how we can expose a microservice to be used by applications or to other microservices, which simplifies how we can perform load balancing between the instances and expose a clear mechanism to access them. Spring Cloud allows us to use Netflix Zuul to easily create a Gateway for our cloud microservices where we can define simple routes for accessing them.

Additionally, Zuul will use NetFlix Ribbon to perform load balancing and Hystrix to create circuit breakers, giving our Gateway a cloud-oriented architecture for our microservices.

In this section, we will create our Gateway and connect it to our microservices.

Creating a Gateway

We can use Spring Initializr to create our Discovery Server by visiting `https://start.spring.io/`.

We have chosen to create a **Maven Project** using **Kotlin** and **Spring Boot 2.0.0 M7**, we choose the Group to be `com.microservices` and the **Artifact** to be `chapter06-gateway`. For **Dependencies**, we have set **Zuul, Eureka Discovery**, and **Config Client**. Now we can click **Generate Project** to download it as a ZIP file. After we unzip it, we can open it with IntelliJ IDEA to start working on our Zuul server.

If our microservice is running, we now try to run the gateway. We will get an error since the `8080` port is already in use. We are going to modify our microservice to run on a random port since it will be exposed later in the gateway.

We will need to modify the `main/resources/application.yml` file in our `microservice` folder:

```
spring:
  application:
    name: "greetings"
eureka:
  client:
    healthcheck:
      enabled: true
server:
  port: 0
```

Now, let's modify our `main/resources/application.yml` gateway:

```
spring:
  application:
    name: "gateway"
```

Let's now start our stack in the right order:

1. Start the Configuration Server
2. Start the Service Discovery Server
3. Start the microservice
4. Start the Gateway server

After these steps, we can navigate to our Eureka dashboard in the
`http://localhost:8761/` URL:

Instances currently registered with Eureka			
Application	**AMIs**	**Availability Zones**	**Status**
DISCOVERY-SERVER	n/a (1)	(1)	**UP** (1) - DESKTOP-2407SAG.home:discovery-server:8761
GATEWAY	n/a (1)	(1)	**UP** (1) - DESKTOP-2407SAG.home:gateway
GREETINGS	n/a (1)	(1)	**UP** (1) - DESKTOP-2407SAG.home:greetings:0

Instances register in Eureka

Now that we can see our components instances registered, let's expose our microservice.

Defining routes

Now that we have our Gateway running, we can use it to route to our services. Let's first enable just adding the `@EnableZuulProxy` annotation in our `Chapter06GatewayApplication` class:

```
package com.microservices.chapter06gateway

import org.springframework.boot.autoconfigure.SpringBootApplication
import org.springframework.boot.runApplication
import org.springframework.cloud.netflix.zuul.EnableZuulProxy

@SpringBootApplication
@EnableZuulProxy
class Chapter06GatewayApplication

fun main(args: Array<String>) {
  runApplication<Chapter06GatewayApplication>(*args)
}
```

If we restart our Gateway, we can use the
`http://localhost:8080/greetings/greetings` URL, and we get the following as an output:

```
secret message
```

How does this actually work? Here's how:

- When entering URL `/greetings/greetings`, Zuul will first look in Eureka for anything registered with the name greetings
- Eureka will return the list of available instances—in our case, just one instance of our microservice
- Zuul will create a circuit breaker using Hystrix for encapsulating all calls to that microservice
- It will use Ribbon to do a round-robin, choosing which instance to call
- Zuul will now remove the name of the services from the URL—in our case, it will become just `/greetings`, and will send it to that instance
- If the call fails, the circuit created by Hystrix will be closed for a few seconds, so further requests will return an error immediately
- Zuul will return the result of the call back to the application that was calling it

Some of these are partially configurable, such as how Ribbon or Hystrix will work. It will probably be a good idea to check the documentation to understand further parameters. One curious thing about this is that the whole microservice is actually redirected; for example, if we use the `http://localhost:8080/greetings/application/health` URL, we will get the output of the actuator health of one of the services. However, Zuul allows us to define our own routes, instead of just redirecting to anything registered in Eureka.

Let's create one new configuration file, `src/resources/config/gateway.yml`, in our `configuration server` project:

```
zuul:
  ignoredServices: '*'
  routes:
    greetings:
      path: /message/**
      serviceId: greetings
```

After restarting the Configuration Server and the Gateway, when we now use the `http://localhost:8080/message/greetings` URL, we will get our greetings message.

Summary

In this chapter, we learned about Cloud-Native microservices. We reviewed how the Spring Cloud Architecture works, and the different patterns that are used. We have also learned how to create the configuration and Service Discovery Servers to support our cloud architecture, and how we can use them in our microservice. Finally, we learned how to create a Gateway that uses all of these components to easily expose our microservices.

In the next chapter, we will learn about Docker containers, and how we can use them for running our microservices.

7
Creating Dockers

Docker is the de facto standard technology for containerizing applications, and containers are one of the key technologies in cloud applications. During this chapter, we will learn what containers actually are, and why we should use them. We will learn how to install a Docker, configure it in our system, and what commands we can use to manage our containers. Then, we will take a look at pulling images from the Docker registry, and running them.

Finally, we will learn how to create Docker containers with our microservices and publish them manually, or integrate them into our Maven lifecycle.

During this chapter, you will learn about:

- Docker containers
- Base images
- Dockerfiles
- Docker command line
- Docker-Maven-plugin

Starting with Docker

Containers are present in almost every modern cloud, and this is because of the benefits they can offer in such architectures. During this section, we will get a deep understanding of containers, and what the key differences are from other approaches. We will install Docker on our system, and understand the basic commands to manage it. Finally, we will pull and run Dockers from the Docker registry.

Understanding containers

Having an application that runs in exactly the same manner in different environments has always been a challenge, especially because environments are not always identical. Our development environment may be completely different to our production servers. In fact, one of the things that is usually really complex when creating a new server is to actually get it configured, patching to the operating system, and to define things as network interfaces or users. To solve some of these issues, **virtual machines** (**VM**) have been used in the industry.

Virtual machines

In virtual machines, we have a server that runs a host operating system, and a component called hypervisor in charge of virtualizing resources and hardware of the machine, such as CPU, or memory. We will start a new virtual machine, which uses the resources that the hypervisor exposes; this includes some mounted spaces to be used as a virtualizing hard drive for the machine.

Then, when the virtual machine starts, it will be like turning on a new computer, from loading the BIOS and booting the operating system on the virtual hard drive that we set up. Then, the operating system will start loading all the required components for virtualized hardware. For that reason, starting a virtual machine is a heavy process that usually takes several minutes. Once the machine is started, we need to configure it as we would configure any server, creating users, configuring the network, installing software, and so on. Configuring a virtual machine is as complex as configuring a real server.

Additional virtual machines allow us to define images, so we can store all our setup and create another server with the same image. But this new server will be identical, so if we need it, for example, for things such as network configuration or users on the machine, we need to configure it again, ensuring that configuration remains challenging. Since virtual machines need to run an operating system, and we need to fully configure it, we can end up with the same problem that we had before - that our VM may not be exactly the same per environment.

So finally, provisioning, configuring, and starting virtual machines is a process that, even with some kind of automation, will take too much time to be viable for a cloud, where we need to create applications at a faster pace. Additionally, virtual machines will be quite resource-intensive, due to the amount of virtualization that a virtual machine requires, and the amount of software that they need to run in each of them, including a whole operating system. Also, the requirements for the server that will host them will be quite demanding.

Containers

The **LXC** (**LinuX Containers**) specification was created with the intention of avoiding some of these problems. The overall intention was to be able to run on a Linux kernel, isolated and contained Linux systems under the same kernel as well as be able to start a new Linux system as a process within another system, with the advantage of sharing some of the already existing operating system resources provided by the kernel. It must also be kept isolated so that if it fails, the kernel is not affected, and neither is the operating system that started the process.

So instead, to have a virtualized system as a hypervisor, we don't really need to virtualize our hardware, and when we start a container, we do not start a brand new server, we just create a process in our server. This makes the container more lightweight and faster to start than any virtual machine, and therefore less resource-intensive. A container can start in seconds, and this is ideal for a cloud application when an instance needs to be created and destroyed in a timely manner.

Docker

Docker originally used the LCX specification, but nowadays it uses RunC, part of the **Open Container Initiative** (**OCI**), and basically shares the same principles that LXC was defining. Docker incorporates the concept of base images where we can define our container based on an existing one, and when defined, we can add the configuration steps that we require, making it more flexible to create applications with.

As an example, we can define a container that includes the Java runtime that we need for our application, then we can define another one based on the previous one that adds our application-specific configuration, and then we can have a third and final container that just adds the software that we require based on the second one. Each of those images will usually be small, consisting of just a few megabytes, and the final result will be an application that starts in seconds and is already configured.

Installing Docker

In order to start this chapter, we will need to have installed **Docker CE** and **Community Edition** in our system, so we can proceed to install the last stable version from their official site choosing our operating systems: `https://www.Docker.com/community-edition`.

Instead of the Docker CE, you can install the older Docker toolbox from their website, `https://www.Docker.com/products/Docker-toolbox`, but we will need the Docker CE for the examples in the next chapters.

> Unfortunately, Docker CE on Windows requires Windows 10 Pro, Enterprise, or Educational, and is not available for older versions or Windows 10 Home.

If you install Docker Toolbox instead of Docker CE, when we refer to localhost, you may need to change it to the IP address of the Docker machine. This can be obtained with the command `Docker-machine ip default`. This command will not work with Docker CE, since the machine is bound to your localhost. After installation, we can check that everything is running alright:

```
docker --version
Docker version 17.09.0-ce, build afdb6d4
```

Starting with Docker

Now that we have our Docker system ready, let's run our first example, just running a simple Docker with the following command:

```
docker run alpine echo hello from a Docker
```

The output should look like this:

```
Unable to find image 'alpine:latest' locally
latest: Pulling from library/alpine
b56ae66c2937: Pull complete
Digest:
sha256:d6bfc3baf615dc9618209a8d607ba2a8103d9c8a405b3bd8741d88b4bef36478
Status: Downloaded newer image for alpine:latest
hello from a Docker
```

What we have done here is we've asked Docker to create or run a Docker-based on an image; in this example, Alpine Linux. Since we haven't provided any version, we will get the latest version of the Alpine Linux image. Additionally, we indicate to Docker that when we run that image it sends some parameters to it, in this case, `echo hello from a Docker`. This has created the Docker, started it, sent the parameters, and then the Docker has terminated.

Let's now run a Docker with an iterative terminal with the following command:

```
docker run -ti ubuntu /bin/bash
```

This should now display like this:

```
Unable to find image 'ubuntu:latest' locally
latest: Pulling from library/ubuntu
ae79f2514705: Pull complete
c59d01a7e4ca: Pull complete
41ba73a9054d: Pull complete
f1bbfd495cc1: Pull complete
0c346f7223e2: Pull complete
Digest:
sha256:6eb24585b1b2e7402600450d289ea0fd195cfb76893032bbbb3943e041ec8a65
Status: Downloaded newer image for ubuntu:latest
root@92665288e3dc:/#
```

This has run another Docker container using Ubuntu as a base image, and attached a terminal connected to the /bin/bash command, so it is effectively a kind of shell session inside of that Docker. We can run commands like ls, or cwd inside the Docker, and if we execute the command exit, our Docker will be terminated.

One interesting concept to understand now is that when we performed Docker run, that Docker was created, and when exited, it stopped, but it still exists and we can resume it again if we want.

First, list all Dockers, including those that are stopped, with the following command:

```
docker ps -a
```

This will give a list of all the existing Dockers with their status, and the Container ID of each of them:

```
CONTAINER ID    IMAGE    COMMAND              STATUS
99f3ec319d74    ubuntu   "/bin/bash"          Exited (0) 26 seconds ago
2caa58b34dd4    alpine   "echo hello from a..."  Exited (0) About a minute
ago
```

So now we can start our Ubuntu image again with:

```
docker start -i  99f3ec319d74
root@92665288e3dc:/#
```

Again, this will open the command line in our Ubuntu container, which has been resumed at the exact point where we stopped it.

Pulling images

When we are running a Docker, we are indicating to the image that we want to run, and then Docker will first try to find it on our system. If it is not present, it will be downloaded from the Docker repository; however, we can download those images before running our Docker using the `pull` command.

For example, let's pull the official Jenkins CI image from Docker by using the following code:

```
docker pull jenkins
```

After some minutes, we should get the downloaded Jenkins image on our system. In this case, it is much slower to pull the image, and this is because the Jenkins image is much more complex than the previously used images:

```
Using default tag: latest
latest: Pulling from library/jenkins
3e17c6eae66c: Pull complete
fdfb54153de7: Pull complete
a4ca6e73242a: Pull complete
93bd198d0a5f: Pull complete
ca4d78fb08d6: Pull complete
ad3d1bdcab4b: Pull complete
4853d1e6d0c1: Pull complete
49e4624ad45f: Pull complete
bcbcd4c3ef93: Pull complete
684fd378d7b5: Pull complete
022bbe93d4a7: Pull complete
b81594f168ea: Pull complete
9d129b450ba7: Pull complete
4440ce182be6: Pull complete
6740814fee7d: Pull complete
569c9d093c48: Pull complete
3476a17f5aaf: Pull complete
b5f15cfc5e79: Pull complete
f09efd2ee9bd: Pull complete
8e110586720b: Pull complete
Digest:
sha256:f369cdbc48c80535a590ed5e00f4bc209f86c53b715851a3d655b70bb1a67858
Status: Downloaded newer image for jenkins:latest
```

Each of those `pull complete` sentences that we see are actually a layer of the Docker image that we are trying to pull. Each layer is the step that the image requires to have actually been created.

Managing images

If we want to know which images we have pulled on our system, we can use the following command:

```
docker images
```

This will list all the images that are available, when they were created, and their size, and we can delete them anytime:

```
REPOSITORY   TAG      IMAGE ID       CREATED       SIZE
ubuntu       latest   20c44cd7596f   3 days ago    123MB
alpine       latest   053cde6e8953   2 weeks ago   3.97MB
```

For example, let's delete the `alpine` image that was pulled when we ran our first example:

```
docker rmi alpine
```

Now, we should have an error, something that looks like this:

```
Error response from daemon: conflict: unable to remove repository reference
"alpine" (must force) - container 2caa58b34dd4 is using its referenced
image 053cde6e8953
```

This is because we cannot delete an image if we have Dockers that actually use them, even if they are stopped. So first, we need to delete those Dockers. Let's list all of them, including the ones that are stopped:

```
docker ps -a
```

In the list, we should see all our Dockers, and in the `IMAGE` column we should see what the images were based on:

```
CONTAINER ID   IMAGE    COMMAND                 STATUS
99f3ec319d74   ubuntu   "/bin/bash"             Exited (0) 26 seconds ago
2caa58b34dd4   alpine   "echo hello from a..."  Exited (0) About a minute
ago
```

We should delete the ones that are based on Alpine:

```
docker rm 2caa58b34dd4
2caa58b34dd4
```

This command just outputs the same CONTAINER ID that we pass to it, then we can delete the image by executing the command again:

```
docker rmi alpine
```

This will display a confirmation that our image has been deleted:

```
Untagged: alpine:latest
Untagged:
alpine@sha256:d6bfc3baf615dc9618209a8d607ba2a8103d9c8a405b3bd8741d88b4bef36
478
Deleted:
sha256:053cde6e8953ebd834df8f6382e68be83adb39bfc063e40b0fc61b4b333938f1
Deleted:
sha256:2aebd096e0e237b4477b81353379722157e6c2d434b9ec5a0d63f2a6f07cf90c2
```

Now, we will list the images again:

```
docker images
```

As a result, we should not get any more images on the Alpine list:

```
REPOSITORY    TAG      IMAGE ID      CREATED      SIZE
ubuntu        latest   20c44cd7596f  3 days ago   123MB
```

Building Dockers with microservices

Now that we have more understanding of how to use Docker, it is time to start creating our images. First, we will create a simple microservice that we will use for this section. Then we will get familiar with the Docker building process, and finally, we will create and run our microservice within a Docker.

Creating an example microservice

In order to create our microservice, we will use Spring Initializr, as we have been doing in previous chapters.

We can start by visiting the URL: `https://start.spring.io/`:

Spring Initializr

We have chosen to create a **Maven Project** using **Kotlin** and **Spring Boot 2.0.0 M7**, and we've chosen the Group to be `com.microservices` and **Artifact** `chapter07`. For **Dependencies**, we have set **Web**. Now we can click on **Generate Project** to download it as a ZIP file. After we unzip it, we can open it with IntelliJ IDEA to start working on our project. After some minutes, our project will be ready and we can open the Maven window to see the different lifecycle phases, Maven plugins, and their goals.

> We cover how to use Spring Initializr, Maven, and IntelliJ IDEA in `Chapter 2`, *Getting Started with Spring Boot 2.0*. You can visit this chapter to understand topics not covered in this section.

Now we will modify our application to create a simple microservice. Open the `Chapter07Application.kt` file from our project window, and modify it by adding a `@RestController`:

```kotlin
package com.microservices.chapter07

import org.springframework.boot.autoconfigure.SpringBootApplication
import org.springframework.boot.runApplication
import org.springframework.web.bind.annotation.GetMapping
import org.springframework.web.bind.annotation.RestController
```

```
@SpringBootApplication
class Chapter07Application

@RestController
class GreetingsController {
  @GetMapping("/greetings")
  fun greetings() = "hello from a Docker"
}

fun main(args: Array<String>) {
    runApplication<Chapter07Application>(*args)
}
```

Let's run to see our microservice start somehow. In the Maven window, just double-click on the **spring-boot** plugin, or just **run** goal from the command line in the microservice folder:

```
mvnw spring-boot:run
```

After some seconds, we will see several log lines, including something like the following:

```
INFO 11960 --- [ main] o.s.b.w.embedded.tomcat.TomcatWebServer : Tomcat
started on port(s): 8080 (http)
INFO 11960 --- [ main] c.m.chapter07.Chapter07ApplicationKt : Started
Chapter07ApplicationKt in 1.997 seconds (JVM running for 8.154)
```

Our service is ready, and we can just navigate to the http://localhost:8080/greetings URL, but it's still not running in a Docker; let's stop with *Ctrl + C*, and continue.

Creating a Dockerfile

In order to create a Docker image, we need to first create a Dockerfile, a file that will include the instructions that we will give to Docker in order to build our image. To create this file, on the top of the **Project** window, right-click on chapter07 and then select in the drop-down menu **New | File**, and type **Dockerfile.** In the next window, click **OK,** and the file will be created.

IntelliJ will recognize that file and offer a plugin to handle it. At the top of the editing window, a message will appear as **Plugins supporting Dockerfile files found.** On the right of this message, we will see **Install Plugins Ignore extension.** Let's click on **Install Plugins** to allow IntelliJ to handle this file. This will require the IDE to restart, and after some seconds it should start again.

Now we can add this to our `Dockerfile`:

```
FROM openjdk:8-jdk-alpine

ENTRYPOINT ["java","-version"]
```

Here, we are telling Docker that our image will be based on Java OpenJDK 8 in Alpine Linux. Then, we configure the entry point of our Docker and the command that will be executed when our Docker runs to be just the `java` command with a parameter, `-version`. Each of the lines on the `Dockerfile` will be a step, one of those layers that our Docker is completed with.

Now, we should open a command line in our `chapter07` directory and run this command to build our image:

```
docker build . -t chapter07
```

This will create output that will look something like this:

```
Sending build context to Docker daemon 2.302MB
Step 1/2 : FROM openjdk:8-jdk-alpine
8-jdk-alpine: Pulling from library/openjdk
b56ae66c2937: Pull complete
81cebc5bcaf8: Pull complete
9f7678525069: Pull complete
Digest:
sha256:219d9c2e4c27b8d1cfc6daeaf339e3eb7ceb82e67ce85857bdc55254822802bc
Status: Downloaded newer image for openjdk:8-jdk-alpine
 ---> a2a00e606b82
Step 2/2 : ENTRYPOINT java --version
 ---> Running in 661d47cd0bbd
 ---> 3a1d8bea31e7
Removing intermediate container 661d47cd0bbd
Successfully built 3a1d8bea31e7
Successfully tagged chapter07:latest
```

What has happened now is that Docker has built an image for us, and the image has been tagged as **chapter07**, since we used the `-t` option. Let's now run it with:

```
docker run chapter07
```

This output should look something like this:

```
openjdk version "1.8.0_131"
OpenJDK Runtime Environment (IcedTea 3.4.0) (Alpine 8.131.11-r2)
OpenJDK 64-Bit Server VM (build 25.131-b11, mixed mode)
```

This has run our Docker image that simply displays the Java version, but we need to add our microservice to it. Before that, let's understand clearly what a Docker is. A `Dockerfile` produces a binary image of a set of commands creating layers for each of them. Those commands are executed at build time to output the desired image. An image will have an entry point, a command that will be executed when we run the image itself.

A Docker is a containerized instance of a particular image. We usually refer to them as containers. When we run them, a copy of the original image is containerized and run through the defined entry point, outputting the results of their execution.

We have just briefly discussed creating Dockerfiles, but it is a technique that we should eventually master. We strongly recommend reviewing the Docker file reference on the Docker page `https://docs.Docker.com/` `engine/reference/builder/`, also see Dockerfile best practices at: `https:/` `/docs.Docker.com/engine/userguide/eng-image/dockerfile_best-` `practices/`.

Dockerize our microservice

In order to create a Docker with our microservice, we first need to package it into a JAR. So let's use Maven to do it, using the package lifecycle:

`mvnw package`

With the package created, now we need to modify our `Dockerfile` to actually use it:

```
FROM openjdk:8-jdk-alpine

ADD target/*.jar microservice.jar

ENTRYPOINT ["java","-jar", "microservice.jar"]
```

We use the `ADD` command to include our microservice JAR from the target folder. We get it from our target directory, and we add it to the Docker as `microservices.jar`. Then, we change our entry point to actually execute our JAR.

Now we can build our image again, repeating the build command:

```
docker build . -t chapter07
```

This should now give the following output:

```
Sending build context to Docker daemon 21.58MB
Step 1/3 : FROM openjdk:8-jdk-alpine
 ---> a2a00e606b82
Step 2/3 : ADD target/*.jar microservice.jar
 ---> 5c385fee6516
Step 3/3 : ENTRYPOINT java -jar microservice.jar
 ---> Running in 11071fdd0eb2
 ---> a43186cc4ea0
Removing intermediate container 11071fdd0eb2
Successfully built a43186cc4ea0
Successfully tagged chapter07:latest
```

However, this build is quicker than before, since the Docker command is an intelligent command; the things that have no changes from our FROM command are cached, and will not be built again.

Now we can run our microservice again by using:

```
docker run chapter07
```

We can now see our Spring Boot application running; however, if we try to navigate in our browser to it, we will not be able to reach it, so let's stop it with *Ctrl + C*.

Sometimes, doing *Ctrl + C* will not stop our Docker from just returning to the terminal. If we really want to completely stop it, we could follow these steps.

First, we should list our Docker with:

```
docker ps
```

This should list our Docker status, and actually, tell us that the Docker is still up:

```
CONTAINER    ID IMAGE    COMMAND               STATUS
d6bd15780353  chapter07  "java -jar microse..."  Up About a minute
```

We can just stop it with the kill command:

```
docker kill d6bd15780353
```

Now, if we repeat our `Docker ps` command again, the Docker should not be shown, but it will if we do a `Docker ps -a`:

```
CONTAINER ID   IMAGE       COMMAND               STATUS
d6bd15780353   chapter07   "java -jar microse..."  Exited (137) 2 minutes ago
```

The status of our Docker has changed from up to existed, as we'd expect.

Running the microservice

The reason we can't access the microservice when we run our previous example is that we need to expose the port that is running on the container outside of it.

So, we need to modify our Docker run command to:

```
docker run -d -p8080:8080 chapter07
```

Now we can just navigate to the URL `http://localhost:8080/greetings`, and we should get the following output:

```
hello from a Docker
```

We have just exposed our Docker internal port `8080`, but the `-p` option allows us to expose a different port too. So inside, the Docker can run on port `8080`, but we can externally run on another port. When we run our microservice via the command line, we actually wait until we press *Ctrl + C* to terminate it. We can instead just run it as a daemon.

 A daemon is a process that runs in the background of our system, so we could continue executing other commands while our process keeps running behind the scenes.

To run a Docker as a daemon, we could use the following command:

```
docker run -d -p8080:8080 chapter07
```

This will run the Docker as a daemon in the background, but it is still accessible. It should be listed when we do the following:

```
docker ps
```

Here, we can get the CONTAINER ID from our running Docker:

```
CONTAINER ID   IMAGE       COMMAND               STATUS
741bf50a0bfc   chapter07   "java -jar microse..."  Up About a minute
```

To see the logs, we can now run the following command:

```
docker logs 741bf50a0bfc
```

This will display the log of a running Docker; however, it will just exit after displaying the current logs. If we can wait for more output, as the Unix command tail does, we can instead do the following:

```
docker logs 741bf50a0bfc -f
```

Publishing Dockers

We have learned how to create Dockers, and how to run them, but these Dockers that we have built are stored in our system. Now we need to publish them so that they are accessible anywhere. During this section, we will learn how to publish our Docker images, and how we can finally integrate Maven with Docker to easily do the same steps for our microservices.

Understanding repositories

In our previous examples, when we built a Docker image, we published it into our local system repository so we can execute Docker run. Docker will be able to find them; this local repository exists only on our system, and most likely we need to have this access to wherever we like to run our Docker.

For example, we may create our Docker in a pipeline that runs on a machine that creates our builds, but the application itself may run in our preproduction or production environments, so the Docker image should be available on any system that we need.

 One of the great advantages of Docker is that any developer building an image can run it from their own system exactly as they would on any server. This will minimize the risk of having something different in each environment, or not being able to reproduce production when you try to find the source of a problem.

Docker provides a public repository, Docker Hub, that we can use to publish and pull images, but of course, you can use private Docker repositories such as Sonatype Nexus, VMware Harbor, or JFrog Artifactory. To learn how to configure additional repositories refer to the repositories documentation.

Creating an account on Docker Hub

To publish Docker images to Docker Hub, we will need to have a Docker.com account. To create one, we can just visit the Docker Hub home page, and in the top-right corner of the screen register for an account:

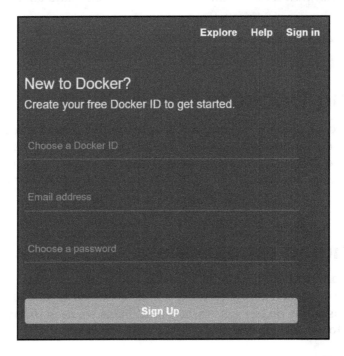

Docker Hub registration

After registering, we need to log into our account, so we can publish our Dockers using the Docker tool from the command line using `Docker login`:

```
docker login
Login with your Docker ID to push and pull images from Docker Hub. If you
don't have a Docker ID, head over to https://hub.Docker.com to create one.
Username: mydockerhubuser
Password:
Login Succeeded
```

When we need to publish a Docker, we must always be logged into the registry that we are working with; remember to log into Docker.

Publishing a Docker

Now we'd like to publish our Docker image to Docker Hub; but before we can, we need to build our images for our repository. When we create an account in Docker Hub, a repository with our username will be created; in this example, it will be `mydockerhubuser`.

In order to build the Docker for our repository, we can use this command from our `microservice` directory:

```
docker build .  -t mydockerhubuser/chapter07
```

This should be quite a fast process since all the different layers are cached:

```
Sending build context to Docker daemon 21.58MB
Step 1/3 : FROM openjdk:8-jdk-alpine
 ---> a2a00e606b82
Step 2/3 : ADD target/*.jar microservice.jar
 ---> Using cache
 ---> 4ae1b12e61aa
Step 3/3 : ENTRYPOINT java -jar microservice.jar
 ---> Using cache
 ---> 70d76cbf7fb2
Successfully built 70d76cbf7fb2
Successfully tagged mydockerhubuser/chapter07:latest
```

Now that our Docker is built, we can push it to Docker Hub with the following command:

```
docker push mydockerhubuser/chapter07
```

This command will take several minutes since the whole image needs to be uploaded. With our Docker published, we can now run it from any Docker system with the following command:

```
docker run mydockerhubuser/chapter07
```

Or else, we can run it as a daemon, with:

```
docker run -d mydockerhubuser/chapter07
```

Integrating Docker with Maven

Now that we know most of the Docker concepts, we can integrate Docker with Maven using the `Docker-Maven-plugin` created by fabric8, so we can create Docker as part of our Maven builds. First, we will move our `Dockerfile` to a different folder. In the IntelliJ **Project** window, right-click on the `src` folder and choose **New | Directory**. We will name it `Docker`. Now, drag and drop the existing `Dockerfile` into this new directory, and we will change it to the following:

```
FROM openjdk:8-jdk-alpine

ADD maven/*.jar microservice.jar

ENTRYPOINT ["java","-jar", "microservice.jar"]
```

To manage the `Dockerfile` better, we just move into our project folders. When our Docker is built using the plugin, the contents of our application will be created in a folder named `Maven`, so we change the `Dockerfile` to reference that folder.

Now, we will modify our Maven `pom.xml`, and add the `Dockerfile-Maven-plugin` in the **build | plugins** section:

```xml
<build>
....
  <plugins>
....
  <plugin>
    <groupId>io.fabric8</groupId>
    <artifactId>Docker-maven-plugin</artifactId>
    <version>0.23.0</version>
    <configuration>
      <verbose>true</verbose>
      <images>
        <image>
          <name>mydockerhubuser/chapter07</name>
          <build>
           <dockerFileDir>${project.basedir}/src/Docker</dockerFileDir>
            <assembly>
              <descriptorRef>artifact</descriptorRef>
            </assembly>
            <tags>
              <tag>latest</tag>
              <tag>${project.version}</tag>
            </tags>
          </build>
          <run>
```

```
            <ports>
              <port>8080:8080</port>
            </ports>
          </run>
        </image>
      </images>
    </configuration>
  </plugin>
 </plugins>
</build>
```

Here, we are specifying how to create our Docker, where the `Dockerfile` is, and even which version of the Docker we are building. Additionally, we specify some parameters when our Docker runs, such as the port that it exposes. If we need IntelliJ to reload the Maven changes, we may need to click on the **Reimport** all maven projects button in the Maven **Project** window.

For building our Docker using Maven, we can use the Maven **Project** window by running the task `Docker: build`, or by running the following command:

mvnw docker:build

This will build the Docker image, but we require to have it before it's packaged, so we can perform the following command:

mvnw package docker:build

We can also publish our Docker using Maven, either with the Maven **Project** window to run the `Docker: push` task, or by running the following command:

mvnw docker:push

This will push our Docker into the Docker Hub, but if we'd like to do everything in just one command, we can just use the following code:

mvnw package docker:build docker:push

Finally, the plugin provides other tasks such as `Docker: run`, `Docker: start`, and `Docker: stop`, which we can use in the commands that we've already learned on the command line.

Summary

By reading this chapter, we now understand what containers are, and what the main differences and advantages are between containers and virtual machines. We have learned how to use Docker to containerize our microservice, and why this will be an advantage for our applications. Finally, we looked at some examples of how we can integrate Docker with our Maven build system.

In the next chapter, we will take a look at how microservices can scale, and to fully understand that concept, we will create our personal cloud using Docker Swarm.

8
Scaling Microservices

As we have discussed in the previous chapters, one of the advantages of the microservice architecture is the capability to be able to scale independently. This will prove to be an excellent asset when we create an application that will use the benefits of cloud computing. In modern architectures, we are no longer attached to a static infrastructure. We deploy our microservices in a cloud, which gives the flexibility to have an optimal number of the instances of our microservices to match our needs, and we build Cloud-Native microservices to smoothly work on those clouds. We discussed this in `Chapter 6`, *Create Cloud-Native Microservices.* You may want to read it again as a refresher for some of the concepts used in this chapter. Having a Cloud-Native microservice requires having a cloud that allows us to manage how we can actually scale them, and how we can control them.

During this chapter, we will learn how we can scale microservices to adapt to our infrastructure for the needs of our applications. We will learn how to set up a cloud in our system that will be used to scale our microservices, and we will learn how we can configure and manage them.

In this chapter, we will learn about:

- Scalable architecture
- Docker swarm
- Services

A scalable architecture

If we need to scale our microservice, we will need to design them in a way that can actually be scaled and to do this, our architecture needs to be able to handle that requirement. In this section, we will try to learn the main concepts that will be used to create a scalable architecture, and how we can apply them in our microservices.

Scaling directions

Applications are not immutable, and they may change during their lifetime, from the requirements that they have, to the number of users that use them. If our application implements more functionality that may require more complex algorithms, resources, or data sources, we may not be able to handle it the same way we originally did.

Additionally, the usage of the application may increase because the number of application users increases or just because they are using it more frequently. In those scenarios, we may need to scale our application, if before we handled 100 transactions per minute, now we may need to do 200. If we were handling 50 concurrent users, we may now need to handle 75. In scenarios such as this, our application needs to be scaled; in order to do so, we could do it in one of two directions, horizontal or vertical.

Vertical scaling

When we scale an application, we can choose to increase the power of the system that it uses, adding more CPU, more memory, or disk space. Basically, we are making our server bigger. This is called vertical scaling.

Of course, we can use this to sale our architecture, but it will have some downsides:

- The scaling is fixed to a certain amount, for example, if we add more RAM it will be always there, used or not used
- We will reach a threshold where the cost of vertical scaling becomes less effective, with a high usage adding more resources to a server that already have plenty of resources to just partially increase its capacity, for example, double the CPU of a server that already has a very powerful CPU
- We can end being tied to a vendor-specific solution that may be far from optimal, for example, buying an enormous system for our database to handle all of the requests for an application in custom hardware that was designed for that purpose

Horizontal scaling

When we scale an application, we can choose to add more servers that handle our scaling demands. Basically, we are adding more servers. This is called horizontal scaling.

This can provide some advantages:

- We can dynamically scale it; today, we can add more servers and tomorrow, remove the ones that we don't need
- The cost of scaling is more effective; we can just add servers according to our demand
- We can create a solution that uses standard and cheap hardware instead of a proprietary big hardware solution, and the cost of maintenance is usually cheaper because of that

But it will present some challenges:

- We can't easily scale applications that are not designed to run on multiple servers
- We will require software and hardware tools to manage our scaling needs

Clouds will help us in this horizontal scaling.

Design for scaling

When we look at each of the individual components of our application, we need to consider whether they are designed for scaling.

We can try to ask each of the components the following questions:

- Does this component need to store and retrieve values that are bound to the server they run? For example, writing or reading in a file on the filesystem?
- Does this component need to synchronize anything with its peers?
- Does this component need an affinity to whoever was calling it before? Imagine that a particular instance always needs to handle the same request from the same customer/user/system.
- Can we stop this component at any time without affecting its peers, or the running requests?

When we answer these questions, we need to think about how we can handle the situations.

One way to deal with this problem is to make stateless components. A component does not require the state to work; each request will handle the parameters that they receive and return the results after processing, and will not need to keep any state on the system. Some applications handle this using an external system to store their state as a database server a stateful component.

So, how can stateful components scale?

Modern databases do scale, either by clustering them into several servers that can synchronize the data as a whole or by clustering or sharding the data among different servers in fractions of data. Either way, we need to be sure that our stateful components, like databases, have the ability to scale and that we can set them up.

Independently scaling

Each component in our architecture should be independently scalable, that means, for example, if one microservice needs to have more instances, we should able to scale it without the need of other parts of the application to scale. For example, if we have a microserver and the database that it uses on the same server, we will always scale them as a whole, and we may not need to. Maybe the microservice doesn't need to be scaled, maybe the database does, so scaling them separately permits optimal scaling. This is probably something that we are already doing if we followed the *Microservice principles* section from Chapter 1, *Understanding Microservices*.

Scaling down

We need to remember that scaling is not only for increasing. Imagine that we are preparing our infrastructure for an online application that we know that will have an additional load on certain dates, for example, on Black Friday or the Christmas season.

We need to design our architecture to scale up on those dates, but also to scale down when they end, or even more optimally, to scale up or down per need, regardless of the date. A way to do this is to do fasten startups and graceful shutdowns. This is something that Spring has already considered when creating Spring Cloud.

Let's look at these concepts:

- **Fast startups**: This means it is able to be ready in a timely manner. Containers, such as Docker, are great for this and will allow us to quickly create new instances of our services to handle our scaling.
- **Graceful shutdown**: When we stop an instance, it isn't as much about the speed as it is about keeping the rest of the system working. For example, if we have a stateful component, it may notify their peers that it is going down so they can handle the state that it was holding. If our instance is registered in a Service Registry, we should notify the Service Registry that the instance is shutting down, so the Service Registry can remove that instance from the list of the available instances from a service.

Creating a Cloud

Now that we understand some concepts about how to handle scaling, we need to have a cloud that we can use to build scalable microservices. In this section, we will learn how we can use Docker swarm to set up a small cloud.

 You will need Docker for Windows or Docker for Mac to continue with this chapter. You can follow the steps described in Chapter 7, *Creating Dockers,* and you can find more information on some of the Docker commands that we will use in this chapter.

Creating a swarm

Docker swarm is a tool provided by Docker that allows us to create a cloud, in a similar way that other tools, such as Kubernetes, do. This is included as part of the current version of Docker. A swarm is like a cluster of Dockers that we can use to create Docker instances, so before anything else, we need to create a new swarm in our system. To do so, we can just create a local swarm with the following command:

```
docker swarm init
```

It should output this message, telling us that our swarm is ready:

```
Swarm initialized: current node (kqhbzwiih5ynqonf2we16cqpn) is now a
manager.

To add a worker to this swarm, run the following command:
```

```
docker swarm join --token
SWMTKN-1-437vu5usnkkvnlb157kmb46gys9784hsnifg79a4lbeu7imv49-85uj1ta34bsu82e
jq0cf1tizc 192.168.65.2:2377

To add a manager to this swarm, run 'docker swarm join-token manager' and
follow the instructions.
```

Now, we can check that our swarm is ready using the following command:

```
docker info
```

This command will output many details of our Docker system, including our Docker swarm details:

```
Swarm: active
 NodeID: kqhbzwiih5ynqonf2we16cqpn
 Is Manager: true
 ClusterID: q5mnpql17drcymadbsy0ri2h5
 Managers: 1
 Nodes: 1
 Orchestration:
  Task History Retention Limit: 5
 Raft:
  Snapshot Interval: 10000
  Number of Old Snapshots to Retain: 0
  Heartbeat Tick: 1
  Election Tick: 3
 Dispatcher:
  Heartbeat Period: 5 seconds
 CA Configuration:
  Expiry Duration: 3 months
  Force Rotate: 0
 Autolock Managers: false
 Root Rotation In Progress: false
 Node Address: 192.168.65.2
 Manager Addresses:
  192.168.65.2:2377
```

Now, our swarm is ready to work.

Adding a service

Docker service is how we can control the Dockers in our cloud. A service is a set of instances of an existing Docker image that we can manage. We will create a new service based on the Docker alpine image with this command:

```
docker service create --replicas 1 --name helloworld alpine ping google.com
```

We can now check how many instances of that service we have in our cloud by using the following command:

```
docker service ls
```

This command should give an output that looks something like:

```
ID              NAME         MODE        REPLICAS   IMAGE
c9f635ec38fb    helloworld   replicated  1/1        alpine:latest
```

And if we want to, we can inspect our services with the following command:

```
docker service inspect --pretty helloworld
```

This should show the following as output:

```
ID: k5krqfpx8e15w91ojmftri9oa
Name: helloworld
Service Mode: Replicated
 Replicas: 1
Placement:
UpdateConfig:
 Parallelism: 1
 On failure: pause
 Monitoring Period: 5s
 Max failure ratio: 0
 Update order: stop-first
RollbackConfig:
 Parallelism: 1
 On failure: pause
 Monitoring Period: 5s
 Max failure ratio: 0
 Rollback order: stop-first
ContainerSpec:
 Image:
alpine:latest@sha256:d6bfc3baf615dc9618209a8d607ba2a8103d9c8a405b3bd8741d88
b4bef36478
 Args: ping google.com
Resources:
```

```
Endpoint Mode: vip
```

Here, we just see the default setting for our service.

Getting logs from a service

Now that we have a service running in our swarm, we may need to retrieve its logs. We can do so with the following command:

```
docker service logs -f helloworld
```

This will output a full set of lines, as in the following example, until we press *Ctrl* + *C*:

```
helloworld.1.ibpnops8gddp@moby | 64 bytes from 216.58.206.78: seq=421
ttl=37 time=10.157 ms
helloworld.1.ibpnops8gddp@moby | 64 bytes from 216.58.206.78: seq=422
ttl=37 time=10.221 ms
helloworld.1.ibpnops8gddp@moby | 64 bytes from 216.58.206.78: seq=423
ttl=37 time=10.158 ms
helloworld.1.ibpnops8gddp@moby | 64 bytes from 216.58.206.78: seq=424
ttl=37 time=10.559 ms
helloworld.1.ibpnops8gddp@moby | 64 bytes from 216.58.206.78: seq=425
ttl=37 time=10.208 ms
helloworld.1.ibpnops8gddp@moby | 64 bytes from 216.58.206.78: seq=426
ttl=37 time=9.969 ms
helloworld.1.ibpnops8gddp@moby | 64 bytes from 216.58.206.78: seq=427
ttl=37 time=13.793 ms
helloworld.1.ibpnops8gddp@moby | 64 bytes from 216.58.206.78: seq=428
ttl=37 time=10.782 ms
helloworld.1.ibpnops8gddp@moby | 64 bytes from 216.58.206.78: seq=429
ttl=37 time=9.776 ms
helloworld.1.ibpnops8gddp@moby | 64 bytes from 216.58.206.78: seq=430
ttl=37 time=11.205 ms
helloworld.1.ibpnops8gddp@moby | 64 bytes from 216.58.206.78: seq=431
ttl=37 time=10.293 ms
helloworld.1.ibpnops8gddp@moby | 64 bytes from 216.58.206.78: seq=432
ttl=37 time=10.612 ms
helloworld.1.ibpnops8gddp@moby | 64 bytes from 216.58.206.78: seq=433
ttl=37 time=10.413 ms
helloworld.1.ibpnops8gddp@moby | 64 bytes from 216.58.206.78: seq=434
ttl=37 time=10.080 ms
helloworld.1.ibpnops8gddp@moby | 64 bytes from 216.58.206.78: seq=435
ttl=37 time=10.448 ms
helloworld.1.ibpnops8gddp@moby | 64 bytes from 216.58.206.78: seq=436
ttl=37 time=9.845 ms
helloworld.1.ibpnops8gddp@moby | 64 bytes from 216.58.206.78: seq=437
```

```
ttl=37 time=10.761 ms
helloworld.1.ibpnops8gddp@moby | 64 bytes from 216.58.206.78: seq=438
ttl=37 time=10.072 ms
```

The interesting thing here is that it will be an aggregate view of all the instances of this service.

Deleting a service

Now, we will try to remove our service. We can do it by using the following command:

```
docker service rm helloworld
```

After removing the service, it will no longer be listed if we use this command:

```
docker service ls
```

Publishing a microservice as a service

Now that our swarm is ready, we can use it to create services that we can use for scaling, but first, we will create a shared registry in our swarm. Then, we will build a microservice and publish it into a Docker. Finally, we will learn how to scale our microservice and how to control it.

Creating a registry

When we create a swarm's service, we specify an image that will be used, but when we ask Docker to create the instances of the service, it will use the swarm master node to do it.

If we have built our Docker images in our machine, they are not available on the master node of the swarm, so it will create a registry service that we can use to publish our images and reference when we create our own services.

First, let's create the registry service:

```
docker service create --name registry --publish 5000:5000 registry
```

Now, if we list our services, we should see our registry created:

```
docker service ls
ID              NAME       MODE        REPLICAS  IMAGE             PORTS
os5j0iw1p4q1    registry   replicated  1/1       registry:latest
*:5000->5000/tcp
```

And if we visit `http://localhost:5000/v2/_catalog`, we should just get:

```
{"repositories":[]}
```

 This Docker registry is ephemeral, meaning that if we stop the service or start it again, our images will disappear. For that reason, we recommend to use it only for development. For a real registry, you may want to use an external service. We discussed some of them in `Chapter 7`, *Creating Dockers*.

Creating a microservice

In order to create a microservice, we will use Spring Initializr, as we have been doing in previous chapters.

We can start by visiting the URL: `https://start.spring.io/`:

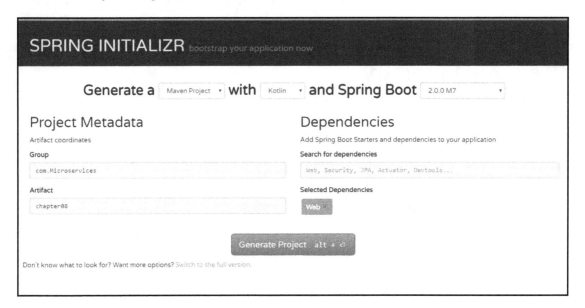

Creating a project in Spring Initializr

We have chosen to create a **Maven Project** using **Kotlin** and **Spring Boot 2.0.0 M7**. We chose the Group to be `com.Microservices` and the **Artifact** to be `chapter08`. For **Dependencies**, we have set **Web**.

Now, we can click **Generate Project** to download it as a zip file. After we unzip it, we can open it with IntelliJ IDEA to start working on our project.

After a few minutes, our project will be ready and we can open the Maven window to see the different lifecycle phases and Maven plugins and their goals.

 We covered how to use Spring Initializr, Maven, and IntelliJ IDEA in `Chapter 2`, *Getting Started with Spring Boot 2.0*. You can check out this chapter to learn about topics not covered in this section.

Now, we will add `RestController` to our project, in IntelliJ IDEA, in the **Project** window. Right-click our `com.Microservices.chapter08` package and then choose **New** | **Kotlin File/Class**. In the pop-up window, we will set its name as `HelloController` and in the **Kind** drop-down, choose **Class**.

Let's modify our newly created controller:

```kotlin
package com.microservices.chapter08

import org.springframework.web.bind.annotation.GetMapping
import org.springframework.web.bind.annotation.RestController
import java.util.*
import java.util.concurrent.atomic.AtomicInteger

@RestController
class HelloController {
  private val id: String = UUID.randomUUID().toString()

  companion object {
    val total: AtomicInteger = AtomicInteger()
  }

  @GetMapping("/hello")
  fun hello() = "Hello I'm $id and I have been called
${total.incrementAndGet()} time(s)"
}
```

This small controller will display a message with a GET request to the /hello URL. The message will display a unique id that we establish when the object is created and it will show how many times it has been called. We have used AtomicInteger to guarantee that no other requests are modified on our number concurrently.

Finally, we will rename application.properties in the resources folder, using *Shift + F6* to get application.yml, and edit it:

```
logging.level.org.springframework.web: DEBUG
```

We will establish that we have the log in the debug level for the Sprint Web Framework, so for the latter, we could view the information that will be needed in our logs. Now, we can run our microservice, either using IntelliJ IDEA Maven **Project** window with the spring-boot:run target, or by executing it on the command line:

```
mvnw spring-boot:run
```

Either way, when we visit the http://localhost:8080/hello URL, we should see something like:

```
Hello I'm a0193477-b9dd-4a50-85cc-9d9405e02299 and I have been called 1
time(s)
```

Doing consecutive calls will increase the number. Finally, we can see at the end of our log that we have several requests. The following should appear:

```
DEBUG 5316 --- [nio-8080-exec-7] o.s.web.servlet.DispatcherServlet :
Successfully completed request
```

Now, we will stop the microservice to create our Docker.

Creating our Docker

Now that our microservice is running, we need to create a Docker. To simplify the process, we will just use Dockerfile. To create this file on the top of the **Project** window, right-click chapter08 and then select **New | File** and type **Dockerfile** in the drop-down menu. In the next window, click **OK** and the file will be created.

Now, we can add this to our Dockerfile:

```
FROM openjdk:8-jdk-alpine

ADD target/*.jar app.jar

ENTRYPOINT ["java","-Djava.security.egd=file:/dev/./urandom","-jar",
"app.jar"]
```

 In this case, we tell the JVM to use dev/urandom instead of dev/random to generate random numbers required by our ID generation and this will make the operation much faster. You may think that urandom is less secure than random, but read this article for more information: https://www.2uo.de/myths-about-urandom/.

From our microservice directory, we will use the command line to create our package:

```
mvnw package
```

Then, we will create a Docker for it:

```
docker build . -t hello
```

Now, we need to tag our image in our shared registry service, using the following command:

```
docker tag hello localhost:5000/hello
```

Then, we will push our image to the shared registry service:

```
docker push localhost:5000/hello
```

Creating the service

Finally, we will add the microservice as a service to our swarm, exposing the 8080 port:

```
docker service create --name hello-service --publish 8080:8080
localhost:5000/hello
```

Now, we can navigate to http://localhost:8888/application/default to get the same results as before, but now we run our microservice in a Docker swarm.

Controlling services

Now that we have our personal cloud running with a microservice as a service, we need to learn how to control it. First, we will look at how we can scale these instances, then at how we can access the logs, and finally, how we can control these instances independently.

Scaling instances

Let's first look at which services we have to run with the following command:

```
docker service ls
```

This should show us our service instances:

```
ID              NAME           MODE         REPLICAS  IMAGE
PORTS
syqgugo598xn    hello-service  replicated   1/1
localhost:5000/hello:latest    *:8080->8080/tcp
os5j0iw1p4q1    registry       replicated   1/1       registry:latest
*:5000->5000/tcp
```

Here, we see that we have 1 replica for `hello-service`. Let's increase it with the following command:

```
docker service scale hello-service=3
```

After a few seconds, we can list our instances again:

```
docker service ls
```

This should now show:

```
ID              NAME           MODE         REPLICAS  IMAGE
PORTS
syqgugo598xn    hello-service  replicated   3/3
localhost:5000/hello:latest    *:8080->8080/tcp
os5j0iw1p4q1    registry       replicated   1/1       registry:latest
*:5000->5000/tcp
```

Now, if we do several requests using `curl`:

```
for i in `seq 1 21`; do curl http://localhost:8080/hello; echo . ; done
```

This should show the following output:

```
Hello I'm c2df911e-b23f-4d5c-abb7-3c0af1075171 and I have been called 1
time(s).
Hello I'm c03dd8f9-ad81-406f-b8d4-9c9afb30f09b and I have been called 1
time(s).
Hello I'm 23b3fc20-e565-46f2-a19a-178b6310de71 and I have been called 1
time(s).
Hello I'm c2df911e-b23f-4d5c-abb7-3c0af1075171 and I have been called 2
time(s).
Hello I'm c03dd8f9-ad81-406f-b8d4-9c9afb30f09b and I have been called 2
time(s).
Hello I'm 23b3fc20-e565-46f2-a19a-178b6310de71 and I have been called 2
time(s).
Hello I'm c2df911e-b23f-4d5c-abb7-3c0af1075171 and I have been called 3
time(s).
Hello I'm c03dd8f9-ad81-406f-b8d4-9c9afb30f09b and I have been called 3
time(s).
Hello I'm 23b3fc20-e565-46f2-a19a-178b6310de71 and I have been called 3
time(s).
Hello I'm c2df911e-b23f-4d5c-abb7-3c0af1075171 and I have been called 4
time(s).
Hello I'm c03dd8f9-ad81-406f-b8d4-9c9afb30f09b and I have been called 4
time(s).
Hello I'm 23b3fc20-e565-46f2-a19a-178b6310de71 and I have been called 4
time(s).
Hello I'm c2df911e-b23f-4d5c-abb7-3c0af1075171 and I have been called 5
time(s).
Hello I'm c03dd8f9-ad81-406f-b8d4-9c9afb30f09b and I have been called 5
time(s).
Hello I'm 23b3fc20-e565-46f2-a19a-178b6310de71 and I have been called 5
time(s).
Hello I'm c2df911e-b23f-4d5c-abb7-3c0af1075171 and I have been called 6
time(s).
Hello I'm c03dd8f9-ad81-406f-b8d4-9c9afb30f09b and I have been called 6
time(s).
Hello I'm 23b3fc20-e565-46f2-a19a-178b6310de71 and I have been called 6
time(s).
Hello I'm c2df911e-b23f-4d5c-abb7-3c0af1075171 and I have been called 7
time(s).
Hello I'm c03dd8f9-ad81-406f-b8d4-9c9afb30f09b and I have been called 7
time(s).
Hello I'm 23b3fc20-e565-46f2-a19a-178b6310de71 and I have been called 7
time(s).
```

If we look at the results, our three microservice instances are being called in a round robin.

 If we try to repeat the same request that we did using cURL using a browser we may always get the same microservice instance instead of a round robin. This is because Docker swarm creates an affinity between our browser, client and the instance that is answering. So, the repeated request from the same browser will get the same instance.

If we want to stop all instances from a microservice, we can just scale it to 0 with the following command:

```
docker service scale hello-service=0
```

Getting logs from a service

If we want to get the logs for our instances, we can use the following command:

```
docker service logs hello-service
```

Or if we want to follow the log, like a tail command will, we can do the following instead:

```
docker service logs -f hello-service
```

Either way, in our logs, we will see something like:

```
hello-service.3.sqmo44zoaqnc@moby ...
hello-service.2.enhf89re1kz9@moby ...
hello-service.2.enhf89re1kz9@moby ...
hello-service.1.suqe3o61n38e@moby ...
hello-service.2.enhf89re1kz9@moby ...
hello-service.2.enhf89re1kz9@moby ...
hello-service.2.enhf89re1kz9@moby ...
hello-service.2.enhf89re1kz9@moby ...
hello-service.2.enhf89re1kz9@moby ...
```

The beginning of each log line indicates the instance where it is coming from. That first element is the instance ID, and we could use it to get the logs from a particular instance.

For example, starting the line with hello-service.3.**sqmo44zoaqnc**@moby, we could get the logs for that instance with the following command:

```
docker service logs -f sqmo44zoaqnc
```

This should output the logs from the third instance.

Controlling the service

We can list the instance of one service with the command:

```
docker service ps hello-service
```

This will output something like:

```
ID             NAME             IMAGE
suqe3o61n38e   hello-service.1  localhost:5000/hello:latest
enhf89re1kz9   hello-service.2  localhost:5000/hello:latest
sqmo44zoaqnc   hello-service.3  localhost:5000/hello:latest
```

We can now open a shell session on those containers with the following command:

```
docker exec -it hello-service.2.enhf89re1kz9cieyvdgmnl911 /bin/sh
```

This will open a terminal to that Docker container, and we need to use the `exit` command to terminate it.

Finally, if we want to, we can delete a service with the following command:

```
docker service rm hello-service
```

With this last command, all service instances will be terminated, and the service will be removed.

> These are just some of the things that we can do with Docker swarm, but we suggest you review their documentation to better understand what this container-managing tool can do. Their official documentation is available at `https://docs.docker.com/engine/swarm/`.

Summary

Now, we understand what a scalable architecture is and the benefits that we can get from it. We learned how to create our own personal cloud using Docker swarm. Finally, we looked at how to scale microservices that are running in our cloud.

In the next chapter, we will move toward production, and our first step is to understand how we can test our microservices using JUnit and the support of Spring Framework.

9
Testing Spring Microservices

Testing is an integral part of software development, not only because it will give us confidence in the correctness of our implementation, but performing testing correctly also allows us to understand that our requirements are met and they provide a living documentation of our code.

Well-written tests can make any complex software understandable; using our domain Ubiquitous language in our tests, we can make the entire team understand our implementation, including the domain experts, which will give inestimable value to our microservices. We learned about domain-driven design and the Ubiquitous language in Chapter 1, *Understanding Microservices*; you can revisit that chapter to refresh some of the concepts that we will use.

Since we will use Spring Framework to build our microservices, we will need to know which components Spring provides for our tests, and in doing so, we will use the industry standard framework for unit testing, JUnit. During this book, we will learn how to use Spring MockMvc for testing our microservices URLs.

However, testing complex software is a challenging task, especially when it depends on other systems, and to help ourselves in this problem, we will learn how we can use Mockito to mock out dependencies or even our Spring beans. Finally, we will learn how we can use Kluent to do fluent tests using Kotlin in a more expressive way to test our microservices.

In this chapter, you will learn about the following topics:

- SpringBootTest
- JUnit
- MockMvc

- Mockito
- MockBean
- Kluent

Understanding SpringBootTest

We have learned how easy it is to create microservices using Spring Framework, but now we need to learn how we can test them, and how Spring can help us. First, we will create a small microservice that will later be used for testing. Then, we will understand what is `SpringBootTest` and how we can test our beans using JUnit. Finally, we will learn how we can test our controller using `MockMvc`.

Creating a simple microservice

In order to create our microservice, we will use Spring Initializr, as we have been doing in the previous chapters.

We can start by visiting `https://start.spring.io/`:

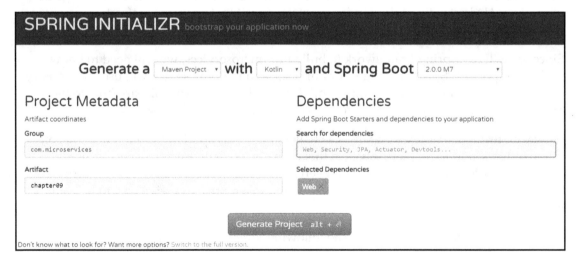

Spring Initializr

We have chosen to create a **Maven Project** using **Kotlin** and **Spring Boot 2.0.0 M7**. We choose **Group** to be `com.microservices` and **Artifact** `chapter09`. For **Dependencies,** we have set **Web**.

Now, we can click on **Generate Project** to download it as a ZIP file; after we unzip it, we can open it with IntelliJ IDEA to start working on our project. After some minutes, our project will be ready, and we can open the Maven window to see the different life cycle phases and Maven plugins and their goals.

 We covered how to use Spring Initializr, Maven, and IntelliJ IDEA in `Chapter 2`, *Getting Started with Spring Boot 2.0*. You can visit this chapter to understand topics not covered in this section.

Now, we will add a `Customer` class to our project. In IntelliJ IDEA, in the **Project** window, right-click on our `com.microservices.chapter09` package and choose **New | Kotlin File/Class** in the pop-up window. We will set the name as `Customer` and in the **Kind** drop-down, choose **Class:**

```
package com.microservices.chapter09

data class Customer(val id: Int, val name: String)
```

We will use this class to hold customer information. Now, let's create a new interface, repeating the following step but choosing **Interface** instead of **Class**. We will name it `CustomerService`:

```
package com.microservices.chapter09

interface CustomerService {
  fun getCustomer(id: Int): Customer?
  fun getAllCustomers(): List<Customer>
}
```

This will be the interface of a service that is in charge of retrieving customers. Now, we will implement it by creating a new class, repeating the previous step, and name it `CustomerServiceImpl`:

```
package com.microservices.chapter09

import org.springframework.stereotype.Service
import java.util.concurrent.ConcurrentHashMap

@Service
class CustomerServiceImpl : CustomerService {
```

```
    companion object {
      private val initialCustomers = arrayOf(Customer(1, "Kotlin"),
          Customer(2, "Spring"),
          Customer(3, "Microservice")
      )
      private val customers = ConcurrentHashMap<Int,
  Customer>(initialCustomers.associateBy(Customer::id))
    }

    override fun getCustomer(id: Int) = customers[id]
    override fun getAllCustomers() = customers.map(Map.Entry<Int,
  Customer>::value).toList()
  }
```

This is a simple implementation of the defined `CustomerService` interface that will just get the value from a `ConcurrentHashMap`.

Finally, we will create a `RestController` that uses our `CustomerService` to return customers in two different GET requests. Repeat the following steps to create a new class named `CustomerController`:

```
package com.microservices.chapter09

import org.springframework.beans.factory.annotation.Autowired
import org.springframework.web.bind.annotation.GetMapping
import org.springframework.web.bind.annotation.PathVariable
import org.springframework.web.bind.annotation.RestController

@RestController
class CustomerController {
  @Autowired
  lateinit var customerService: CustomerService

  @GetMapping("/customer/{id}")
  fun getCustomer(@PathVariable id: Int) = customerService.getCustomer(id)

  @GetMapping("/customers")
  fun getCustomers() = customerService.getAllCustomers()
}
```

Now, we can run our microservice either using the IntelliJ IDEA Maven **Project** window with the `spring-boot:run` target, or by executing the following on the command line:

```
mvnw spring-boot:run
```

Either way, when we visit `http://localhost:8080/customers`, we can see something like this:

```
[
 {
  "id":1,
  "name":"Kotlin"
 },
 {
  "id":2,
  "name":"Spring"
 },
 {
  "id":3,
  "name":"Microservice"
 }
]
```

Also, if we visit `http://localhost:8080/customer/1`, we can instead get the following:

```
{
 "id":1,
 "name":"Kotlin"
}
```

> Many of the things that we have used in this example have been covered in `Chapter 2`, *Getting Started with Spring Boot 2.0*, and `Chapter 3`, *Creating RESTful Services*. You may need to revisit them to understand it further.

Understanding SpringBootTest

When we create a Spring Boot application using Spring Initializr; it will already contain a test that uses `SpringBootTest`. In our example, we can just open the `Chapter09ApplicationTests` file, which is under the `src/test/kotlin/com/microservices/chapter09` path:

```
package com.microservices.chapter09

import org.junit.Test
import org.junit.runner.RunWith
import org.springframework.boot.test.context.SpringBootTest
import org.springframework.test.context.junit4.SpringRunner

@RunWith(SpringRunner::class)
```

```
@SpringBootTest
class Chapter09ApplicationTests {

  @Test
  fun contextLoads() {
  }

}
```

This is a JUnit test that uses `SpringBootTest` to test that the Spring application can run. Let's understand it in detail. First, we indicate to JUnit, which is the runner, that we will be using the `@RunWith` annotation in our tests. Spring provides a JUnit runner named `SpringRunner`; this will make it that when our test runs, Spring will launch the Spring Boot application, and in doing so, our Spring Application Context will load and our beans will be created; basically, we start our microservice for our tests.

Then, we can see that we have defined a test annotating a method with the `@Test` annotation, but this test, named `contextLoads`, does nothing, and this is because it is a simple text that will run using the `SpringBootTest`, and if for any reason, the context cannot load, or the application cannot start, that test will fail. It may look strange to have such an empty test, but if we change something in our service, for example, creating an incorrect bean, a wrong configuration, and so on, that test will fail, and we can use it to just check that our Spring application is set up correctly. Now, we can run our test either using the IntelliJ IDEA Maven **Project** window with the `test` life cycle or by executing the following on the command line:

```
mvnw test
```

Either way, at the end, you will see some statistics about our `Tests` run in the log:

```
[INFO]
[INFO] Results:
[INFO]
[INFO] Tests run: 1, Failures: 0, Errors: 0, Skipped: 0
[INFO]
```

However, IntelliJ IDEA provides an interface to quickly run the test. With our test open, we can click on the green arrow in the `Chapter09ApplicationTests` class or in the `contextLoads` method to run the same test:

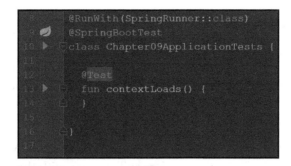

IntelliJ run test arrows

When we click on those arrows in the bottom-center of the screen, we will see the window with the test result indicating which test has passed, colored in green, and which tests have failed, in red, and the log for each of them:

tests results window

If a test fails, we can double-click on its name to actually go to the line that has failed in our test code. Additionally, we will see the log of that test execution on the test results window.

If we want to run all the tests of our project, we can right-click on the **Project** window in the src/test/Kotlin folder and choose **Run All Tests**, and this is something that we should do from time to time—not just run the test that we are working on, since our changes may cause other tests to fail.

Testing beans

In Spring microservices, we create beans that will be used by other components within the application, and as they need to be tested, we can create a JUnit test that uses them. In our example, we have created an interface named `CustomerService` that has been implemented by the `CustomerServiceImpl` class, which is annotated with the `@Service` annotation; this has created a bean in our context that we can test.

First, let's open our `CustomerServiceImpl` class and select **class**. We can select the class name and press *Shift + Ctrl + T*. A new window will appear with the title **Choose Test** for `CustomerServiceImpl` with an option to **Create New Test**. Selecting that option will bring up the **Create Test** window:

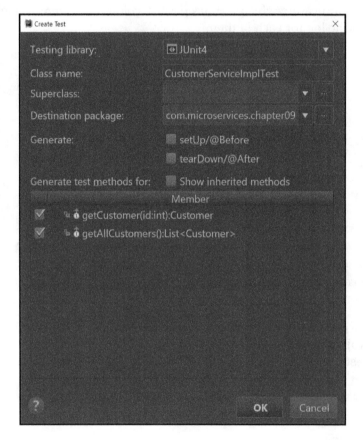

Create Test Window

By default, this window will indicate the testing library to be `JUnit 4` and the class name as `CustomerServiceImplTest`. We will mark the methods that we would like to add tests for `getCustomer` and `getAllCustomers` and click on **OK**. This will generate the new `CustomerServiceImplTest` class in the `src/test/kotlin/com/microservices/chapter09web` path. Let's open it:

```kotlin
package com.microservices.chapter09

import org.junit.Test

class CustomerServiceImplTest {
  @Test
  fun getCustomer() {
  }

  @Test
  fun getAllCustomers() {
  }
}
```

We can run those tests, as we did before, by clicking on the green arrow on the left of the `CustomerImplTest` text class, and two tests will run with a green status. Those are JUnit tests, but not `SpringBootTest`, so let's modify them so that they will be as follows:

```kotlin
package com.microservices.chapter09

import org.junit.Test
import org.junit.runner.RunWith
import org.springframework.boot.test.context.SpringBootTest
import org.springframework.test.context.junit4.SpringRunner

@RunWith(SpringRunner::class)
@SpringBootTest
class CustomerServiceImplTest {
  @Test
  fun getCustomer() {
  }

  @Test
  fun getAllCustomers() {
  }
}
```

We can run the test again either by clicking on the green arrow on the test results window or again, as we did earlier, on the arrow in the class name in the main editor; either way, it should be green.

 Not every test needs to be a `SpringBootTest`, but when we are trying to test Spring components, we must make them. However, if you have a plain class that has no dependency to have the Spring context or application, you don't need to create a `SpringBootTest`.

Now, we should get our service in our test. Since this is a `SpringBootTest`, we can get it autowired:

```
@RunWith(SpringRunner::class)
package com.microservices.chapter09

import org.junit.Test
import org.junit.runner.RunWith
import org.springframework.beans.factory.annotation.Autowired
import org.springframework.boot.test.context.SpringBootTest
import org.springframework.test.context.junit4.SpringRunner

@RunWith(SpringRunner::class)
@SpringBootTest
class CustomerServiceImplTest {
  @Autowired
  lateinit var customerServiceImpl: CustomerServiceImpl

  @Test
  fun getCustomer() {
    customerServiceImpl.getCustomer(1)

  }

  @Test
  fun getAllCustomers() {
    customerServiceImpl.getAllCustomers()
  }
}
```

Before advancing further, we need to consider what we are trying to test—is it the service implementation or the service interface?

Testing the implementation, we see that if we change the implementation to something else, we either need to rewrite the test or change it; if we test the interface regardless of the implementation, our test will still be valid. However, we keep a separate test for the implementation that will test the concrete implementation details, but not the interface.

So, we will change this test to test the interface. First, select the `CustomerServiceImplTest` class in the editor window, click on *Shift* + *F6* to rename it to `CustomerServiceTest`, and then edit it:

```
package com.microservices.chapter09

import org.junit.Test
import org.junit.runner.RunWith
import org.springframework.beans.factory.annotation.Autowired
import org.springframework.boot.test.context.SpringBootTest
import org.springframework.test.context.junit4.SpringRunner

@RunWith(SpringRunner::class)
@SpringBootTest
class CustomerServiceTest {
  @Autowired
  lateinit var customerService: CustomerService

  @Test
  fun getCustomer() {
    customerService.getCustomer(1)

  }

  @Test
  fun getAllCustomers() {
    customerService.getAllCustomers()
  }
}
```

Now, we can run our tests again and they should work correctly. However, in our test, we are not really doing much apart from purely invoking the methods of the service. We need to validate the results that we expect, and we can use assertions for that:

```
package com.microservices.chapter09

import org.junit.Assert
import org.junit.Test
import org.junit.runner.RunWith
import org.springframework.beans.factory.annotation.Autowired
import org.springframework.boot.test.context.SpringBootTest
```

```
import org.springframework.test.context.junit4.SpringRunner

@RunWith(SpringRunner::class)
@SpringBootTest
class CustomerServiceTest {
  @Autowired
  lateinit var customerService: CustomerService

  @Test
  fun getCustomer() {
    val customer = customerService.getCustomer(1)
    Assert.assertNotNull(customer)
    Assert.assertEquals(customer?.name, "Kotlin")
  }

  @Test
  fun getAllCustomers() {
    val customers = customerService.getAllCustomers()
    Assert.assertEquals(customers.size, 3)
  }
}
```

 Assert allow us to specify an assertion message. For example, we can change our asserts to be `assertNotNull(customer, "customer is null");` in that way, we will get more meaningful messages when the test fails.

First, we added some assertions to our test. We verify that we get a customer and their name is Kotlin, and for the other method, we just check that we get 3 customers back. However, we can do static imports to the assert methods to get the more clear code and rename our test to have something more meaningful in what we try to test, not how we test it:

```
package com.microservices.chapter09

import junit.framework.Assert.assertEquals
import junit.framework.Assert.assertNotNull
import org.junit.Test
import org.junit.runner.RunWith
import org.springframework.beans.factory.annotation.Autowired
import org.springframework.boot.test.context.SpringBootTest
import org.springframework.test.context.junit4.SpringRunner

@RunWith(SpringRunner::class)
@SpringBootTest
class CustomerServiceTest {
```

```kotlin
@Autowired
lateinit var customerService: CustomerService

@Test
fun `we should get a customer with a valid id`() {
  val customer = customerService.getCustomer(1)
  assertNotNull(customer)
  assertEquals(customer?.name, "Kotlin")
}

@Test
fun `we should get all customers`() {
  val customers = customerService.getAllCustomers()
  assertEquals(customers.size, 3)
}
}
```

If we run them now, our test result window should display:

More expressive results in the test window

What happens if we change our assert to be invalid? For example, changing one assert to be `assertEquals(customer?.name, "Java")`. If we run the test now, we will see this:

Test failure

Let's revert it and continue to test our controllers.

 We have not covered any invalid scenarios in this test, such as giving an ID that does not exist, but a complete test should take care of those, and naming them correctly will make it really easy to understand our intention in each test.

Using MockMvc

So far, we have tested our beans, but we need to test how our controller answers our HTTP requests. For example, what happens when we do an HTTP GET request from the /customers URL? To test this, we need a way to test each of our requests. Spring provides a class named MockMvc that simulates our server in a way that we can test our requests.

First, go to the CustomerController class. Select it in the **Project** window, and then select the class name in the editor. Press *Shift + Ctrl + T* and choose to **Create New Test.** This will be automatically named as CustomerControllerTest. We do not need to choose any options on **Create Test window**, just click on **OK.**

Now, we need to add our MockMvc object to the class:

```
package com.microservices.chapter09

import org.junit.Test
import org.junit.runner.RunWith
import org.springframework.beans.factory.annotation.Autowired
import
org.springframework.boot.test.autoconfigure.web.servlet.AutoConfigureMockMv
c
import org.springframework.boot.test.context.SpringBootTest
import org.springframework.test.context.junit4.SpringRunner
import org.springframework.test.web.servlet.MockMvc

@RunWith(SpringRunner::class)
@SpringBootTest
@AutoConfigureMockMvc
class CustomerControllerTest {
  @Autowired
  lateinit var mockMvc: MockMvc

  @Test
  fun `mock mvc should be configured`() {
  }
}
```

First, we have set our test class to be a SpringBootTest that uses the SpringRunner. Then, we have autowired MockMvc. When our first test runs, we should not get any errors; we can delete this first test since we don't really need it.

Now, let's try to make a test carry out a GET request in our /customer URL by adding a test for it in our CustomerControllerTest class:

```
package com.microservices.chapter09

import org.junit.Test
import org.junit.runner.RunWith
import org.springframework.beans.factory.annotation.Autowired
import
org.springframework.boot.test.autoconfigure.web.servlet.AutoConfigureMockMv
c
import org.springframework.boot.test.context.SpringBootTest
import org.springframework.test.context.junit4.SpringRunner
import org.springframework.test.web.servlet.MockMvc
import
org.springframework.test.web.servlet.request.MockMvcRequestBuilders.get
import
org.springframework.test.web.servlet.result.MockMvcResultMatchers.status
import
org.springframework.test.web.servlet.result.MockMvcResultHandlers.print

@RunWith(SpringRunner::class)
@SpringBootTest
@AutoConfigureMockMvc
class CustomerControllerTest {
  @Autowired
  lateinit var mockMvc: MockMvc

  @Test
  fun `mock mvc should be configured`() {
  }

  @Test
  fun `we should GET a customer by id`() {
    mockMvc.perform(get("/customer/1"))
        .andExpect(status().isOk)
        .andDo(print())
  }
}
```

We use `mockMvc` to perform a GET request to our `/customer/1` URL and then check that we get **200 OK** as the HTTP response status. Finally, we have to just ask `mockMvc` to print the request and response in our log. Our test should run and additionally, we should see this within the log lines of the test:

```
MockHttpServletResponse:
          Status = 200
   Error message = null
         Headers = {Content-Type=[application/json;charset=UTF-8]}
    Content type = application/json;charset=UTF-8
            Body = {"id":1,"name":"Kotlin"}
   Forwarded URL = null
  Redirected URL = null
         Cookies = []
```

However, we haven't checked the actual response. We can perform XPath-like queries in the output JSON using the `jsonPath` method:

```kotlin
package com.microservices.chapter09

import org.junit.Test
import org.junit.runner.RunWith
import org.springframework.beans.factory.annotation.Autowired
import org.springframework.boot.test.autoconfigure.web.servlet.AutoConfigureMockMvc
import org.springframework.boot.test.context.SpringBootTest
import org.springframework.test.context.junit4.SpringRunner
import org.springframework.test.web.servlet.MockMvc
import org.springframework.test.web.servlet.request.MockMvcRequestBuilders.get
import org.springframework.test.web.servlet.result.MockMvcResultHandlers.print
import org.springframework.test.web.servlet.result.MockMvcResultMatchers.jsonPath
import org.springframework.test.web.servlet.result.MockMvcResultMatchers.status

@RunWith(SpringRunner::class)
@SpringBootTest
@AutoConfigureMockMvc
class CustomerControllerTest {
  @Autowired
  lateinit var mockMvc: MockMvc

  @Test
  fun `mock mvc should be configured`() {
```

```
  }

  @Test
  fun `we should GET a customer by id`() {
    mockMvc.perform(get("/customer/1"))
        .andExpect(status().isOk)
        .andExpect(jsonPath("\$.id").value(1))
        .andExpect(jsonPath("\$.name").value("Kotlin"))
        .andDo(print())
  }
}
```

Here, we first use the `$.id` path to get our customer `id`. Remember that we need to escape the `$` character with `\$` because `$` is used in Kotlin String interpolations.

Then, to compare the values, we will use the `value` method.

Now, let's try to test our `/customers` URL to get the list of customers adding a new test:

```
package com.microservices.chapter09

import org.junit.Test
import org.junit.runner.RunWith
import org.springframework.beans.factory.annotation.Autowired
import org.springframework.boot.test.autoconfigure.web.servlet.AutoConfigureMockMvc
import org.springframework.boot.test.context.SpringBootTest
import org.springframework.test.context.junit4.SpringRunner
import org.springframework.test.web.servlet.MockMvc
import org.springframework.test.web.servlet.request.MockMvcRequestBuilders.get
import org.springframework.test.web.servlet.result.MockMvcResultHandlers.print
import org.springframework.test.web.servlet.result.MockMvcResultMatchers.jsonPath
import org.springframework.test.web.servlet.result.MockMvcResultMatchers.status

@RunWith(SpringRunner::class)
@SpringBootTest
@AutoConfigureMockMvc
class CustomerControllerTest {
  @Autowired
  lateinit var mockMvc: MockMvc

  @Test
```

```
fun `mock mvc should be configured`() {
}

@Test
fun `we should GET a customer by id`() {
  mockMvc.perform(get("/customer/1"))
       .andExpect(status().isOk)
       .andExpect(jsonPath("\$.id").value(1))
       .andExpect(jsonPath("\$.name").value("Kotlin"))
       .andDo(print())
}

@Test
fun `we should GET a list of customers`() {
  mockMvc.perform(get("/customers"))
       .andExpect(status().isOk)
       .andExpect(jsonPath("\$").isArray)
       .andExpect(jsonPath("\$[0].id").value(1))
       .andExpect(jsonPath("\$[0].name").value("Kotlin"))
       .andExpect(jsonPath("\$[1].id").value(2))
       .andExpect(jsonPath("\$[1].name").value("Spring"))
       .andExpect(jsonPath("\$[2].id").value(3))
       .andExpect(jsonPath("\$[2].name").value("Microservice"))
       .andDo(print())
  }
}
```

In this final test, we check that there's actually an array in the result, and each value is the element that we were expecting.

Mocking beans

Testing complex systems can be challenging, especially when we are dealing with dependencies. If our software depends on an external system such as a database or another service backend, it's hard to make our test without predicting the results from something that is not in our control. We can use a mechanism to prevent this from affecting us. We can use mocks that will mimic the expected output from another system.

Making our tests repeatable is a must in modern software development. Mocking will allow us to always get the same result, regardless of how many times, or in what order, our tests run.

Why we mock

Let's go back to our previous test, where we tested our `CustomerController` in our `CustomerControllerTest` class, and let's review our `/customers` test:

```
@Test
fun `we should GET a list of customers`() {
  mockMvc.perform(get("/customers"))
      .andExpect(status().isOk)
      .andExpect(jsonPath("\$").isArray)
      .andExpect(jsonPath("\$[0].id").value(1))
      .andExpect(jsonPath("\$[0].name").value("Kotlin"))
      .andExpect(jsonPath("\$[1].id").value(2))
      .andExpect(jsonPath("\$[1].name").value("Spring"))
      .andExpect(jsonPath("\$[2].id").value(3))
      .andExpect(jsonPath("\$[2].name").value("Microservice"))
      .andDo(print())
}
```

Imagine that our customers are actually behind a database—a database that may be modified externally or outside of our tests—then our test will fail if we actually don't get that specific list of customers. We can minimize this problem if we create our own independent database when we run our tests, only for our testing purposes, but then what could happen if our test database is modified within our own tests?

We can have tests that insert customers or delete them. Depending on the order that we run our tests in, the results will change, and our tests need to be repeatable, always getting the same results. We can also solve this by deleting or inserting the data that we need in the database before each test, but let's think about it.

Our controller tests are trying to test what our controller does. If we delegate the responsibility of having data in the database in a certain way before our tests, we are leaking the knowledge of the implementation of our service into our controller test. Due to the implementation of the service is why we know that we use a database and that knowledge should not be transferred somewhere else.

If we change our implementation to be in a different database tomorrow, will we change our tests to insert the data differently?

Our tests should say what they expect from the service, regardless of their implementation; for that, we can use mocks.

There is a whole debate in the industry about the needs, or not, to have mocked in well-written software, but that is not a trivial discussion. It's true that having excessive use of mocks in the software may hint a wrong design in our application, but this is something that we should master with time and experience.

Setting up a mock

Spring uses `Mockito` for mocking, the most widely used Java library for mocking objects in the JVM, and provides an annotation to use it easily with our Spring context. We will modify our `CustomerControllerTest` class to first add a `Mock` to our `CustomerService` bean:

```
package com.microservices.chapter09

import org.junit.Test
import org.junit.runner.RunWith
import org.springframework.beans.factory.annotation.Autowired
import
org.springframework.boot.test.autoconfigure.web.servlet.AutoConfigureMockMv
c
import org.springframework.boot.test.context.SpringBootTest
import org.springframework.boot.test.mock.mockito.MockBean
import org.springframework.test.context.junit4.SpringRunner
import org.springframework.test.web.servlet.MockMvc
import
org.springframework.test.web.servlet.request.MockMvcRequestBuilders.get
import
org.springframework.test.web.servlet.result.MockMvcResultHandlers.print
import
org.springframework.test.web.servlet.result.MockMvcResultMatchers.jsonPath
import
org.springframework.test.web.servlet.result.MockMvcResultMatchers.status

@RunWith(SpringRunner::class)
@SpringBootTest
@AutoConfigureMockMvc
class CustomerControllerTest {
  @Autowired
  lateinit var mockMvc: MockMvc

  @MockBean
  lateinit var customerService: CustomerService

  . . . . .
```

}

In this change, we use the `@MockBean` Spring annotation to indicate to our `SpringBootTest`, `CustomerControllerTest`, that we would like to inject a `MockBean` into the Spring context for `CustomerService`. When we run our test and any component of our application is requesting the `CustomerService` bean, for example, as our `CustomerController` uses `@Autowired`, it will get the `Mock` that we just defined instead of the real object.

Returning mocked values

Now that we have our `CustomerService` mocked, we can define what value should be returned for our test.

We will modify the test to get a list of customers:

```
package com.microservices.chapter09

import org.junit.Test
import org.junit.runner.RunWith
import org.mockito.BDDMockito.given
import org.mockito.Mockito.reset
import org.springframework.beans.factory.annotation.Autowired
import
org.springframework.boot.test.autoconfigure.web.servlet.AutoConfigureMockMvc
import org.springframework.boot.test.context.SpringBootTest
import org.springframework.boot.test.mock.mockito.MockBean
import org.springframework.test.context.junit4.SpringRunner
import org.springframework.test.web.servlet.MockMvc
import
org.springframework.test.web.servlet.request.MockMvcRequestBuilders.get
import
org.springframework.test.web.servlet.result.MockMvcResultHandlers.print
import
org.springframework.test.web.servlet.result.MockMvcResultMatchers.jsonPath
import
org.springframework.test.web.servlet.result.MockMvcResultMatchers.status

@RunWith(SpringRunner::class)
@SpringBootTest
@AutoConfigureMockMvc
class CustomerControllerTest {
...............
```

```
@Test
fun `we should GET a list of customers`() {
  given(customerService.getAllCustomers())
      .willReturn(listOf(Customer(1, "test"), Customer(2, "mocks")))

  mockMvc.perform(get("/customers"))
      .andExpect(status().isOk)
      .andExpect(jsonPath("\$").isArray)
      .andExpect(jsonPath("\$[0].id").value(1))
      .andExpect(jsonPath("\$[0].name").value("test"))
      .andExpect(jsonPath("\$[1].id").value(2))
      .andExpect(jsonPath("\$[1].name").value("mocks"))
      .andDo(print())

  reset(customerService)
  }
}
```

Here, we use the `Mockito` BDD-style functions to set up our mock. We said that using our `customerService` bean when calling the `getAllCustomers` method will return that specific list of customers. Then, our test can verify those particular values. Finally, we reset the `Mock` to prevent other tests from getting affected by this particular setup. Now, let's modify our test for a particular customer, where we will set up to return values based on the input parameters:

```
@Test
fun `we should GET a customer by id`() {
  given(customerService.getCustomer(1))
      .willReturn(Customer(1, "mock customer"))

  mockMvc.perform(get("/customer/1"))
      .andExpect(status().isOk)
      .andExpect(jsonPath("\$.id").value(1))
      .andExpect(jsonPath("\$.name").value("mock customer"))
      .andDo(print())

  reset(customerService)
  }
```

In this test, we set up our `Mock` to return a mocked customer only when we get a parameter, that is, an `id` equal to 1; then, we verify that we get the customer values.

 When we are testing these requests in the controller, we are testing how the controller works, how it gets the output of the service, and how it transforms it into our HTTP response, regardless of the implementation of the service.

Verifying Mock invocation

Using `Mockito` allows us to verify the invocation of our mock. We can use it to validate that our controller actually invoked the method of the service, and also know with which parameter it's used.

First, we will verify our customer list test:

```
package com.microservices.chapter09

import org.junit.Test
import org.junit.runner.RunWith
import org.mockito.BDDMockito.given
import org.mockito.BDDMockito.then
import org.mockito.Mockito.reset
import org.mockito.Mockito.times
import org.springframework.beans.factory.annotation.Autowired
import
org.springframework.boot.test.autoconfigure.web.servlet.AutoConfigureMockMv
c
import org.springframework.boot.test.context.SpringBootTest
import org.springframework.boot.test.mock.mockito.MockBean
import org.springframework.test.context.junit4.SpringRunner
import org.springframework.test.web.servlet.MockMvc
import
org.springframework.test.web.servlet.request.MockMvcRequestBuilders.get
import
org.springframework.test.web.servlet.result.MockMvcResultHandlers.print
import
org.springframework.test.web.servlet.result.MockMvcResultMatchers.jsonPath
import
org.springframework.test.web.servlet.result.MockMvcResultMatchers.status

@RunWith(SpringRunner::class)
@SpringBootTest
@AutoConfigureMockMvc
class CustomerControllerTest {
.........
  @Test
  fun `we should GET a list of customers`() {
    given(customerService.getAllCustomers())
        .willReturn(listOf(Customer(1, "test"), Customer(2, "mocks")))

    mockMvc.perform(get("/customers"))
        .andExpect(status().isOk)
        .andExpect(jsonPath("\$").isArray)
        .andExpect(jsonPath("\$[0].id").value(1))
```

```
        .andExpect(jsonPath("\$[0].name").value("test"))
        .andExpect(jsonPath("\$[1].id").value(2))
        .andExpect(jsonPath("\$[1].name").value("mocks"))
        .andDo(print())

    then(customerService).should(times(1)).getAllCustomers()
    then(customerService).shouldHaveNoMoreInteractions()

    reset(customerService)
    }
}
```

Here, we ask `Mockito` to verify that our `getAllCustomers` service method has been invoked only one time and that after that, there are no more iterations of our customer service.

Finally, we can apply similar verification to our test to get a single customer `ID`:

```
@Test.
fun `we should GET a customer by id`() {
  given(customerService.getCustomer(1))
        .willReturn(Customer(1, "mock customer"))

  mockMvc.perform(get("/customer/1"))
        .andExpect(status().isOk)
        .andExpect(jsonPath("\$.id").value(1))
        .andExpect(jsonPath("\$.name").value("mock customer"))
        .andDo(print())

    then(customerService).should(times(1)).getCustomer(1)
    then(customerService).shouldHaveNoMoreInteractions()

    reset(customerService)
  }
```

What is interesting here is that when we verify that the `getCustomer` has been invoked, we can check which parameters have been used. This may not look as important with this example since it is a direct mapping from the request parameter into the service parameter, but it can be really important later on.

For example, if we receive some parameters in our request and then call different methods in the service with different values, and even if the service calls other methods with other parameters, we can just get the whole execution of our Mock verified. At the very end, what we are trying to test here is that our controller uses the service as it should, calling the right methods with the right parameters, and so on.

Fluent tests

When we do these tests, it is really important to do them in a way that everyone can understand, and have these tests that can be easily read is something really important for our applications. As we said earlier, we can even use our Ubiquitous language in our tests so that anyone in the team can understand them, including our domain experts. There is a Kotlin library named `Kluent` that allows us to do fluent tests, taking advantage of some of the benefits of the Kotlin programming language. More details are available at: `https://markusamshove.github.io/Kluent/`.

Adding Kluent

First, we will add `Kluent` as a dependency in our Maven POM. Go to the **Project** window and open `pom.xml` in the root folder of the project. `Kluent` is hosted in bintray JCenter, so we need to add that repository to our POM. Find the tag repositories and add another one at the end of the existing repositories:

```
....
<repositories>
....
  <repository>
    <id>jcenter</id>
    <url>http://jcenter.bintray.com</url>
    <snapshots>
      <enabled>true</enabled>
      <updatePolicy>never</updatePolicy>
      <checksumPolicy>warn</checksumPolicy>
    </snapshots>
    <releases>
      <enabled>true</enabled>
      <checksumPolicy>warn</checksumPolicy>
    </releases>
  </repository>
</repositories>
....
```

Now, go to the `dependencies` section and add `Kluent` as a `dependency` within the `dependencies` tags:

```
....
<dependencies>
....
  <dependency>
```

```
        <groupId>org.amshove.kluent</groupId>
        <artifactId>kluent</artifactId>
        <version>1.30</version>
        <scope>test</scope>
    </dependency>
</dependencies>
....
```

When we added this dependency, we set the scope to be tested since we do not require this dependency to be included in the application binary, just for our tests. Now, in IntelliJ IDEA, we need to reimport the POM. Go to the Maven **Project** window and click on the first button in the toolbar, that is, **Reimport All Maven Projects**.

Testing our services expressively

Now, that we have Kluent, let's modify our tests. First, we will work on CustomerServiceTest.

We will modify our test for getting one valid customer, which was written as shown:

```
@Test
fun `we should get a customer with a valid id`() {
  val customer = customerService.getCustomer(1)
  assertNotNull(customer)
  assertEquals(customer?.name, "Kotlin")
}
```

We can change our assertNotNull assertion to use shouldNoteNull, a high-level function that we can use in an object:

```
package com.microservices.chapter09

import junit.framework.Assert.assertEquals
import org.amshove.kluent.shouldNotBeNull
import org.junit.Test
import org.junit.runner.RunWith
import org.springframework.beans.factory.annotation.Autowired
import org.springframework.boot.test.context.SpringBootTest
import org.springframework.test.context.junit4.SpringRunner

@RunWith(SpringRunner::class)
@SpringBootTest
class CustomerServiceTest {
  @Autowired
  lateinit var customerService: CustomerService
```

```
@Test
fun `we should get a customer with a valid id`() {
  val customer = customerService.getCustomer(1)
  customer.shouldNotBeNull()
  assertEquals(customer?.name, "Kotlin")
}

. . . . . . . . . .
}
```

However, `Kluent` allows us to use better functions, including spaces, for readability:

```
package com.microservices.chapter09

import junit.framework.Assert.assertEquals
import org.amshove.kluent.`should not be null`
import org.junit.Test
import org.junit.runner.RunWith
import org.springframework.beans.factory.annotation.Autowired
import org.springframework.boot.test.context.SpringBootTest
import org.springframework.test.context.junit4.SpringRunner

@RunWith(SpringRunner::class)
@SpringBootTest
class CustomerServiceTest {
  @Autowired
  lateinit var customerService: CustomerService

  @Test
  fun `we should get a customer with a valid id`() {
    val customer = customerService.getCustomer(1)
    customer.`should not be null`()
    assertEquals(customer?.name, "Kotlin")
  }

. . . . . . . . .
}
```

Then, we can check our name parameter:

```
package com.microservices.chapter09

import junit.framework.Assert.assertEquals
import org.amshove.kluent.`should be`
import org.amshove.kluent.`should not be null`
import org.junit.Test
import org.junit.runner.RunWith
import org.springframework.beans.factory.annotation.Autowired
```

```
import org.springframework.boot.test.context.SpringBootTest
import org.springframework.test.context.junit4.SpringRunner

@RunWith(SpringRunner::class)
@SpringBootTest
class CustomerServiceTest {
  @Autowired
  lateinit var customerService: CustomerService

  @Test
  fun `we should get a customer with a valid id`() {
    val customer = customerService.getCustomer(1)
    customer.`should not be null`()
    customer?.name `should be` "Kotlin"
  }

  .......
}
```

This is a test that we can easily understand, and we use a Kotlin Influx function for more readability.

Let's now work on our second test:

```
@Test
fun `we should get all customers`() {
  val customers = customerService.getAllCustomers()
  assertEquals(customers.size, 3)
}
```

We can replace that with the following:

```
package com.microservices.chapter09

import org.amshove.kluent.`should be`
import org.amshove.kluent.`should equal to`
import org.amshove.kluent.`should not be null`
import org.junit.Test
import org.junit.runner.RunWith
import org.springframework.beans.factory.annotation.Autowired
import org.springframework.boot.test.context.SpringBootTest
import org.springframework.test.context.junit4.SpringRunner

@RunWith(SpringRunner::class)
@SpringBootTest
class CustomerServiceTest {
  @Autowired
  lateinit var customerService: CustomerService
```

```
@Test
fun `we should get a customer with a valid id`() {
  val customer = customerService.getCustomer(1)
  customer.`should not be null`()
  customer?.name `should be` "Kotlin"
}

@Test
fun `we should get all customers`() {
  val customers = customerService.getAllCustomers()
  customers.size `should equal to` 3
}
}
```

We can use other methods, even if we don't need them, to see other features from Kluent:

```
package com.microservices.chapter09

import org.amshove.kluent.*
import org.junit.Test
import org.junit.runner.RunWith
import org.springframework.beans.factory.annotation.Autowired
import org.springframework.boot.test.context.SpringBootTest
import org.springframework.test.context.junit4.SpringRunner

@RunWith(SpringRunner::class)
@SpringBootTest
class CustomerServiceTest {
  @Autowired
  lateinit var customerService: CustomerService

  @Test
  fun `we should get a customer with a valid id`() {
    val customer = customerService.getCustomer(1)
    customer.`should not be null`()
    customer?.name `should be` "Kotlin"
  }

  @Test
  fun `we should get all customers`() {
    val customers = customerService.getAllCustomers()
    customers.size `should equal to` 3
    customers.size `should be greater than` 0
    customers.size `should be less or equal to` 3
    customers.size `should be in range` 1..3
  }
}
```

Testing our controller expressively

We will now work on our `CustomerControllerTest` to make it more expressive.

First, let's look at our original test for the list of customers:

```
@Test
fun `we should GET a list of customers`() {
  given(customerService.getAllCustomers())
      .willReturn(listOf(Customer(1, "test"), Customer(2, "mocks")))

  mockMvc.perform(get("/customers"))
      .andExpect(status().isOk)
      .andExpect(jsonPath("\$").isArray)
      .andExpect(jsonPath("\$[0].id").value(1))
      .andExpect(jsonPath("\$[0].name").value("test"))
      .andExpect(jsonPath("\$[1].id").value(2))
      .andExpect(jsonPath("\$[1].name").value("mocks"))
      .andDo(print())

  then(customerService).should(times(1)).getAllCustomers()
  then(customerService).shouldHaveNoMoreInteractions()

  reset(customerService)
}
```

`Kluent` provides methods for `Mockito` as well:

```
package com.microservices.chapter09

import org.amshove.kluent.*
import org.junit.Test
import org.junit.runner.RunWith
import org.mockito.BDDMockito.given
import org.mockito.BDDMockito.then
import org.mockito.Mockito.reset
import org.mockito.Mockito.times
import org.springframework.beans.factory.annotation.Autowired
import org.springframework.boot.test.autoconfigure.web.servlet.AutoConfigureMockMvc
import org.springframework.boot.test.context.SpringBootTest
import org.springframework.boot.test.mock.mockito.MockBean
import org.springframework.test.context.junit4.SpringRunner
import org.springframework.test.web.servlet.MockMvc
import org.springframework.test.web.servlet.request.MockMvcRequestBuilders.get
```

```
import
org.springframework.test.web.servlet.result.MockMvcResultHandlers.print
import
org.springframework.test.web.servlet.result.MockMvcResultMatchers.jsonPath
import
org.springframework.test.web.servlet.result.MockMvcResultMatchers.status

@RunWith(SpringRunner::class)
@SpringBootTest
@AutoConfigureMockMvc
class CustomerControllerTest {
..........
  @Test
  fun `we should GET a list of customers`() {
    When calling customerService.getAllCustomers() `it returns`
        listOf(Customer(1, "test"), Customer(2, "mocks"))

    mockMvc.perform(get("/customers"))
        .andExpect(status().isOk)
        .andExpect(jsonPath("\$").isArray)
        .andExpect(jsonPath("\$[0].id").value(1))
        .andExpect(jsonPath("\$[0].name").value("test"))
        .andExpect(jsonPath("\$[1].id").value(2))
        .andExpect(jsonPath("\$[1].name").value("mocks"))
        .andDo(print())

    Verify on customerService that customerService.getAllCustomers()
     was called
    `Verify no further interactions` on customerService

    reset(customerService)
  }
.........
}
```

Now, our test fluently expresses what the mocks will do; let's modify our other test:

```
@Test
fun `we should GET a customer by id`() {
  When calling customerService.getCustomer(1) `it returns`
      Customer(1, "mock customer")

  mockMvc.perform(get("/customer/1"))
      .andExpect(status().isOk)
      .andExpect(jsonPath("\$.id").value(1))
      .andExpect(jsonPath("\$.name").value("mock customer"))
      .andDo(print())
```

```
    Verify on customerService that customerService.getCustomer(1) was
    called
    `Verify no further interactions` on customerService

    reset(customerService)
}
```

However, we can see that there is some code still not as expressive as the rest, so we can create our infix function and high-level functions for that purpose. We can add this at the top of the file, where our `CustomerControllerTest` is present:

```
package com.microservices.chapter09

import org.amshove.kluent.*
import org.junit.Test
import org.junit.runner.RunWith
import org.mockito.Mockito.reset
import org.springframework.beans.factory.annotation.Autowired
import
org.springframework.boot.test.autoconfigure.web.servlet.AutoConfigureMockMv
c
import org.springframework.boot.test.context.SpringBootTest
import org.springframework.boot.test.mock.mockito.MockBean
import org.springframework.test.context.junit4.SpringRunner
import org.springframework.test.web.servlet.MockMvc
import org.springframework.test.web.servlet.ResultActions
import org.springframework.test.web.servlet.ResultHandler
import org.springframework.test.web.servlet.ResultMatcher
import
org.springframework.test.web.servlet.request.MockMvcRequestBuilders.get
import org.springframework.test.web.servlet.result.JsonPathResultMatchers
import
org.springframework.test.web.servlet.result.MockMvcResultHandlers.print
import
org.springframework.test.web.servlet.result.MockMvcResultMatchers.jsonPath
import
org.springframework.test.web.servlet.result.MockMvcResultMatchers.status

class WithKeyword {
  infix fun `json path`(expression: String) = jsonPath("\$" + expression)
}

val With = WithKeyword()

class ThatKeyword {
  infix fun `status is http`(value : Int) = status().`is`(value)
}
```

```
val That = ThatKeyword()

infix fun JsonPathResultMatchers.`that the value is`(value: Any) =
this.value(value)
infix fun ResultActions.`and expect`(matcher: ResultMatcher) =
this.andExpect(matcher)
infix fun ResultActions.`and then do`(handler: ResultHandler) =
this.andDo(handler)
infix fun MockMvc.`do a get request to`(uri: String) =
this.perform(get(uri))

@RunWith(SpringRunner::class)
@SpringBootTest
@AutoConfigureMockMvc
class CustomerControllerTest {
}
```

Here, we have defined some functions to make our test more readable. Let's use them in the test for getting one customer:

```
@Test
fun `we should GET a customer by id`() {
  When calling customerService.getCustomer(1) `it returns`
      Customer(1, "mock customer")

  (mockMvc `do a get request to` "/customer/1"
      `and expect` (That `status is http` 200)
      `and expect` (With `json path` ".id" `that the value is` 1)
      `and expect` (With `json path` ".name" `that the value is`
      "mock customer")
      ) `and then do` print()

  Verify on customerService that customerService.getCustomer(1) was
  called
  `Verify no further interactions` on customerService

  reset(customerService)
}
```

Now, we can modify the other test to use the same functions:

```
@Test
fun `we should GET a list of customers`() {
  When calling customerService.getAllCustomers() `it returns`
      listOf(Customer(1, "test"), Customer(2, "mocks"))

  (mockMvc `do a get request to` "/customers"
      `and expect` (That `status is http` 200)
```

```
           `and expect` (With `json path` "[0].id" `that the value is` 1)
           `and expect` (With `json path` "[0].name" `that the value is`
       "test")
           `and expect` (With `json path` "[1].id" `that the value is` 2)
           `and expect` (With `json path` "[1].name" `that the value is`
       "mocks")
           ) `and then do` print()

    Verify on customerService that customerService.getAllCustomers()
     was called
     `Verify no further interactions` on customerService

    reset(customerService)
    }
```

Now, with these changes, we should have something more readable and understandable in our tests.

This is just an introductory chapter to testing microservices. There is an extended range of tools that we can use to improve our testing capabilities. We recommend the readers of this book to find out more about Maven Surefire from `http://maven.apache.org/surefire/maven-surefire-plugin/` and about Maven Failsafe from `http://maven.apache.org/surefire/maven-failsafe-plugin/`; both can be easily integrated with Kotlin microservices that are built with Maven.

Summary

We have learned how we can test our microservices, and now we have a powerful set of tools and resources to use, such as JUnit, `SpringBootTest`, or `MockMvc`. We understood how we can use mocks to concentrate our tests on the functionally that they need to check and not in the dependencies that they require. Finally, we learned how to write easily readable tests with fluent language using `Kluent`. However, we need to continue on our road to reach production with our microservices.

In the next chapter, we will discuss how we can monitor our microservices and the importance of this for a production-ready service. Then, we will learn how we can customize the information that we can expose to monitoring and operation systems and what Spring Framework has to help us in our monitoring.

10
Monitoring Microservices

When we move to production of our microservices, it does not matter how good our code was, how well we designed our architecture, or how many tests we have done, our microservices will fail. Since our microservices will eventually fail, we need to know when, and we need to provide the tools so that we can handle that situation.

In this chapter, we will discuss why monitoring is a critical part of any production-ready system, and how we can provide microservices that can be monitored and controlled. To experiment with this problem, we will create a microservice that can, and eventually will fail. Then, we will learn what SpringBoot Actuator can do, and how we can customize it for our needs. We will understand what microservices instrumentation is and how we can use it. We will create our own JMX Management Beans for providing tools to manage our production-ready microservice.

In this chapter, you will learn about the following:

- Monitoring
- SpringBoot Actuator
- Instrumentation
- JMX
- JConsole
- Management Beans

Understanding monitoring

This section will give an overview of what monitoring actually is and why it is important for delivering a quality production service. We will learn what alerting can do, and how we can use it effectively. Then, we will learn about how we can recover from failures. Finally, we will build a small microservice that will eventually fail, and we will use this to cover more topics in this chapter.

What is monitoring?

The best way to understand and react to failures in a production-ready system is to know what is actually happening. For this, we have to monitor our microservices. Microservices are a complicated set of software, from the code that we write to the libraries that we use, and they utilize, directly or indirectly, hardware resources such as memory or CPU.

They usually depend on other systems, even when we try to minimize the coupling on our architecture, from the servers or clouds that they run on, to databases or services they use. Monitoring provides understandable and measurable data that we can use to learn what is happening with our microservice.

It can be from simple data points, such as how much memory our microservice uses, to more complicated details, such as how many failures occur when we are performing a particular operation, for example, failures when adding new customers into our database. And sometimes, we can provide simple values on a particular time or event, or as a flow of information that we can feed into other analytics or an MI system to understand changes, trends, or even patterns in our monitoring data.

Nowadays, it is more common to integrate our monitoring feeds into systems that can explore that information using advanced analytics capabilities. In these systems, the data can be explored and analyzed, or even used for machine learning algorithms to predict what can happen in our system, and how we should handle it.

This is a trend that will increase and has already proven to be a successful practice in the industry. Think about creating these feeds, even if you don't need them right now, for having the information stored and available can be very valuable in the future.

But monitoring is not only about our own microservice; all the different elements in our architecture and system should provide meaningful monitoring that can be used to understand the current status of our application. Finally, monitoring should be visible, as we can have a rich set of data, but if it is not actually visible it may be worthless; having dashboards or control panels that can constantly provide this information is as important as having the information available.

Alerting

Having that information available allows us to alert on failures or problems in our applications so we can react to that situation. And those alerts can either be visualized in our control panels or dashboards, notified to individuals or groups, or even to the system that will handle them automatically. But to do that effectively, we need to define those alerts when we create our microservices.

Try to think about these elements when you're defining your alerts:

- **Have meaningful information**: It is not good enough to just provide a "System Failure" message, give a context to the problem, or hints about how to handle it, for example, "Failure connecting to the customer database".
- **Conditions which trigger it**: Is it just because we have one particular problem or failure? Is it because there are more than 10? Is it because it is critical? Is it because we group them with other problems?
- **Contextualize information**: What or where was that problem actually happening, such as the server that is producing the alert, or the one that it was connecting to.
- **Try to provide a summary and a breakdown of the detail**: We don't need a massive amount of information to just understand what alerts we have, but we need details if we want to explore them further.
- **Make them classifiable**: Think about how to categorize or group them.
- **Have a meaningful severity**: If all are defined as high, they may be wrong.
- **Traceable**: Always record the time and occurrence of the alert.
- **Authenticity**: Is this really an alert? If an alert requires nothing to be done, is this really something that you want to alert?

Alerts can also be used as another feed to the analytics system and can be used to create detailed information on volumes, trends, and even predict problems. As before, we should think about these feeds, eventually, the effort will pay off.

Recovering

Having a good monitoring system and alerts in place will help us to understand when something is wrong, such as failures in our systems, but then we need to understand how we can handle these situations. When something is failing, we need to provide mechanisms to recover from that failure. Some of these can be automatically handled and recovered, and some may need manual intervention.

We cannot be so naive as to think that everything can be handled automatically, for example, if a hard drive is broken we can automatically do many things, such as switching off the server or system that is used, move data to another server or volumes, or so on, but eventually someone needs to manually replace that hard drive or even the system that it was on.

And in those cases, we need to provide tools in our microservice to handle those recoveries. For example, if our database connections are failing, we need to be able to connect back when the problem is solved, and to handle some of those cases, we may need to provide tools that help to manage our microservice.

Some of these tools can be built into our microservice itself, and some others may need to be created separately, or we can even use already existing tools within our system to handle some of this recovery. It may be a good idea to have these tools integrated with our alert and monitoring control panel or dashboard, so as to have a centralized view of the operation of our production-ready microservices.

Building a failing microservice

Now that we have a clear understanding of monitoring, let's create a microservice that will eventually fail. To create our microservice, we will use Spring Initializr as we have done in previous chapters.

We can start by visiting: `https://start.spring.io/`.

Spring Initializr

We have chosen to create a **Maven Project** using **Kotlin** and **Spring Boot 2.0.0 M7** we choose the **Group** to be `com.microservices` and the **Artifact** to be `chapter10`. For **Dependencies,** we have set **Web** and **Actuator**. Now, we can click on **Generate Project** to download it as a ZIP file and after we unzip it, we can open it with IntelliJ IDEA to start working on our project. After a few minutes, our project will be ready and we can open the Maven window to see the different life cycle phases and Maven plugins and their goals.

> We cover how to use Spring Initializr, Maven, and IntelliJ IDEA in `Chapter 2`, *Getting Started with Spring Boot 2.0*. You can visit this chapter to understand topics not covered in this section.

Now, we will create a service interface in our project, in IntelliJ IDEA. In the **Project** window, right-click on our package `com.microservices.chapter10` and then choose **New | Kotlin File/Class**, in the pop-up window. We will set the name as `GreetingsService` and in the **Kind** drop-down, choose **Interface:**

```
package com.microservices.chapter10

interface GreetingsService {
  fun getGreeting(): String
}
```

This will be the interface of a service that is in charge of retrieving customers. Now, we will implement it to create a new class, repeating the previous step and naming it GreetingsServiceImpl:

```
package com.microservices.chapter10

import org.springframework.stereotype.Service
import java.util.*

@Service
class GreetingsServiceImpl : GreetingsService {
  companion object {
    private val greetingsMessages = arrayOf("Hello", "Olá", "Namaste",
"Hola")
  }

  fun random(max: Int): Int = Random().nextInt(max) + 1

  override fun getGreeting(): String = greetingsMessages[random(4)]
}
```

This is a simple implementation of the service that will return a different random message every time it is invoked, but it has a failure. The function that we have created named random will return a number from 1 to 4, but arrays start on the element 0, so it should return from 0 to 3; this will cause our service to fail randomly with a java.lang.ArrayIndexOutOfBoundsException.

Can this not be caught by a test? Probably, but depending on the tests that we created, we may get a surprise in production, in any case, we created it this way for demonstration purposes. Finally, we will create a RestController that uses our GreetingsService to return the messages in a GET request. Repeat the following steps to create a new class named GreetingsController class:

```
package com.microservices.chapter10

import org.springframework.beans.factory.annotation.Autowired
import org.springframework.web.bind.annotation.GetMapping
import org.springframework.web.bind.annotation.RestController

@RestController
class GreetingController {
  @Autowired
  lateinit var greetingService: GreetingsService

  @GetMapping("/hello")
  fun message() = greetingService.getGreeting()
```

```
}
```

This controller will just return a random message invoked through the URL,
`http://localhost:8080/hello`.

 Many of the things that we have used in this example have been covered in `Chapter 2`, *Getting Started with Spring Boot 2.0*, and `Chapter 3`, *Creating RESTful Services*. You may need to re-visit them to understand it further.

Now, we can run our microservice, either using the IntelliJ IDEA Maven **Project** window with the `spring-boot:run` target, or by executing the command line:

```
mvnw spring-boot:run
```

Either way, when we visit the URL `http://localhost:8080/hello`, we will get a random message or an error.

SpringBoot Actuator

SpringBoot includes a number of additional features to help you monitor and manage your application when it's pushed to production, with a component name SpringBoot Actuator that enables production-ready features for Spring Boot applications. You can find more information about it in the official documentation: `https://docs.spring.io/spring-boot/docs/2.0.0.M7/reference/htmlsingle/#production-ready`.

The Actuator includes a number of additional features to help you monitor and manage your application when it's pushed to production. You can choose to manage and monitor your application using HTTP endpoints and with JMX. Additionally, auditing, health, and metrics gathering can be automatically applied to your application. In this section, we will learn how to use and configure it in our microservices monitoring.

Enabling SpringBoot Actuator

We already included SpringBoot Actuator as a dependency when we were using Spring Initializr, and if we open our `pom.xml`, we should see it added as a `dependency`:

```
.....
<dependencies>
 <dependency>
   <groupId>org.springframework.boot</groupId>
```

```
    <artifactId>spring-boot-starter-actuator</artifactId>
  </dependency>
  . . . . .
  </dependencies>
```

Now, we will open our `resources` folder in IntelliJ IDEA using the **Project** window expanding `main | src | resources`. Now we will click on the file named `application.properties` and we will press *Shift + F6* to rename it to `application.yml`, and then we will edit it:

```
management:
  endpoints:
    web:
      expose: ["health", "metrics", "trace"]
```

We have enabled some endpoints for Actuator so that we can use it to explore the health status.

After running our microservice again, we can explore its status in the URL `http://localhost:8080/actuator/health`; this will provide a response about the status of the microservice:

```
{
  "status": "UP",
  "details": {
    "diskSpace": {
      "status": "UP",
      "details": {
        "total": 126967869440,
        "free": 9880883200,
        "threshold": 10485760
      }
    }
  }
}
```

This is the health endpoint that provides status information. We can use this to monitor our microservice, but there are many more endpoints that we can explore.

Understanding Actuator's endpoints

We have just used the status endpoint to retrieve information, but there are others that we can use for monitoring microservices:

- `health`: Shows application health information, in detail
- `metrics`: Shows "metrics" information for the current application
- `trace`: Displays trace information (by default, the last 100 HTTP requests)

There are more endpoints in SpringBoot Actuator and you can get the full list in the official documentation available on the Spring Boot project website: `https://docs.spring.io/spring-boot/`.

Health endpoint

The health endpoint will provide detailed status information of our microservice; it is available in the URL `http://localhost:8080/actuator/health`:

```
{
  "status": "UP",
  "details": {
    "diskSpace": {
      "status": "UP",
      "details": {
        "total": 126967869440,
        "free": 10007228416,
        "threshold": 10485760
      }
    }
  }
}
```

SpringBoot gets information through health indicators, a specialized object that will provide information about one specific area of concern. By default, these are the ones autoconfigured by SpringBoot:

- `CassandraHealthIndicator`: Checks that a Cassandra database is UP
- `DiskSpaceHealthIndicator`: Checks for low disk space
- `DataSourceHealthIndicator`: Checks that a connection to DataSource can be obtained
- `ElasticsearchHealthIndicator`: Checks that an Elasticsearch cluster is UP

- `JmsHealthIndicator`: Checks that a JMS broker is UP
- `MailHealthIndicator`: Checks that a mail server is UP
- `MongoHealthIndicator`: Checks that a Mongo database is UP
- `Neo4jHealthIndicator`: Checks that a Neo4j server is UP
- `RabbitHealthIndicator`: Checks that a Rabbit server is UP
- `RedisHealthIndicator`: Checks that a Redis server is UP
- `SolrHealthIndicator`: Checks that a Solr server is UP

If any of these default indicators are not UP, our health endpoint will reflect it, so will the status, and for each of them, it will show the detailed information available. In our example, the only indicator available is the `DiskSpaceHealthIndicator`, since we did not use any other system in our microservice.

The disk space health indicator will check periodically if we have enough free space in our disk/file system to return its health information. Additionally, it provides the details of the current free space, the total size, and the threshold that it will use to fail.

Metrics endpoint

The metrics endpoint available in the URL `http://localhost:8080/actuator/metrics/` provides statistics on our microservice. If we invoke this URL, we can see the following names; each of them will be a metric that we can use to get more information on:

```
{
  "names": [
    "jvm.buffer.memory.used",
    "jvm.memory.used",
    "jvm.buffer.count",
    "logback.events",
    "process.uptime",
    "jvm.memory.committed",
    "jvm.buffer.total.capacity",
    "jvm.memory.max",
    "system.cpu.count",
    "process.start.time"
  ]
}
```

If we like to get details on the JVM memory used, we can use the URL
`http://localhost:8080/actuator/metrics/jvm.memory.used`:

```
{
    "name": "jvm.memory.used",
    "measurements": [
      {
        "statistic": "Value",
        "value": 195595240
      }
    ],
    "availableTags": [
      {
        "tag": "area",
        "values": [
          "heap",
          "heap",
          "heap",
          "nonheap",
          "nonheap",
          "nonheap"
        ]
      },
      {
        "tag": "id",
        "values": [
          "PS Old Gen",
          "PS Survivor Space",
          "PS Eden Space",
          "Code Cache",
          "Compressed Class Space",
          "Metaspace"
        ]
      }
    ]
}
```

Trace endpoint

The trace endpoint available in the URL `http://localhost:8080/actuator/trace`
provides detailed information of the latest 100 HTTP responses that our microservice has
returned.

For example, this can be one response within our trace endpoint:

```json
{
  "timestamp": 1512029264243,
  "info": {
    "method": "GET",
    "path": "/hello",
    "headers": {
      "request": {
        "host": "localhost:8080",
        "connection": "keep-alive",
        "cache-control": "max-age=0",
        "user-agent": "Mozilla/5.0 (Windows NT 10.0; Win64; x64)
        AppleWebKit/537.36 (KHTML, like Gecko) Chrome/62.0.3202.94
        Safari/537.36",
        "upgrade-insecure-requests": "1",
        "accept":
        "text/html,application/xhtml+xml,application/xml;q=0.9,
        image/webp,image/apng,*/*;q=0.8",
        "accept-encoding": "gzip, deflate, br",
        "accept-language": "en-GB,en;q=0.9,es;q=0.8"
      },
      "response": {
        "Content-Type": "text/html;charset=UTF-8",
        "Content-Length": "7",
        "Date": "Thu, 30 Nov 2017 08:07:43 GMT",
        "status": "200"
      }
    },
    "timeTaken": "1"
  }
}
```

We can see very detailed information, including the various headers in the request and response.

Defining health indicators

Probably the most valuable endpoint is health, but the default indicators that it use may not be enough for our microservice. It's our responsibility to define custom indicators that will return the status of our microservices with accuracy and to consider what we really need to check so that we know the health of our microservice. We will create a health indicator that will check if our GreetingsService actually works.

Let's create a new class named `GreetingsServiceHealthIndicator`:

```
package com.microservices.chapter10

import org.springframework.beans.factory.annotation.Autowired
import org.springframework.boot.actuate.health.AbstractHealthIndicator
import org.springframework.boot.actuate.health.Health
import org.springframework.stereotype.Component

@Component
class GreetingsServiceHealthIndicator : AbstractHealthIndicator() {

  @Autowired
  lateinit var greetingsService : GreetingsService
  override fun doHealthCheck(builder: Health.Builder) {
    val lastMessage = try {
      val message = greetingsService.getGreeting()
      builder.up()
      message
    }catch (exception : Exception){
      builder.down()
      "ERROR:$exception"
    }
    builder.withDetail("lastMessage", lastMessage)
  }
}
```

This health indicator, that must extend `AbstractHealthIndicator`, overrides the method `doHealthCheck`. We will use the passed `builder` object to construct our health status so as to get a message from the `greetingsService` and set our build to up or down status.

This indicator will be picked up by the SpringBoot Actuator and will be used in our health endpoint.

If we now query the health endpoint several times through its URL `http://localhost:8080/actuator/health`, we will get this message if the service is working:

```
{
  "status": "UP",
  "details": {
    "greetingsService": {
      "status": "UP",
      "details": {
        "lastMessage": "Namaste"
      }
    },
```

```
      "diskSpace": {
        "status": "UP",
        "details": {
          "total": 126967869440,
          "free": 9991962624,
          "threshold": 10485760
        }
      }
    }
  }
}
```

And we will get this other message when our service is not working:

```
{
  "status": "DOWN",
  "details": {
    "greetingsService": {
      "status": "DOWN",
      "details": {
        "lastMessage": "ERROR:java.lang.ArrayIndexOutOfBoundsException: 4"
      }
    },
    "diskSpace": {
      "status": "UP",
      "details": {
        "total": 126967869440,
        "free": 9998520320,
        "threshold": 10485760
      }
    }
  }
}
```

This is an oversimplified example, probably it would be a good idea if we used a circuit breaker such as hystrix to close future calls of the service until it's really back, but for the purpose of this chapter, it should be good enough.

 Defining the right indicators and how to implement them may be a challenging task, but one that will pay off in the long run when we have microservices that can tell us if they are actually working or not.

Protecting Actuator endpoints

One of the things that we need to consider is when we enable our Actuator endpoints. They are open for use in those particular URLs by anyone that can access them, and that may not be ideal as they can provide sensitive information that we may not want to be used.

First, we can change their default URL and port by editing our `application.yml`:

```
management:
  endpoints:
    web:
      base-path: "/management"
      expose: ["health", "metrics", "trace"]
  server:
    port: 8089
```

Now, our URLs have changed to be like `http://localhost:8089/management/health`, and with this, we have to hide our Actuator endpoints in a production setup. We can even block the access to those URLs and ports outside our internal trusted zones.

To secure our endpoint further, we can use Spring Security and add roles and users to access the Actuator endpoints, but this is more complex than the intended scope of this chapter. Please review the official documentation of SpringBoot and Spring Security to understand this further: `https://spring.io/projects`.

Java Managing Extensions

Since our Kotlin microservices run in the JVM, we can use the **Java Managing Extensions** (**JMX**) to provide our monitoring information to external systems. But enabling JMX will also allow us to define custom tools that we can use to either retrieve custom information of our microservice or even act on them, for example, allow us to recover from a failure.

Understanding JMX

Since Java 6 JMX is shipped with the Java SDK, it allows Java programs to provide monitoring information to other systems and to enable the administration of our Java applications.

This is a very powerful feature that most third-party monitoring tools can use to retrieve information on our microservices.

JMX also allows us to expose management beans that invoke certain functionalities of our application externally; this could be used to provide operations that support our applications such as restarting certain services or changing internal behaviors.

Basically, JMX will act as an interface to systems that need to access our application, providing a standard mechanism that is widely used in the industry for supporting Java applications.

Using JMX

Java JDK ships with a JMX console that we can use by typing in our command line:

```
jconsole
```

This program is actually available under our JDK directory in the bin folder, and launching it will show a window like this:

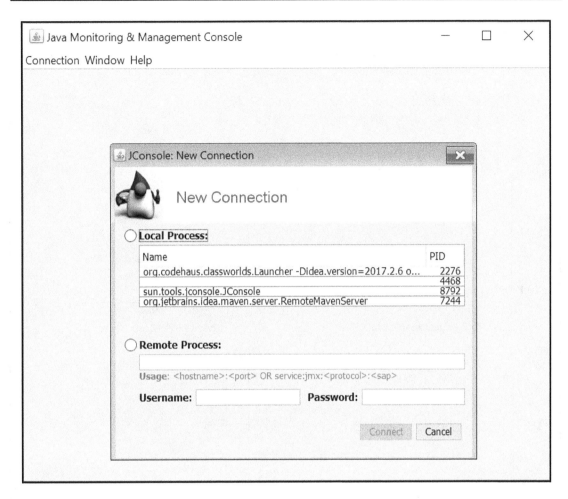

Java JMX console

When this window is shown, it will ask us to create a new connection. We can just use **Local Process** to select our Java application. If we are running our microservice from IntelliJ IDEA, we should choose the process `org.codehaus.classworlds.Launcher`. If we are running from the command line, we should choose `org.apache.maven.wrapper.MavenWrapperMain` instead.

Either way, when we choose it, we should see the **Overview** window:

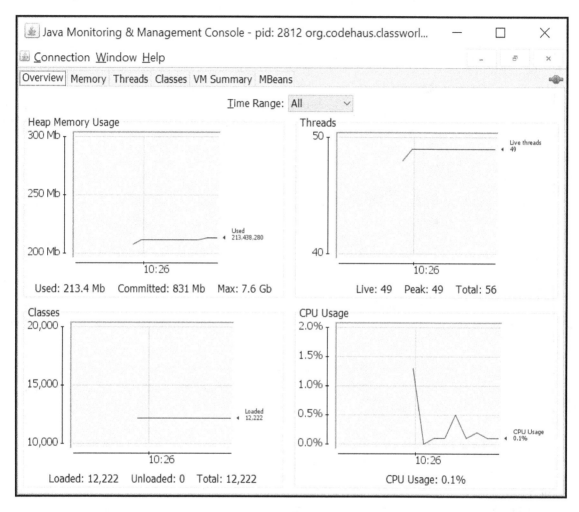

JConsole Overview window

This window provides a small dashboard of some of the microservice statistics and metrics and we can use it for a while, but probably we need to create our own dashboards. We have additional tabs to get more detailed information, but we will focus on the last tab, **MBeans**, the management beans. The management beans provide services that we can use to either retrieve data or even invoke operations. SpringBoot Actuator has already defined some of them:

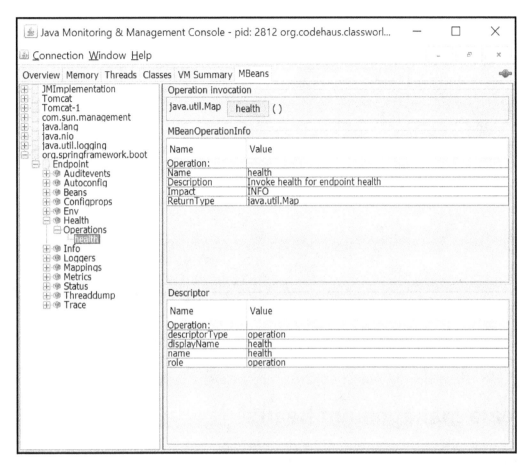

SpringBoot Actuator Management Beans

 In the same way that we enable the Actuator endpoints, we can enable or disable which MBeans are available in JMX. Refer to the SpringBoot Actuator Documentation for further details.

We can invoke the health operation by just clicking on the right side of the window on the **health** button, and this will give us the details in a new window:

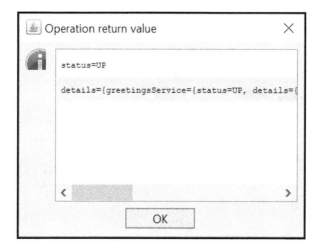

Health operation result

With this, we can execute the different SpringBoot Actuators MBeans to operate our microservice.

Create management beans

If we explore the existing MBeans in our microservice, there are plenty of them, but it may be possible to create our own to provide either information or tools for managing our microservice.

We will create a new class and name it GreetingsMBean:

```
package com.microservices.chapter10

import org.springframework.beans.factory.annotation.Autowired
import org.springframework.jmx.export.annotation.ManagedOperation
import org.springframework.jmx.export.annotation.ManagedOperationParameter
import org.springframework.jmx.export.annotation.ManagedOperationParameters
import org.springframework.jmx.export.annotation.ManagedResource
import org.springframework.stereotype.Component

@Component
@ManagedResource(objectName =
"com.microservices:type=greetings,name=GetHello",
```

```
      description = "Get greetings")
class GreetingsMBean {
  @Autowired
  lateinit var greetingsService: GreetingsService

  @ManagedOperation(description = "Returns a greeting message")
  @ManagedOperationParameters(ManagedOperationParameter(description =
"provide a name",
      name = "name"))
  fun hello(name: String) = try {
    greetingsService.getGreeting() + " $name!"
  } catch (exception: Exception) {
    "oh $name, we get an error: $exception"
  }
}
```

Now, we can invoke it by using our JMX console:

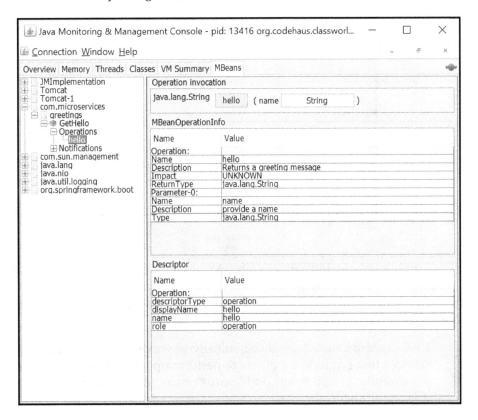

MBean interface

First, we set our parameter **name**, for example, as `Spring`, typing in the box where we see `String` near the **name** parameter, and now we can click on the **hello** button and if the service works, we will get the following:

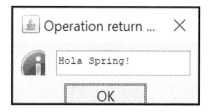

Hello returns a message

But if the service fails, instead we should get:

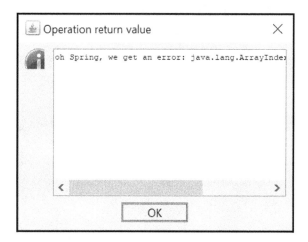

Hello returns an error

This is a very simple example, but MBeans allows us to do more advanced operations. For example, we can create an operation that will help us recover from a failure, things like reconnecting to a database, or restarting our circuit breaker, things that will allow us to recover from failures.

 JMX can also be used programmatically so we can write applications or services that can monitor others to perform operations on them, but most importantly, to add to our dashboards or control centers to allow us to operate our microservices.

Summary

Now, we understand in detail why we should monitor our microservices to make them production ready. We have done a deep dive into alerts to understand how we can define them correctly. Then, we have learned how we can use SpringBoot Actuator and how we can customize it. Finally, we learned what JMX actually is and how we can create management beans to allow us to operate our microservices.

Now that we have our microservice ready to reach production, we will need to learn how we can deploy it. In the next chapter, we will learn how we can deploy our microservices in a production system. We will use OpenShift online to create a cloud application and learn how we can set up a Git repository to automatically deploy our microservices, whenever they change.

11
Deploying Microservices

To have our microservices ready in our production environments, we need to deploy them, and this task may look trivial, but it can become an impediment to delivering the pace and speed required by our application. In this chapter, we will be using OpenShift Online to understand how we can easily and effectively deploy microservices, and how this can be done in such a way that allows us to deliver the best quality at the best speed. To help us in this task, we will be using Git, the industry standard control version system, to simplify our deployments.

In this chapter, you will learn about:

- OpenShift Online
- Git
- GitHub
- Deployments
- Webhooks

Setting things up

Before we can deploy our application, we need to have the right access and tools ready for the task. In this section, we will create a GitHub account, that we can use as a repository for our microservices. For publishing our microservice code into GitHub, we will install and configure Git on our system. Then, we will create an OpenShift account that we will use to create a cloud application and link our OpenShift account to our GitHub account. Finally, we will install and configure the OpenShift command line tools to use in our examples.

Creating a GitHub account

In this chapter, we will use GitHub as the platform for storing our Git repositories. This will be required to deploy our microservices. If you already have a GitHub account you can skip this step.

First, visit the GitHub main site `http://github.com`; in the center of the screen, you will find a form to create an account. Enter your details and click on the **Sign up for GitHub** button:

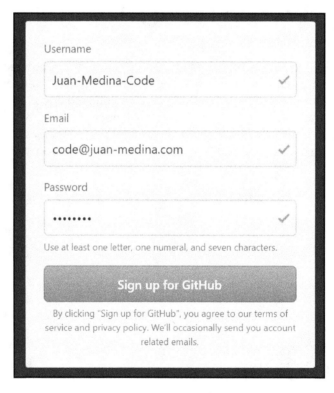

Signing up for a GitHub Account

In the next step, we will be asked to **Choose a personal plan**, we will go with the **Unlimited public repositories for free** option and click on the **Continue** button:

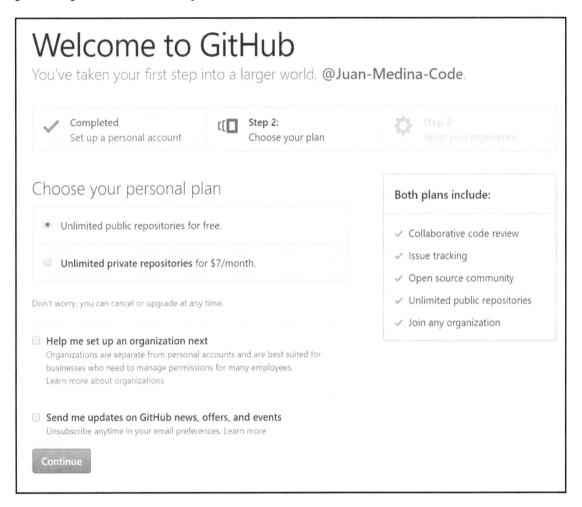

Choosing a personal plan

Finally, they will ask us to tailor our experience, but we can skip this by clicking on **skip this step**:

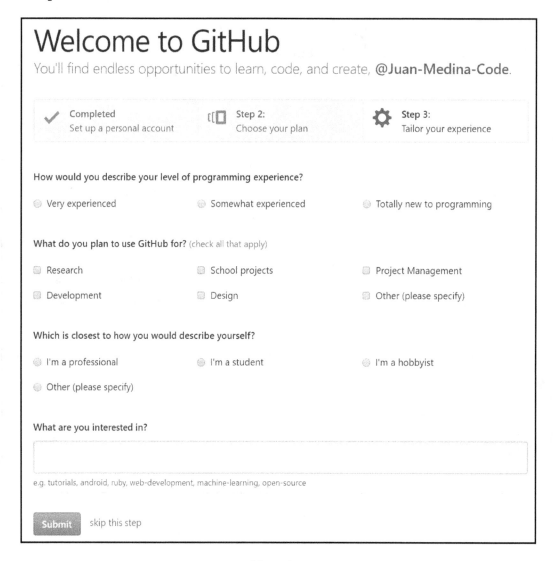

Tailor experience

Now, we should receive an email to verify our email account. Just click on the link provided in the email and everything should be ready to work.

Installing Git

We will get Git installed on our system in order to execute the examples later on, as we will use it to publish our code in GitHub. If you have a Windows system, we recommend you download Git for Windows from their website `https://git-scm.com/download/win` and complete the default installation. Mac already ships with a Git client provided by Apple, however, we recommend you download and use the Git Mac client from their website `https://git-scm.com/download/mac` and complete the default installation.

Now that we have Git installed, we can verify the installation by opening a command line and executing:

```
git --version
```

In Windows, you may need to execute the program Git Bash, available on the **Programs Menu**, to perform Git commands, depending on how you have installed Git for Windows. This should display the version of Git that we just installed, but now we need to configure it. We will need to set up what is going to be our name and email when we use Git by using the commands for changing the username and email, as you have set them up in GitHub:

```
git config --global user.name "Juan Medina Code"
git config --global user.email "code@juan-medina.com"
```

Create an OpenShift account

Now, we will proceed to create an OpenShift Online account by going to their web page, `https://manage.openshift.com/`. Click on the **Sign up** link on the bottom-left side of the screen:

OpenShift Online main page

In the next screen, in the **LOG IN USING SOCIAL ACCOUNT** section, we will click on the **GITHUB** button:

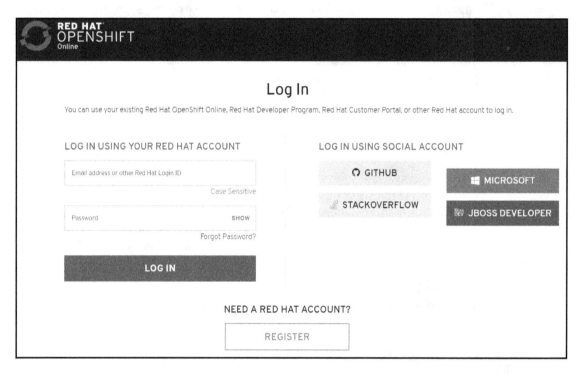

Log In screen

Then a new screen will appear, asking us to **Authorize Red Hat Developers** to get our email address. We will click on the **Authorize redhat-developer** button:

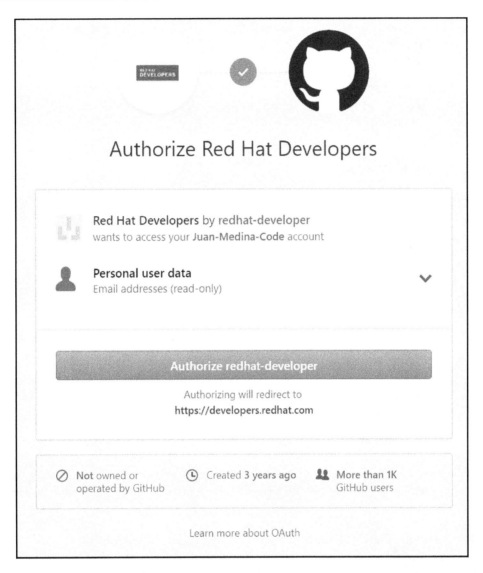

Authorize redhat-developer

Now, we will be asked to verify our account details with a form that we should fill in with the same email that we used in our GitHub account, and set a password for login into OpenShift Online:

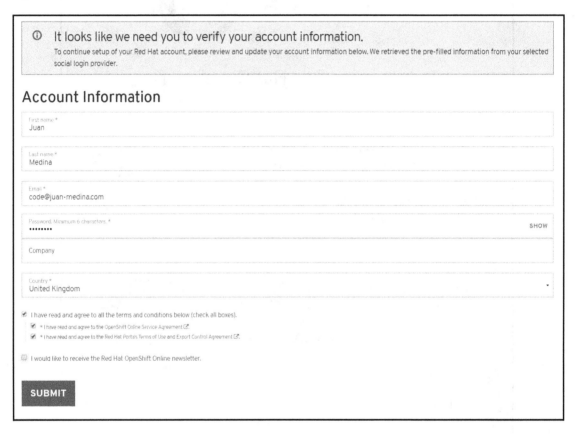

Account Information

After clicking on the **SUBMIT** button, we should get an email with a link to verify our email address, and when we click on that link, we should see a screen to verify the plan for our application. We may choose to use the free Starter plan, which may have some restrictions but will be okay for our examples, by clicking on the **FREE** button:

Plans	Cluster Regions	Confi
1	2	3

Select a Plan

Starter

For individual learning and experimenting.

1 Project

1GiB Memory Included

1GiB Terminating Memory Included ❶

1GiB Storage Included

Resource Hibernation ❶

FREE

Pro

For professional projects and hosting.

10 Projects

2GiB Memory Included
Up to 48GiB Memory Available

2GiB Terminating Memory Included ❶
Up to 20GiB Terminating Memory Available

Up to 100GiB Storage

Always On, Unlimited Usage

Invite Collaborators to Projects

Supports Custom Domains

Scheduled Jobs

Starting at $50.00/Month

Select a Plan screen

Then, a new page will load, asking us to choose the region for our applications. We may choose any of them by clicking on the links available on the screen:

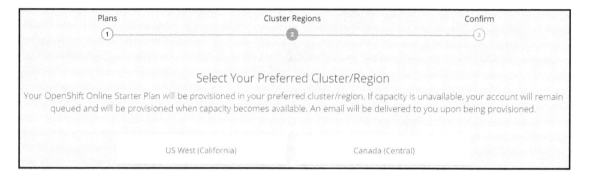

Choosing region

Finally, the confirmation screen will show up and we can click on the **Confirm Subscription** button to complete the account creation. After a few minutes, we should receive a new email welcoming us to OpenShift Online and providing a link to the console. In my example, I received the link to `https://console.starter-ca-central-1.openshift.com`. We can open this URL to verify that we can log in to our account.

Downloading the OpenShift client

If we log into our OpenShift account on the top-right corner of the screen, we can see a Help icon. Click on that icon; a pop-up menu should display with an option labeled as **Command Line Tools**:

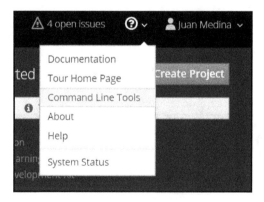

Clicking on that allows us to download the OpenShift Command Line client. We can choose from different operating systems, and after downloading it, unzip it and then add it to our system path.

Now, we should be able to use the `oc login` command in our command line:

```
oc login https://api.starter-ca-central-1.openshift.com
Authentication required for
https://api.starter-ca-central-1.openshift.com:443 (openshift)
Username: code@juan-medina.com
Password:
Login successful.

You don't have any projects. You can try to create a new project, by
running

    oc new-project <projectname>

Welcome! See 'oc help' to get started.
```

Building our application

In order to have a microservice ready to be deployed, first we need to build it, and for that, we will use some of the knowledge that we have gained during the course of the chapters in this book. We will use Spring Boot to create a microservice that will have some tests using SpringBootTest and MockMVC, then, we will upload our microservice to GitHub so that it is available for the next sections on this chapter.

Creating an example microservice

Now that we have our tools ready, we should create our microservice, and we will use Spring Initializr as we have done in previous chapters.

We can start by visiting the URL: `https://start.spring.io/`:

Spring Initializr

We have chosen to create a **Maven Project** using **Kotin** and **Spring Boot 2.0.0 M7**. We choose the **Group** to be `com.microservices` and the **Artifact** to be `chapter11`. For **Dependencies**, we have set **Web**. Now, we can click on **Generate Project** to download it as a ZIP file, and after we unzip it, we can open it with IntelliJ IDEA to start working on our project. After a few minutes, our project will be ready and we can open the Maven window to see the different life cycle phases and Maven plugins and their goals.

> We cover how to use Spring Initializr, Maven, and IntelliJ IDEA in `Chapter 2`, *Getting Started with Spring Boot 2.0.* You can visit this chapter to understand topics not covered in this section.

Now, we will create a data `class` in our project, in IntelliJ IDEA, in the **Project** window, right-click on our package `com.microservices.chapter11` in the `src/main/kotlin` folder, and then choose **New | Kotlin File/Class.** In the pop-up window, we will set the name as `Customer` and in the **Kind** drop-down, choose **Class**:

```
package com.microservices.chapter11

class Customer(val id: Int, val name: String)
```

This will be the class that will hold customer data in our microservice. Now, create a new class repeating the previous steps and name it `CustomerController`:

```kotlin
package com.microservices.chapter11

import org.springframework.web.bind.annotation.GetMapping
import org.springframework.web.bind.annotation.PathVariable
import org.springframework.web.bind.annotation.RestController
import java.util.concurrent.ConcurrentHashMap

@RestController
class CustomerController {
  companion object {
    val initialCustomers = arrayOf(Customer(1, "Kotlin"),
        Customer(2, "Spring"),
        Customer(3, "Microservice"))
    val customers = ConcurrentHashMap<Int, Customer>
    (initialCustomers.associateBy(Customer::id))
  }

  @GetMapping("/customers")
  fun getCustomers() = customers.values.toList()

  @GetMapping("/customer/{id}")
  fun getCustomer(@PathVariable id: Int) = customers[id]
}
```

This controller will be just an individual customer when we use the URL `/customer/{id}` or will return all when we use the URL `/customers`.

 Many of the things that we have used in this example have been covered in our Chapter 2, *Getting Started with Spring Boot 2.0*, and Chapter 3, *Creating RESTful Services*. You may need to re-visit them to understand it further.

Now, we can run our microservice, either using the IntelliJ IDEA Maven **Project** window with the `spring-boot:run` target, or by executing in the command line:

mvnw spring-boot:run

Either way, when we visit the URL `http://localhost:8080/customers`, we will get our list of customers:

```
[
  {
    "id": 1,
    "name": "Kotlin"
  },
  {
    "id": 2,
    "name": "Spring"
  },
  {
    "id": 3,
    "name": "Microservice"
  }
]
```

If we use the URL for a customer, for example, `http://localhost:8080/customer/1`, we will get that customer instead:

```
{
  "id": 1,
  "name": "Kotlin"
}
```

Now, the main functionality of our microservice is ready.

Adding tests

Our microservice is ready but we have no test to validate it. We should have it verified so that our software works before deploying it into production, so let's do some tests.

Now, we will create a `SpringBootTest` in our project, in IntelliJ IDEA. In the **Project** window, right-click on our package `com.microservices.chapter11` in the `src/test/kotlin` folder and then choose **New** | **Kotlin File/Class**. In the pop-up window, we will set the name as `CustomerControllerTest` and in the **Kind** drop-down, choose **Class**:

```
package com.microservices.chapter11

import org.junit.Test
import org.junit.runner.RunWith
import org.springframework.beans.factory.annotation.Autowired
import
```

```
org.springframework.boot.test.autoconfigure.web.servlet.AutoConfigureMockMv
c
import org.springframework.boot.test.context.SpringBootTest
import org.springframework.test.context.junit4.SpringRunner
import org.springframework.test.web.servlet.MockMvc
import
org.springframework.test.web.servlet.request.MockMvcRequestBuilders.get
import
org.springframework.test.web.servlet.result.MockMvcResultHandlers.print
import
org.springframework.test.web.servlet.result.MockMvcResultMatchers.jsonPath
import
org.springframework.test.web.servlet.result.MockMvcResultMatchers.status

@RunWith(SpringRunner::class)
@SpringBootTest
@AutoConfigureMockMvc
class CustomerControllerTest {
  @Autowired
  lateinit var mockMvc: MockMvc

  @Test
  fun `we should get the customer list`() {
    mockMvc.perform(get("/customers"))
        .andExpect(status().isOk)
        .andExpect(jsonPath("\$[0].id").value(1))
        .andExpect(jsonPath("\$[0].name").value("Kotlin"))
        .andExpect(jsonPath("\$[1].id").value(2))
        .andExpect(jsonPath("\$[1].name").value("Spring"))
        .andExpect(jsonPath("\$[2].id").value(3))
        .andExpect(jsonPath("\$[2].name").value("Microservice"))
        .andDo(print())
  }

  @Test
  fun `we should get a customer by id`() {
    mockMvc.perform(get("/customer/1"))
        .andExpect(status().isOk)
        .andExpect(jsonPath("\$.id").value(1))
        .andExpect(jsonPath("\$.name").value("Kotlin"))
        .andDo(print())
  }
}
```

We have just created a couple of tests for our two URLs, using Spring `MockMvc`.

 Most of the elements on those tests, we'll discuss in `Chapter 9`, *Testing Spring Microservices*. You may need to re-visit that chapter to fully understand it.

Now we can run our test, either using IntelliJ IDEA Maven **Project** window with the **verify** lifecycle, or in the command line by executing:

```
mvnw verify
```

Either way, we should get a `BUILD SUCCESS` message and the log lines:

```
[INFO] Results:
[INFO]
[INFO] Tests run: 3, Failures: 0, Errors: 0, Skipped: 0
[INFO]
[INFO] -------------------------------------------------------------
----
[INFO] BUILD SUCCESS
[INFO] -------------------------------------------------------------
----
[INFO] Total time: 16.984 s
[INFO] Finished at: 2017-12-09T13:00:36+00:00
[INFO] Final Memory: 40M/813M
[INFO] -------------------------------------------------------------
----
```

You may wonder why we have run three tests, and this is because Spring Initializr already created one default test when creating our initial project.

Uploading to GitHub

Now that our microservice is ready, we can upload it to GitHub, but first, we need to create a project on GitHub itself. Log in to your account at `https://github.com/login`, and a page will appear.

Click on the **Start a Project** button to create our first project. This window will appear:

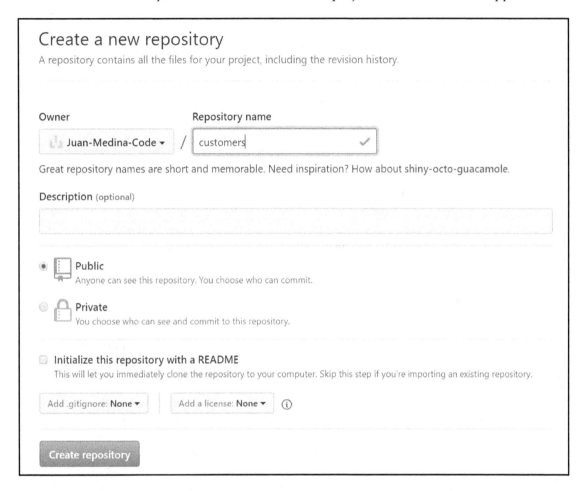

We need to choose a **Repository name** and just click on the **Create repository** button.

In the next window, we will see the Git URL for our newly created repository:

Save that URL because we will need it later on in the chapter. Now, we will need to use some Git commands so open our command line; remember that if you are using Windows, you may need to open the Git Bash program instead of the normal command line. Navigate to our `microservice` folder using the command line, the same one that our `pom.xml` is added to. Let's first initialize our Git repository with the command:

```
git init
```

Now, we will connect our folder to the GitLab project. We need the Git URL that we used before to execute this command on the command line:

```
git remote add origin https://github.com/Juan-Medina-Code/customers.git
```

Now, we can add all the files for our microservice to our local Git repository, and push it to the server.

 Git works with the concept of having a local repository in your computer and synchronizes with a remote repository in a server. You can work with your files, adding them, updating, or committing changes and then pushing to the server when you want the changes to be published, or pulling down from the server to synchronize changes that you may not yet have in your local repository.

First, we will add our files using the command:

```
git add .
```

Then we can commit, staging all the changes in our local Git repository, with a message using the command:

```
git commit -m "first commit to github"
```

Finally, pushing them into GitHub with the command:

```
git push origin master
```

This command will ask us to input our username, that is, our email and our password, and after we input these, we can see that our code is uploaded:

```
Username for 'https://github.com': code@juan-medina.com
Password for 'https://code@juan-medina.com@github.com':
Counting objects: 28, done.
Delta compression using up to 12 threads.
Compressing objects: 100% (19/19), done.
Writing objects: 100% (28/28), 47.84 KiB | 0 bytes/s, done.
Total 28 (delta 0), reused 0 (delta 0)
To https://github.com/Juan-Medina-Code/customers.git
 * [new branch] master -> master
```

With this push, our project should be available on the GitHub project site. In this example, it will be `https://github.com/Juan-Medina-Code/customers`:

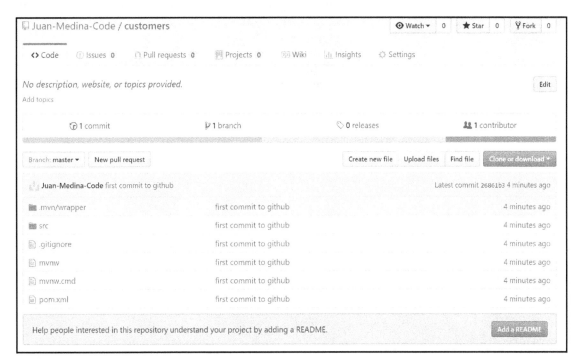

Project on GitHub

Now, we have our microservice code uploaded and ready for the next sections of the chapter.

Publishing to OpenShift

When we have the code for our microservice ready, and our tests are completed, we are ready to start doing our deployment into production. In this section, we will learn how easily we can deploy our microservice in OpenShift Online and how we can manage it. Then, we will update our microservice code and trigger new deployments to complete the life cycle of deployments of our application.

Creating an application

In order to deploy our microservice, first we need to create an application in OpenShift Online, so we will log in to the OpenShift Online console. Remember that we got an URL in an email at the beginning of this chapter (in our example, it was `https://console.starter-ca-central-1.openshift.com`). Let's open it in our browser.

We may be asked to log in with our credentials, so let's introduce the one that we set up at the beginning of the chapter. The `Catalog` should appear, showing different application templates to choose from:

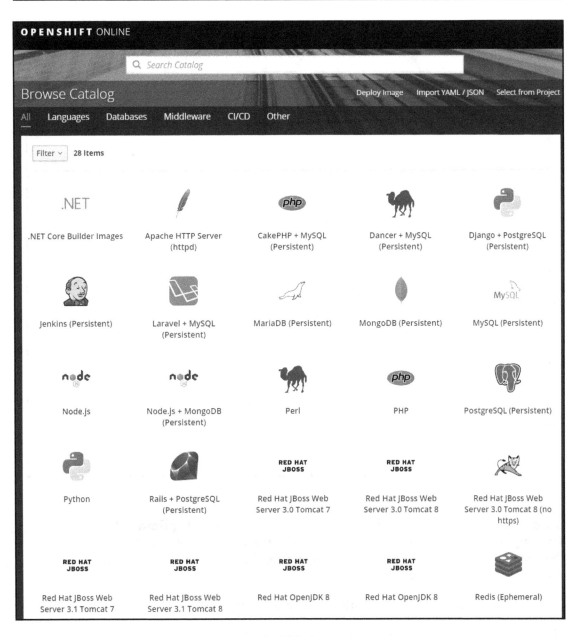

OpenShift Catalog

We will choose the second **Red Hat OpenJDK 8** application by clicking on that icon. A new window should appear:

OpenJDK 8 template

If we have chosen correctly, we should see in the description, **Application template for Java applications built using S2I**. S2I means Source To Image, and it basically means that this template will create a docker image of our application using the source code that's provided.

Now, we can click on the **Next >** button to go to the next page.

Here, we will have a form to fill in with different values:

- **Project Name:** Our project in OpenShift; we will choose `kotlin-microservices`

- **Project Display Name**: How it will be shown on the OpenShift console; we will choose `Kotlin Microservices`
- **Application Name**: What is going to be the name of our application in the project; this will be `customers`
- **Git Repository URL**: This is our Git URL that we have used before: `https://github.com/Juan-Medina-Code/customers.git`
- **Git Reference**: We will leave this as it is `master`
- **Context Directory**: Allows us to specify a folder in our Git repository, we should clear the field and leave it empty

We can leave the rest of the fields as they are and just click on the **Create** button:

Filling the form

Now, the Window will display a message that will say: **A new Java application has been created in your project**. We can close that window and see on the top right side of the screen that a new icon has appeared for our project:

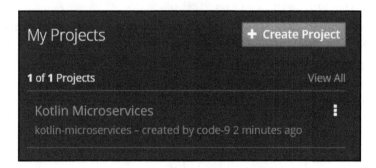

Project in dashboard

Now, OpenShift is building and deploying our microservice, and this will take several minutes. Internally this is what OpenShift will do:

- Pull our software from GitHub
- Call maven to package our application into a JAR
- Create a docker image including OpenJDK 8 and our application
- Publish that docker image in the internal OpenShift registry
- Deploy the image into a pod; this is how an instance is named on OpenShift
- Create a service, an internal HTTP route for our microservice
- Create a route, an external HTTP route that will expose our microservice externally

When all these steps are done, we click on the Kotlin microservices link and we should see a new page:

Application deployed in OpenShift Online

We can see that on the right side of the screen we get a URL for our microservice, an URL that we can use as before to test our microservice. In our example, it will be `http://customers-kotlin-microservices.193b.starter-ca-central-1.openshiftapps.com/customers`.

Managing our application

Now that our application is running, we can manage through the OpenShift web console, or by using the command-line tools. On the web console, on the top left menu, we can select **Application | Pods** to see the instances of our microservices. It should show:

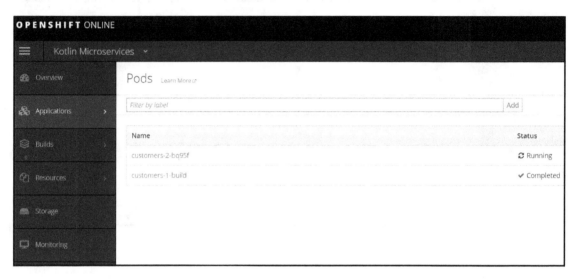

OpenShift pods

We can see here that there are two pods, one that was used to build our application, and another that is our application which is actually running. If we click on it, a new page should be displayed. In the new window, click on the tab **logs**.This should show us the log for our microservice.

Alternatively, we can use the command `oc`, OpenShift command line tools, to see the logs, but remember that first, we need to have it installed and log in on OpenShift as we have done at the beginning of the chapter.

First, we will use the `oc` command to change to our current project:

```
oc project kotlin-microservices
Now using project "kotlin-microservices" on server
"https://api.starter-ca-central-1.openshift.com:443".
```

Then, we can list the `pods`:

```
oc get pods
NAME READY STATUS RESTARTS AGE
customers-1-build 0/1 Completed 0 14m
customers-2-bq95f 1/1 Running 0 6m
```

Finally, we can get the log for our microservice pod with the command:

```
oc logs customers-2-bq95f
```

This will display the last entries in our microservice log as the web interface did previously.

> OpenShift is a really complex tool that has a dozen of tools and option. You may want to fully explore them in the excellent online documentation available on: `https://docs.openshift.com/online/welcome/index.html`.

Updating the application

Now, we will make a small change in our application. Open again our project using IntelliJ IDEA, and then open our `CustomerController` class:

```kotlin
package com.microservices.chapter11

import org.springframework.web.bind.annotation.GetMapping
import org.springframework.web.bind.annotation.PathVariable
import org.springframework.web.bind.annotation.RestController
import java.util.concurrent.ConcurrentHashMap

@RestController
class CustomerController {
  companion object {
    val initialCustomers = arrayOf(Customer(1, "Kotlin"),
        Customer(2, "Spring"),
        Customer(3, "Microservice"),
        Customer(4, "OpenShift"))
    val customers = ConcurrentHashMap<Int, Customer>
    (initialCustomers.associateBy(Customer::id))
  }

  @GetMapping("/customers")
  fun getCustomers() = customers.values.toList()

  @GetMapping("/customer/{id}")
```

```
    fun getCustomer(@PathVariable id: Int) = customers[id]
}
```

We have added one more customer to our microservice, but then we need to change our test because they will fail if not, and we should always run our test before deploying our software.

Having a pipeline will prevent us from actually deploying code that does not pass our test, and this is great for delivering high-quality software. In the next chapter, we will discuss this further.

We will modify our `CustomerControllerTests` class:

```
package com.microservices.chapter11

import org.junit.Test
import org.junit.runner.RunWith
import org.springframework.beans.factory.annotation.Autowired
import org.springframework.boot.test.autoconfigure.web.servlet.AutoConfigureMockMvc
import org.springframework.boot.test.context.SpringBootTest
import org.springframework.test.context.junit4.SpringRunner
import org.springframework.test.web.servlet.MockMvc
import org.springframework.test.web.servlet.request.MockMvcRequestBuilders.get
import org.springframework.test.web.servlet.result.MockMvcResultHandlers.print
import org.springframework.test.web.servlet.result.MockMvcResultMatchers.jsonPath
import org.springframework.test.web.servlet.result.MockMvcResultMatchers.status

@RunWith(SpringRunner::class)
@SpringBootTest
@AutoConfigureMockMvc
class CustomerControllerTest {
  @Autowired
  lateinit var mockMvc : MockMvc

  @Test
  fun `we should get the customer list`(){
    mockMvc.perform(get("/customers"))
        .andExpect(status().isOk)
        .andExpect(jsonPath("\$[0].id").value(1))
        .andExpect(jsonPath("\$[0].name").value("Kotlin"))
```

```
          .andExpect(jsonPath("\$[1].id").value(2))
          .andExpect(jsonPath("\$[1].name").value("Spring"))
          .andExpect(jsonPath("\$[2].id").value(3))
          .andExpect(jsonPath("\$[2].name").value("Microservice"))
          .andExpect(jsonPath("\$[3].id").value(4))
          .andExpect(jsonPath("\$[3].name").value("OpenShift"))
          .andDo(print())
    }

    @Test
    fun `we should get a customer by id`(){
      mockMvc.perform(get("/customer/1"))
          .andExpect(status().isOk)
          .andExpect(jsonPath("\$.id").value(1))
          .andExpect(jsonPath("\$.name").value("Kotlin"))
          .andDo(print())
    }
}
```

Now, we can run our test, either using the IntelliJ IDEA Maven **Projects** window with the **verify** lifecycle, or in the command line by executing:

```
mvnw verify
```

Either way, we should get a BUILD SUCCESS message:

```
[INFO] Results:
[INFO]
[INFO] Tests run: 3, Failures: 0, Errors: 0, Skipped: 0
[INFO]
[INFO] ------------------------------------------------------------------------
[INFO] BUILD SUCCESS
[INFO] ------------------------------------------------------------------------
[INFO] Total time: 5.959 s
[INFO] Finished at: 2017-12-09T13:07:04+00:00
[INFO] Final Memory: 29M/416M
[INFO] ------------------------------------------------------------------------
```

Now, we can push our change to Git, and then go to the OpenShift web interface, or use the command line, to ask the platform to deploy our software again. But it would be great if we could just push to our Git and our software is deployed again automatically. OpenShift can do that; let's review how.

First, in the OpenShift console menu, navigate and select the option **Builds | Builds**. A new page will load with a list of builds and we can click on **customers** to show the details for building our microservice.

In this new page, we can navigate to the tab **Configuration**:

Build configuration

On the right side of the page, we can see the **Triggers** section. Let's copy the **GitHub Webhook URL**. Now we can go to our GitHub project page and click on the **Settings** tab, then on the left side of the page, click on the **Webhooks** option:

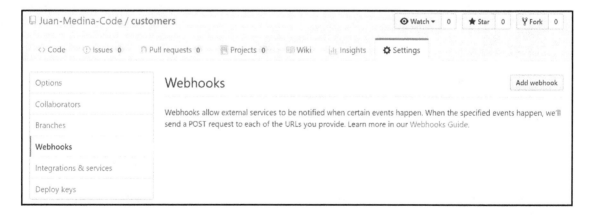

Now we can click on the **Add webhook** button and a new page will load to enter the details:

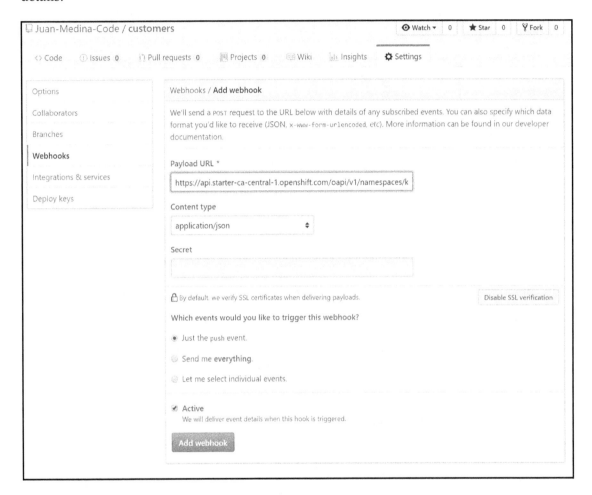

In this new window, we should set in the **Payload URL,** the one that we copy on the OpenShift build configuration. We should set the content type to be `application/JSON` and finally, we should set to just trigger push events, selecting the **Just the push event** option. Then, we can click on the **Add webhook** button.

Now, let's push our software, open the command line to run some Git commands, and navigate to our microservice folder. First, we can double-check which file has changed with the command:

```
git status
On branch master
Changes not staged for commit:
  (use "git add <file>..." to update what will be committed)
  (use "git checkout -- <file>..." to discard changes in working
  directory)

        modified:
src/main/kotlin/com/microservices/chapter11/CustomerController.kt
        modified:
src/test/kotlin/com/microservices/chapter11/CustomerControllerTest.kt
```

Let's add our changes. This time, we can add reviewing by using the command:

```
git add -p
```

This will ask file-by-file if we want to add the change previewing the difference with the original file. To accept the change, we will type Y and press *Enter.*

Now, we will add a commit for this change:

```
git commit -m "updating customers"
```

Finally, we will push the changes to GitHub:

```
git push origin master
```

If we go back to OpenShift Online to the **Builds** section, a new **Builds** should show as running:

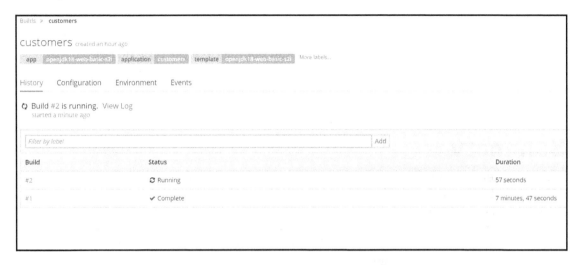

New build running

After a few minutes, our application should be deployed again and available in the previously used URL `http://customers-kotlin-microservices.193b.starter-ca-central-1.openshiftapps.com/customers`, but this time it should return:

```
[
  {
    "id": 1,
    "name": "Kotlin"
  },
  {
    "id": 2,
    "name": "Spring"
  },
  {
    "id": 3,
    "name": "Microservice"
  },
  {
    "id": 4,
    "name": "OpenShift"
  }
]
```

We have just deployed a change in our microservice by just doing a `git push`. Not bad, but not as good as having a pipeline that will also run the test before actually deploying the software.

 If you want to learn more about how to create a fully functional pipeline using Git and OpenShift, you could use the example provided by Travis CI in this guide: `https://docs.travis-ci.com/user/deployment/openshift/`.

Summary

In this chapter, we have learned how easily we can deploy microservices into production systems, and how we can configure and use Git as a repository for our microservice code. We learned how we can create cloud applications in OpenShift Online and how we can deploy our microservices on this platform. Finally, we learned how we can integrate GitHub and OpenShift Online in our projects so that we automatically deploy our microservices when they change.

In the next chapter, we will discuss industry best practices when creating Kotlin microservices. We will cover some of the Kotlin best practices so that we make use of its advantages. Then, we do a deep dive into the Spring application context to create best-in-class Spring applications. To have code that we can easily manage, we will propose a better layering structure for our microservices code. Then, we will try to review how we can do effective testing when creating microservices. Finally, we will discuss how we should handle Continuous Integration and Continuous Delivery.

12

Best Practices

During the course of this book, we have learned a vast set of technologies and tools that allowed us to create microservices with Kotlin using the Spring Framework; however, this is not a simple task. When we apply what we have learned in our own project, there will always be an infinite amount of approaches that we could choose, and some may work better than others.

In this chapter, we will try to learn industry best practices, which will allow us to improve the overall quality of our microservices. In this chapter, you will learn more about:

- Kotlin idioms
- Spring Context
- Layering
- Testing
- Continuous Integration
- Continuous Delivery

Using Kotlin idioms

Kotlin provides a set of idioms that allows us to drastically reduce the amount of boilerplate code. Boilerplate refers to sections of code that have to be included in many places with little or no alteration. In this section, we will learn some of the most used idioms.

Inferred types

We may have a function written that returns a value, such as:

```
fun lower(name : String) : String {
  val lower : String = name.toLowerCase()
  return "$name in lower case is: $lower"
}
```

Here, we are explicitly indicating the type of the result of the function and the internal variable that we use inside.

In Kotlin, we could infer the type of the variable:

```
fun lower(name : String): String {
  val lower = name.toLowerCase()
  return "$name in lower case is: $lower"
}
```

And even the return type of our function could be inferred:

```
fun lower(name : String) = "$name in lower case is: ${name.toLowerCase()}"
```

This will be extremely useful as the code that we created with the inferred type did not need to change if we change the type it uses. Let's clarify this with an example:

```
fun foo() : String {
  return "14"
}

fun bar() : String {
  val value : String = foo()
  return value
}
```

If we change our `foo` method to:

```
fun foo() : Int {
  return 14
}
```

Our `bar` method needs to be changed to:

```
fun bar() : Int {
  val value : Int = foo()
  return value
}
```

However, if our methods were declared like:

```
fun foo() = "14"

fun bar() = foo()
```

Then we could simply change the result of foo without affecting bar:

```
fun foo() = 14

fun bar() = foo()
```

Expressions

Considering that we have a simple function to return some value:

```
fun oddOrEven(number: Int): String {
  if(number % 2 == 0)
    return "odd"
  else
    return "even"
}
```

It could be used as an expression:

```
fun oddOrEven(number: Int): String {
  return if(number % 2 == 0)
    "odd"
  else
    "even"
}
```

And, of course, we could infer the type:

```
fun oddOrEven(number: Int) =
    if (number % 2 == 0)
      "odd"
    else
      "even"
```

Other statements could be used as an expression, for example, if we have this function:

```
fun fizzBuzz(number: Int): String {
  if (number % 15 == 0) {
    return "FizzBuzz"
  } else if (number % 3 == 0) {
    return "Fizz"
```

```
    } else if (number % 5 == 0) {
      return "Buzz"
    } else {
      return number.toString()
    }
  }
```

We could convert it into an expression:

```
fun fizzBuzz(number: Int) =
    if (number % 15 == 0) {
      "FizzBuzz"
    } else if (number % 3 == 0) {
      "Fizz"
    } else if (number % 5 == 0) {
      "Buzz"
    } else {
      number.toString()
    }
```

But Kotlin has the when expression that could be used in the same way as Java switch/case:

```
fun fizzBuzz(number: Int) =
    when {
      number % 15 == 0 -> "FizzBuzz"
      number % 3 == 0 -> "Fizz"
      number % 5 == 0 -> "Buzz"
      else -> number.toString()
    }
```

This could be applied to other expressions such as try/catch:

```
fun calculate(number1: Int, number2: Int) =
    try {
      number1 / number2
    } catch (ex: Exception) {
      0
    }
```

Default parameters

Kotlin allows us to specify default parameters when declaring functions:

```
fun compute(number1: Int, number2: Int = 2, number3: Int = 5) = number1 *
number2 * number3
```

This could be used as:

```
println(compute(7))
println(compute(7, 2))
println(compute(7, 2, 8))
println(compute(number1 = 8, number3 = 4))
```

Lambda

Considering that we just use a range of numbers that we cycle in a loop:

```
fun printNumbers(){
  val range = 1..10
  for(i in range){
    println(i)
  }
}
```

We could use a lambda to access them:

```
fun printNumbers(){
  val range = 1..10
  range.forEach { i -> println(i) }
}
```

But lambda could be easily shortened with the inferred `it` object:

```
fun printNumbers(){
  val range = 1..10
  range.forEach { println(it) }
}
```

And we don't really need a variable for `it`, so we could simplify it with:

```
fun printNumbers() {
  (1..10).forEach { println(it) }
}
```

But since we just print the elements of `forEach`, we could just use a method reference instead of the lambda:

```
fun printNumbers() {
   (1..10).forEach(::println)
}
```

These were just some examples of some of the Kotlin idioms, but there are dozens more, and we strongly recommend you check the official Kotlin documentation to review them all to keep you up to date with new additions that appear as the language evolves: `https://kotlinlang.org/docs/reference/idioms.html`.

Managing the Spring context

The Spring application context is where our beans are referenced to be used in our application, and managing it correctly is not a simple task. When we have dozens of beans created, where and how we access them is important, and we could end up in a situation that we refer to as an incorrect bean.

In this section, we will discuss ways to handle this complexity.

Constructor injection

In this book, we have used `@Autowired` in our examples to illustrate how we ask Spring to inject a bean into our application.

Consider this example of two services and a controller that uses them:

```
import org.springframework.beans.factory.annotation.Autowired
import org.springframework.stereotype.Service
import org.springframework.web.bind.annotation.*

@Service
class AccountService {
   fun getAccountsByCustomer(customerId: Int): List<Account>
       = listOf(Account(1, 125F), Account(2, 500F))
}

@Service
class CustomerService {
   @Autowired
```

```
  private lateinit var accountService: AccountService

  fun getCustomer(id: Int): Customer {
    val accounts = accountService.getAccountsByCustomer(id)
    return Customer(id, "customer$id", accounts)
  }
}

@RestController
class CustomerController {
  @Autowired
  private lateinit var customerService: CustomerService

  @GetMapping("/customer/{id}")
  fun getCustomer(@PathVariable id: Int) = customerService.getCustomer(1)
}
```

CustomerController injects the CustomerService bean using the @AutoWired
annotation, and CustomerService injects the AccountService using the @Autowired
annotation as well.

These services use a couple of data classes that we created for this example:

```
data class Account(val id : Int, val balance : Float)
data class Customer(val id : Int, val name : String, val accounts:
List<Account>)
```

Instead of using @AutoWired, we could inject our services as part of the constructor of the
classes:

```
import org.springframework.stereotype.Service
import org.springframework.web.bind.annotation.*

@Service
class AccountService {
  fun getAccountsByCustomer(customerId: Int): List<Account>
      = listOf(Account(1, 125F), Account(2, 500F))
}

@Service
class CustomerService(val accountService: AccountService) {
  fun getCustomer(id: Int): Customer {
    val accounts = accountService.getAccountsByCustomer(id)
    return Customer(id, "customer$id", accounts)
  }
}
```

```
@RestController
class CustomerController(val customerService: CustomerService) {
  @GetMapping("/customer/{id}")
  fun getCustomer(@PathVariable id: Int) = customerService.getCustomer(1)
}
```

When Spring is creating our `CustomerController`, it will detect that the parameter in the constructor, `CustomerService`, is actually a bean that exists in the context so it will inject while creating the `CustomerController`. Exactly the same will happen when the `CustomerService` is created with the `AccountService` being injected.

This will improve a couple of things; first, it will become clearer what is required in our components just by looking at the constructor, the second autowired required a `var`, a mutable object, with constructor injection we could use `val`, an immutable object that could not be changed later on.

 Having our objects as immutable allows us to prevent problems when creating concurrent applications such as microservices. They could also have a positive impact on performance.

Explicit context configuration

So far, we have used `@Component` or `@Service` to declare our beans that later on, when the SpringBoot application starts, will add to the Spring context by the component scan. However, we may want to explicitly declare our beans using a `Configuration` class:

```
import org.springframework.context.annotation.Bean
import org.springframework.context.annotation.Configuration

@Configuration
class ContextConfiguration {
  @Bean
  fun accountService() = AccountService()

  @Bean
  fun customerService(accountService: AccountService) =
CustomerService(accountService)

  @Bean
  fun customerController(customerService: CustomerService) =
CustomerController(customerService)
}
```

Since we now have a constructor injection, we need to specify our bean declaration to receive as a parameter the bean that we need, so we could send it to the constructor of the method. Then, we could remove the @Service from our service since we don't need the component scan created then:

```
class AccountService {
    fun getAccountsByCustomer(customerId: Int): List<Account>
        = listOf(Account(1, 125F), Account(2, 500F))
}

class CustomerService(val accountService: AccountService) {
    fun getCustomer(id: Int): Customer {
        val accounts = accountService.getAccountsByCustomer(id)
        return Customer(id, "customer$id", accounts)
    }
}
```

Finally, we could move the application class and the ContextConfiguration class to a separate package, which will prevent the component scan from picking any other annotated class and adding it as a bean, and to do this, we have an explicit context configuration that tells us exactly what we need in our context:

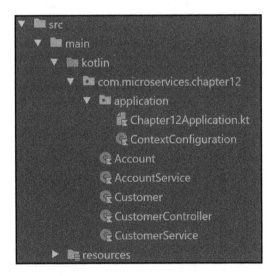

Application package

In this example, the component scan loads our ContextConfiguration class when the application is launched and then we will create our beans.

Having an explicit context allows us to avoid situations that could be very complicated to handle, such as getting the right bean when we have a large number of classes. We are not saying that we need to avoid the component scan completely, but we need to use it cautiously.

Decouple services

One thing that we may overlook is that our controller and service have a dependency on the actual implementation. This means that if we have an implementation change tomorrow, for example, moving from a database into a different mechanism, we need to change who uses it, so to avoid that, we will create interfaces for them.

First, we will rename our `CustomerService` to `CustomerServiceImpl`, and our `AccountService` to `AccountServiceImpl`; then, we will create our interfaces:

```
interface AccountService {
  fun getAccountsByCustomer(customerId: Int): List<Account>
}

class AccountServiceImpl : AccountService {
  override fun getAccountsByCustomer(customerId: Int): List<Account>
      = listOf(Account(1, 125F), Account(2, 500F))
}

interface CustomerService {
  fun getCustomer(id: Int): Customer
}

class CustomerServiceImpl(val accountService: AccountService) :
CustomerService {
  override fun getCustomer(id: Int): Customer {
    val accounts = accountService.getAccountsByCustomer(id)
    return Customer(id, "customer$id", accounts)
  }
}
```

Now, we have to change our `CustomerController` and `ContextConfiguration` to refer to the interfaces:

```
import org.springframework.context.annotation.Bean
import org.springframework.context.annotation.Configuration
import org.springframework.web.bind.annotation.*

@RestController
```

```
class CustomerController(val customerService: CustomerService) {
  @GetMapping("/customer/{id}")
  fun getCustomer(@PathVariable id: Int) = customerService.getCustomer(1)
}

@Configuration
class ContextConfiguration {
  @Bean
  fun accountService() : AccountService = AccountServiceImpl()

  @Bean
  fun customerService(accountService: AccountService) : CustomerService =
    CustomerServiceImpl(accountService)

  @Bean
  fun customerController(customerService: CustomerService) =
CustomerController(customerService)
}
```

Now, if we need to change our implementation of the services, we only need to change our context configuration; the rest of the application will be unchanged. Another effect on this change is that now our services may not have any Spring dependent code, and this could be great as if tomorrow we need to move them to a different framework, we may do it seamlessly.

> Remember that avoiding coupling should be one of our principles when we create microservices, as it is in any software that we build.

Layering the application

When our application grows, it is going to be more complex to manage the large number of classes that we may end up with. And if we haven't taken care of our application structure, we may end in a situation that may not find the class that we need when we are looking for it.

In this section, we will propose a structure for layering our application and packaging the classes.

Understanding our classes

Let's first look at our current classes in our project:

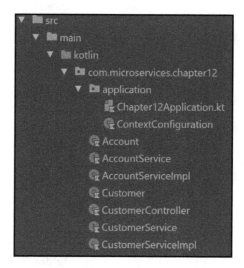

Current application structure

Currently, if we look at the preceding image of our classes to understand what domain they may refer to, we could divide them into two domains:

- Customer-related classes
- Account-related classes

But if we look at the same image to understand what our classes are, we can classify them into various groups:

- Application classes
- Context configuration classes
- Data classes
- Services interfaces
- Services implementation classes
- Controllers classes

Let's think how we can arrange them using those groups and domains.

Domains

We can create two domains and place our classes inside, and we already have an `application` package that we could use to store our application classes that don't belong to a particular domain:

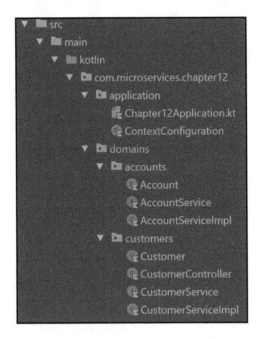

This does look better, however, we may not need to have a `domains` package, though it may be handy if we have more things to add to our structure.

Splitting

Now, we could split them into the domain based on what they are used for:

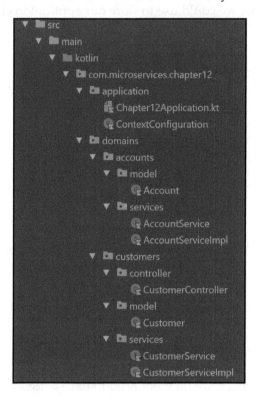

final packages

We have created separate packages for:

- `model`: Our domain model objects such as our data classes
- `services`: Our services with the business logic on that domain, we may want to split the implementation
- `controllers`: Our controllers that expose our model and use the services

Each of these packages could grow if there are more model, services, or controllers classes to add.

Having our application layered in a way that we can understand is key for our microservice, however, no structure is perfect and you should decide which way you want to structure yours. It may differ from this structure, but remember that it is not only for you, anyone in your project should understand the used structure and if you are thinking about making your project or application **Open Source Software (OSS)**, you may want to add this to your contributing documentation.

Testing effectively

Testing is one of the most important elements of modern software development, and you should take care of it right at the beginning when you start to design your microservice. In this section, we will try to guide you with some suggestions on how to effectively test your microservice, however, really understanding testing requires a deeper look that you should cover eventually.

Understanding type of tests

There are several kinds of tests that you can carry out on microservices, but here are some of the most common ones that you should understand:

- Unit tests
- Integration tests
- E2E tests

This is important to us because we should name our test according to what they are, either by naming the test class with the name of the type of test or classifying the package that refers to that type of test.

For example, if we have one Integration test for our controller that is named `CustomerControllerTest`, we could name it `CustomerControlIntegrationTest`, `CustomerControllerIT`, or leave it in the package `com.microservices.test.integration`.

Classifying our test correctly allows us to easily understand what kind of test it is when a test fails.

Let's review the different types of test so we have a clear understanding of how to name or place ours.

Unit tests

They should focus on testing small units (typically a class or a complex algorithm). They should be tested in isolation and independent of other units. They should be fast, not more than a few seconds to provide immediate feedback. With these tests, we could refactor our code with confidence, making small changes and running the tests constantly.

Integration tests

Integration tests test different components of our software to test if they work correctly in combination. Our classes may work in isolation, but they may fail when tested together.

E2E tests

End-to-End (E2E) tests try to prove that each complete functionality works, from an end-user perspective. If we are running a microservice that exposes an API, we may test the different methods as we would do with an external application that was invoking us.

Other tests

There are many other types of tests, but they maybe be a subcategorization of the previously defined types. Here are some examples:

- **System test**: An Integration test that tries to check if the integration with another system actually works
- **Acceptance or functional test**: These are usually E2E tests that we use to validate that our software is working as the user specified
- **Smoke or sanity test**: Usually an Integration or E2E test, created to verify that the most important parts of our application are still working before releasing the software
- **Security tests**: Usually an E2E or Integration test that tries to prove how secure our software is

Testing pyramid

When we test our microservices, we may choose to use a different kind of test, but many parts of the software could be tested in different kinds of tests. For example, when we create a customer, we may test this using a **Unit** test on the service that creates them, however, we could also test it using an **Integration** test or even an **E2E** test. It is a common understanding in the industry that we should approach testing using the test pyramid that indicates how many tests of each type we should have:

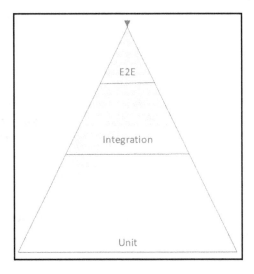

Test pyramid

The overall idea is that we should do as much testing as we can using a Unit test, this will provide more immediate feedback. Unit tests are easy to develop and maintain and we can go there with all different kinds of conditions and scenarios that our unit allows us. However, we may also need to test how our units are integrated, so we need an Integration test that only tests that integration, and all the logic that is already tested in the unit should be retested.

For example, if you do a Unit test for a service covering all the different business rules that return just a result of an error, in an Integration test, for a component that uses the service, you should only test that result or error from the service and not duplicate all the tests done previously in the Unit tests. Finally, we should carry out our E2E test covering the complete scenarios, not just those defined in our requirements, regardless of how they are implemented.

The Google Testing blog suggests a 70/20/10 split: 70% Unit tests, 20% Integration tests, and 10% End-to-End tests, you may consider these numbers when doing testing for your microservices. Refer to the following site for more details: `https://testing.googleblog.com/2015/04/just-say-no-to-more-end-to-end-tests.html`.

Test Driven Development

We should try to do **Test Driven Development (TDD)** when we create our microservices. TDD will not only help us to ensure that our microservices are tested correctly, it will guide the design of our microservices to a better implementation. The overall idea for doing TDD is that you start writing a test first that will fail since there is no code for it yet, this test will be red. Then you move to implement just the minimum code to make the test pass, the test will be green. Then you refactor your code to improve it and rerun the test to check that it is working again, and if not, fix it. You then write another test, for example, to make another change in your code and repeat the cycle as before. These short cycles of red-green-refactor are what makes a TDD great.

For a microservice, you may start doing a test for a controller that may not exist, then implement the controller to return just the data, then you may create a test for a service that will do what the controller needs, and implement the service. Next, you could move to modify your controller and you would still have the test originally created to verify that everything works as defined.

Other great advantages of this are that whatever you need in your application, it will become apparent when you need it rather than creating a service (and related components) before they are required; this is a great way to do lean software development.

Unfortunately, we could not cover the full scope of TDD during this book, but we encourage you to find out more about it and try to bring this discipline when you write your own microservices. You could look at this small article from Martin Fowler's blog to get you started, `https://martinfowler.com/bliki/TestDrivenDevelopment.html,` but we really recommend that you read Kent Beck's book, *Test-Driven Development*.

Behavior-Driven Development

You can also use **Behavior-Driven Development (BDD)** when you carry out tests on your microservices. BDD is a software development process that emerged from TDD, with ideas from domain-driven design and object-oriented analysis and design to provide software development and management teams with shared tools and a shared process to collaborate on software development.

The idea is that the requirements from your software are created by the team, including the domain experts defining how the application should behave. This is done using a behavioral specification that uses the ubiquitous language from our domain model.

This is an example of such a specification:

```
Story: Get a customer from the API

As a user of the API
In order to been able to get customers
I want to query them

Scenario 1: Get a customer that does exist
Given that I've the id from a customer
and the customer exists
When I query the customers API
and I use the customer id
Then I should get the customer details.

Scenario 2: Get a customer that does not exist
Given that I've the id from a customer
and the customer doest not exists
When I query the customers API
and I use the customer id
Then I should get a not found response
```

This describes our requirements that it will be written before we build our microservices, and since we will use our ubiquitous language, the whole team could work together defining the specification. Then, we can use tools such as **Cucumber** to literally read that specification and create a test that validates it. Finally, we can use TDD for the code that makes those test pass and do our red-green-refactor cycles. Making tests like this will be great as we will have tests that everyone can contribute to, including our domain –JVM:reference">experts and the team as a whole.

Cucumber–JVM provides an excellent framework for doing BDD tests, and since they run in the JVM, we could create them in Kotlin. Refer to the following website for more details: `https://cucumber.io/docs/reference/jvm`.

Handling CI and CD

Adding Continuous Integration and Continuous Delivery to our microservice will allow us to deliver our application at the fastest pace with great quality and is something that we should look for when we create our microservices. In this section, we will discuss some practices that you should consider when doing Continuous Integration and Continuous Delivery.

Continuous Integration

Maintaining your software working is not always easy, especially when you have several developers working on the same code base. **Continuous Integration** (**CI**) allows us to minimize the problems when working with our software. The main idea behind CI is that every single time that we push code to our repository, our tests runs, and this allows us to know if the change that we just made has broken our application, even if what is broken was not actually in the code that was modified.

This minimizes the problems of integrating software in a code base if someone pushes a piece of software that is faulty, we can fix it and get it back working. And this is something that we should target to do all the time, as having a working software on our repository allows us to release as often as we can to get feedback, and feedback is what makes software better.

We may think that we shouldn't commit software until everything is ready, and that has been proved to be a painful approach which pushes dozen of changes to our code base to find out that it could not integrate with the rest. This is something that we should avoid. CI allows us to integrate the software while we are writing it, so we never end up in the situation where we have software completed that actually is not, because it is not working with the rest of our code base.

Try to commit small, and try to commit often; this allows you to go back and fix things until they are integrated without too much effort.

Continuous Delivery

If we have CI working, we are only one step away from **Continuous Delivery (CD)**, but sometimes that step is not a short step. However, we should always try to move in that direction regardless. We could have a working software in our integration environment, but if it takes weeks to be available at our end, we are not giving the users the value that our application should give.

In CD, we will try to automate the whole process to get our software from our code base into a live application, with all the steps that we could need. This could go from having our infrastructure created and configured, to our application being tested, deployed, or even verified and a range of things in-between, with the minimum, or non-manual intervention. The goal is simple from a developer pushing a change in our repository to getting the application live to end users.

> Nothing is really done until it is available to end users. This is how we give value to our applications, and we like to do it often, and for the best quality, we must do CD.

Pipeline

To do proper CI and CD, we need a pipeline tool that allows us to handle this process, something that enables us to pick up our changes, build our software, run the test, deploy the application, or any steps that require in-between. And if something fails, our pipeline could notify us, so we can react and correct the problem.

There is a huge range of tools to do pipelines, but we recommend you look at tools such as Jenkins (probably the most popular tool), or others such as Concourse, Bamboo Gitlab CI, Travis CI, Drone, and many more.

> Do not just go to Jenkins because it is what everyone else does. There are many tools and many of them as good or even better than Jenkins; try some of them.

Dashboard

Having a pipeline running is great, but if our build is not working, or our tests aren't running, we need to know about it and react. Most pipelines provide systems which give notifications, for example, sending emails or posting in programs like Slack, but most of them provide tools to create a dashboard as well.

A dashboard from a pipeline should visualize the different stages that we do, from building our software to launching our test or deployments, and usually are color coded with the standard work green, broken red. If we have a dashboard, we could just display it somewhere that the team could use to see if the pipeline is working and fix it where needed. Our pipeline dashboard could also be easily integrated with our application monitoring to have a centralized view of what is going on with our application.

It is a whole team responsibility to fix broken builds, and we need to encourage them to understand why. It is in our application's best interest to have a pipeline working so that we can deliver often and with confidence to our end users.

Summary

During the course of this book, we have covered what microservices are, and the benefits that they bring to our applications. Now we can design them with the best principles in the industry that allow us to have an architecture that evolves as our products do. We learned how the Spring Framework could easily be integrated with Kotlin, providing excellent tools to build microservices. During this process, we realized the advantages of using a modern programming language such as Kotlin to deliver high-quality software. And remember that we have just started creating some RESTFul APIs that eventually can become reactive microservices used in a NoSQL database such as MongoDB with the best performance of non-blocking operations. Then, we learned how to create containers and clouds, and how we can scale our applications when required.

But we need software that gives us confidence, so we learned how our tests not only give a guarantee that our requirements are met, but they act as a live documentation that anyone in our team can use to understand our applications. And when our application reaches production, we can use what we have learned to have production-ready alerts and monitoring that could be used to control and manage our microservices, even in the worst scenarios. Finally, we learned how we can use industry best practices when creating microservices in Kotlin to provide the best value to our end users.

At this point, you should be more than ready to start building your own microservices with Kotlin and the Spring Framework with the best techniques available to you.

Other Books You May Enjoy

If you enjoyed this book, you may be interested in these other books by Packt:

Mastering Android Development with Kotlin
Miloš Vasić

ISBN: 978-1-78847-369-9

- Understand the basics of Android development with Kotlin
- Get to know the key concepts in Android development
- See how to create modern mobile applications for the Android platform
- Adjust your application's look and feel
- Know how to persist and share application database
- Work with Services and other concurrency mechanisms
- Write effective tests
- Migrate an existing Java-based project to Kotlin

Spring 5.0 Microservices - Second Edition
Rajesh R V

ISBN: 978-1-78712-768-5

- Familiarize yourself with the microservices architecture and its benefits
- Find out how to avoid common challenges and pitfalls while developing microservices
- Use Spring Boot and Spring Cloud to develop microservices
- Handle logging and monitoring microservices
- Leverage Reactive Programming in Spring 5.0 to build modern cloud native applications
- Manage internet-scale microservices using Docker, Mesos, and Marathon
- Gain insights into the latest inclusion of Reactive Streams in Spring and make applications more resilient and scalable

Leave a review - let other readers know what you think

Please share your thoughts on this book with others by leaving a review on the site that you bought it from. If you purchased the book from Amazon, please leave us an honest review on this book's Amazon page. This is vital so that other potential readers can see and use your unbiased opinion to make purchasing decisions, we can understand what our customers think about our products, and our authors can see your feedback on the title that they have worked with Packt to create. It will only take a few minutes of your time, but is valuable to other potential customers, our authors, and Packt. Thank you!

Index

D

data classes, Kotlin documentation
  reference 84
deployment models, for cloud applications
  about 35
  hybrid cloud 36
  private cloud 35
  public cloud 36
deserialization
  about 113
  complex objects 114, 115
  object validation 115
  request, into object 113
DevOps 8
Discovery Server
  connecting to 224
Docker CE 235
Docker Hub
  account, creating on 248
Docker
  about 233, 235
  building, with microservices 240
  example, running 236
  images, managing 239
  images, pulling 238
  installing 235
  integrating, with Maven 250
  publishing 247, 249
Dockerfile
  creating 242, 244
Domain-Driven Design (DDD)
  about 24, 25
  bounded context 25, 26
  context mapping 26, 27
  ubiquitous language 25
  using, in microservices 27
domains 375
downstream 20

E

End-to-End (E2E) tests 378
endpoints, SpringBoot Actuator
  health endpoint 313
  metrics endpoint 314

reference 313
  trace endpoints 315
Enterprise Software Bus (ESB) 13
errors
  capturing, on Handlers 164
  handling 116
  publishing 166
Eureka 211
example microservice
  creating 240, 241, 339, 341

F

fallbacks 21
fluent tests 295
Flux
  using, in service 136
functional test 378
functional web programming
  using 142

G

Gateway
  about 208, 227
  creating 228
  routes, defining 229
generated project files, Spring Initializr
  Gitignore 48
  Maven files 47
  resource files 48
  source files 48
Git for Windows
  download link 333
Git Mac client
  reference 333
Git
  installing 333
GitHub account
  creating 330
  setting up 331, 332
GitHub
  reference 330

S